D0948368

NGOs, the UN,
and Global Governance

Emerging Global Issues
Thomas G. Weiss, Series Editor

Published in association with the
Thomas J. Watson Jr. Institute for International Studies,
Brown University

NGOs, the UN, and Global Governance

■

edited by
Thomas G. Weiss
Leon Gordenker

LYNNE
RIENNER
PUBLISHERS

BOULDER
LONDON

Published in the United States of America in 1996 by
Lynne Rienner Publishers, Inc.
1800 30th Street, Boulder, Colorado 80301

and in the United Kingdom by
Lynne Rienner Publishers, Inc.
3 Henrietta Street, Covent Garden, London WC2E 8LU

Library of Congress Cataloging-in-Publication Data
NGOs, the United Nations, and global governance / edited by Thomas G.
  Weiss and Leon Gordenker.
      p.   cm.
  Includes bibliographical references and index.
  ISBN 1-55587-613-7 (hardcover : alk. paper)
  ISBN 1-55587-626-9 (pbk. : alk. paper)
  1. Non-governmental organizations. 2. United Nations.
3. International cooperation. 4. International organization.
I. Weiss, Thomas George. II. Gordenker, Leon, 1923–   .
JX1995.N48   1996
361.7'7—dc20   96-411
                                                            CIP

British Cataloguing in Publication Data
A Cataloguing in Publication record for this book
is available from the British Library.

Printed and bound in the United States of America

⊗ The paper used in this publication meets the requirements
   of the American National Standard for Permanence of
   Paper for Printed Library Materials Z39.48-1984.

 5 4 3 2 1

Contents

Foreword *Boutros Boutros-Ghali*   7
Preface *Thomas G. Weiss*   13

■ **Part 1   Theoretical Framework**

1   Pluralizing Global Governance: Analytical Approaches
     and Dimensions
     Leon Gordenker and Thomas G. Weiss   17

■ **Part 2   NGOs in Action**

2   Reality Check: Human Rights NGOs Confront Governments
     at the UN
     Felice D. Gaer   51
3   NGOs and the UN System in Complex Humanitarian Emergencies:
     Conflict or Cooperation?
     Andrew S. Natsios   67
4   The Bureaucracy and the Free Spirits: Stagnation and Innovation
     in the Relationship Between the UN and NGOs
     Antonio Donini   83
5   Greening the UN: Environmental Organisations and the
     UN System
     Ken Conca   103
6   IGO-NGO Relations and HIV/AIDS: Innovation or Stalemate?
     Christer Jönsson and Peter Söderholm   121
7   Engendering World Conferences: The International Women's
     Movement and the UN
     Martha Alter Chen   139

■ **Part 3   Cross-Cutting Themes and Processes**

8 Scaling Up the Grassroots and Scaling Down the Summit:
    The Relations Between Third World NGOs and the UN
    Peter Uvin   159

9 Coordinate? Cooperate? Harmonise? NGO Policy and
    Operational Coalitions
    Cyril Ritchie   177

10 Partners in Development? The State, NGOs, and the UN in
    Central America
    Peter Sollis   189

■ **Part 4   Conclusions**

11 NGO Participation in the International Policy Process
    Leon Gordenker and Thomas G. Weiss   209

List of Acronyms   223
Annotated Bibliography   227
About the Authors   241
Index   245
About the Book   249
Books in the Series   250

Foreword

BOUTROS BOUTROS-GHALI

It is my distinct pleasure to write a few words at the outset of this important volume dealing with the formal and informal interactions between nongovernmental organizations and the United Nations.

Until recently, the notion that the chief executive of the United Nations would have taken this issue seriously might have caused astonishment. The United Nations was considered to be a forum for sovereign states alone. Within the space of a few short years, however, this attitude has changed. Nongovernmental organizations are now considered full participants in international life. This change is largely due to the quick succession of historical events that we have witnessed in recent years. The fall of the Berlin Wall shattered the ideological screen that had concealed the reality of international relations. Political, economic, social, and cultural phenomena have been revealed in their true dimensions and in their profound complexity.

Today, we are well aware that the international community must address a human community that is transnational in every way. For a long time, the international order was regarded as political and firmly established. Now we must learn to accept and to deal with a world that is both social and mobile. The movement of people, information, capital, and ideas is as important today as the control of territory was yesterday. We therefore must build a framework that takes into account not only political issues, but economic behavior and social and cultural aspirations as well.

Nongovernmental organizations are a basic form of popular participation and representation in the present-day world. Their participation in international organizations is, in a way, proof of this. It is therefore not surprising that in a short time we have witnessed the emergence of so many new NGOs, which continue to increase in number on every continent.

In France, 54,000 new associations have been established since 1987. In Italy, 40 percent of all associations have been set up within the last 15 years. This phenomenon is also occurring in developing countries. Within a short space of time 10,000 NGOs have been established in Bangladesh, 21,000 in the Philippines, and 27,000 in Chile. In Eastern Europe, since the fall of communism,

7

nongovernmental organizations have been playing an increasingly important role in people's lives.

This development is inseparable from the aspiration for freedom that in various forms is today shaking international society. Democratization, and the democratization of the international system, are important subjects on the international agenda today; that is why I welcome the publication of this book by the Academic Council on the United Nations System (ACUNS) as an important contribution to the debate on these subjects. The United Nations is the obvious forum for conciliation not only among governments, but also between governments and nongovernmental organizations.

This volume represents a particulary ambitious and innovative approach to the subject. We are aware of what some nongovernmental organizations do in social, cultural, and humanitarian fields, as well as their work to protect human rights and to promote development. But we do not often have occasion to think about what these organizations can do for international peace and security. And we too rarely think about the taxonomy of linkages—formal and informal, in education, advocacy, and operations—between NGOs and the UN system as a whole.

For my part, I am convinced that NGOs have an important role to play in the achievement of the ideal established by the Charter of the United Nations: the maintenance and establishment of peace. We all know that states play the preponderant role in this area. We all know that the Charter confers upon the Security Council the primary responsibility for the maintenance of peace. But I have sought, in *An Agenda for Peace,* to emphasize as clearly as possible that "peace in the largest sense cannot be accomplished by the United Nations system or by Governments alone. Nongovernmental organizations, academic institutions, parliamentarians, business and professional communities, the media and the public at large must all be involved."

This is the point I wish to stress. To paraphrase an old saying: peace is too important to be entrusted to states alone. I believe NGOs can pursue their activities on three fronts. In the search for peace, they must obtain the means—and we must help them to do so—to engage in assistance, mobilization, and democratization activities, all at the same time. I would like to consider these three types of activity.

With regard to assistance, nongovernmental organizations have a key role to play—and many are already doing so. Today, the mandates of the United Nations operations go far beyond the standard definition of "peacekeeping" employed in the past.

These operations reflect recent international developments, in that conflicts increasingly are taking place within, rather than between, countries. Every day the UN deals with civil wars, secessions, partitions, ethnic clashes, and tribal conflicts. It will be understood how difficult the world organization's mission then becomes, obliged as it is to respect the fragile balance between the sovereignty of states and a mandate to intervene.

Moreover, the role of these operations is no longer confined to simply deploying a neutral presence between two belligerent parties. The aim of the new operations is the making, and indeed the building, of peace. This can involve electoral assistance, humanitarian aid, administrative activities, the rebuilding of roads and bridges, rural demining operations, the promotion of democracy, and the protection of human rights.

In *An Agenda for Peace* I stated explicitly that "this wider mission for the world organization will demand the concerted attention and effort of individual states, of regional and nongovernmental organizations, and of all of the United Nations system." Indeed, the vast enterprise of building peace presupposes that NGOs will be involved at every stage.

In the field of preventive diplomacy and because of their familiarity with the situation on the ground, nongovernmental organizations are well placed to play a part in early warning by drawing the attention of governments to nascent crises and emerging conflicts. With regard to peacemaking, there is wide recognition of the humanitarian and social work done by NGOs, generally under perilous and difficult conditions. Lastly, with regard to post-conflict peace building, they can do a good deal to help fragile governments and destitute populations find the confidence and resources to make peace last.

The NGO community is extremely varied. Many legitimate—and sometimes contradictory—objectives are being pursued by this galaxy of nonstate actors. New ideas and approaches are being tested all the time. I welcome this. However, in the arena of peace and security, it is essential that the activities of nongovernmental organizations and those of the UN should be complementary, or at least compatible. We can all readily recall the difficulties, misunderstandings, and differences that have arisen from time to time between the world organization and certain NGOs in the context of specific operations. Today it must be stated quite clearly that we must all make an honest and fundamental reappraisal. We want not to lay blame at anyone's door, but to avoid any repetition of events that undermine peace—the objective that together we pursue.

Perhaps the United Nations has not yet fully appreciated the importance of the role of NGOs in the field. Perhaps it does not cooperate enough with institutions on the spot that can provide essential support. But NGOs must also understand the political complexity of any peacekeeping operation. Perhaps in their desire to resolve problems urgently, they do not appreciate how much time is needed to settle any conflict. Perhaps their involvement in activities sometimes prevents them from grasping all particular aspects of a conflict. Perhaps on occasion they are too quick to point the finger, whereas the overriding aim is to reconcile the belligerents. Moreover, the roles—and perspectives—of the UN organization and of the NGOs must be kept distinct. The UN cannot and should not act as an NGO, and vice versa.

I believe that the time has now come to tackle these problems so that we—international civil servants and NGO personnel—together can act still more effectively to promote peace. I have asked my own staff to undertake in-depth analyses of how to better coordinate our common activities. I am confident that NGOs themselves, and especially research efforts like this one, will contribute to these analyses.

This is my sincere expectation. Yet I hope for still more. NGOs must also undertake essential mobilization activities. The mobilization of states and public opinion by NGOs is an essential element in international activities to promote peace. In some cases, the end of the Cold War has had untoward effects. Certain regions of the world have suddenly lost strategic interest for the great powers. As a result, these powers have been sorely tempted to leave those regions to their own devices—to let them sink into economic underdevelopment, or to founder in political disorder.

As Secretary-General of the United Nations, I know that it is sometimes difficult to convince states to commit themselves to essential peacekeeping activities. For them to commit personnel, matériel, and money in the service of peace and in the framework of UN activities, it is often necessary for national public opinion to lead the way. Nongovernmental organizations, in most cases, have helped to clear the way. I wish to state, as clearly as possible—I need the mobilizing power of NGOs.

But here again, each of us must consider the matter in depth. Just as the UN must constantly strive to transcend partisan differences in order to uphold the higher interests of peace, NGOs must secure and maintain their independence with regard to all states—this is a basic condition for their credibility. Nongovernmental organizations are infinitely diverse by virtue of their size, statutes, fields of activity, methods, means, and objectives. It is understandable that states are sometimes tempted to try to utilize or control NGOs in order to place them indirectly in the service of their own national policies.

It is equally obvious that to carry out fully their role as a stimulus for the international community in promoting peace, NGOs, particularly those involved in providing assistance, must not mix humanitarianism and politics. I know that this is not an easy task. It entails constant and continual work. But I also know that I can rely on NGOs to be vigilant. For, let me repeat, independence is essential for NGOs to be able to be full participants in the international peace and policy processes.

Indeed, the mobilization mission that the international community fully expects of nongovernmental organizations will be possible only if the organizations are in their totality representative of international society. In other words, this mobilization can be truly meaningful only if it is based on a third element: activities for democratization.

In *An Agenda for Peace* I had occasion to reflect on the necessary democratization of international relations and of the United Nations. I stressed that, for me, "democracy at all levels is essential to attain peace." Democracy must be the guiding principle both in relations between states and within states themselves. And I believe that nongovernmental organizations have a major role to play in the democratization process. As I said at the outset, the international order in which we conduct our work today is radically different from that of those who drafted the Charter. We find ourselves today within a world system that has profound doubts about its own structures and, strangely, about the most fundamental of these: the very notion of the state. Undoubtedly, the twentieth century will not only have been the century of the downfall of empires—the consequences of which we have yet to fully experience or sustain—but also the century in which doubt was cast on the exclusive claims of the state to jurisdiction over the lives of citizens.

Some peoples seek to reconcile the rational nature of the state with the urges of micronationalism. Elsewhere, it is the very substance of the state that is collapsing. Social integration has become more difficult even within Western societies. Decaying institutions have led to the resurgence or rebirth of primitive ties of solidarity, many of which, alas, seem prone to engender fanaticism and a desire to exclude.

Accordingly, it is necessary to provide men and women in today's world with a framework that will enable them, amidst the practical challenges of their own concrete situations, to mobilize themselves in favor of the great ideals of the international community. It is NGOs that, in most cases, make it possible for these complex and often diffuse aspirations to take form, and to flourish. They float new ideas and approaches. They push and embarrass governments and international secretariats to do their jobs. NGOs also carry out an essential representational role, an essential part of the legitimacy without which no international activity can be meaningful. Often, it is nongovernmental organizations that, on a day-to-day basis, link democracy and peace.

Indeed, the democratic imperative is inseparable from the activities that we must carry out to promote peace. In my opinion, diplomacy that consolidates peace and democracy is of the utmost importance at the close of the twentieth century. I pay close attention to independent analyses and ideas about how to strengthen the link between peace and democracy, and I commend ACUNS for its insights into a research area that cries out for more attention.

I am convinced that, just as human rights are universal, democracy also can be adapted to all cultures. As human rights are the common language of mankind, democracy is the political expression of our common heritage. It must be understood that democracy is not a model to be copied from certain states but a goal to be reached by all peoples.

Nongovernmental organizations have a crucial role to play in this area. They can help develop effective ways of spreading the ideas of peace and democracy. They have issues of justice very high up on their agenda. They can take part in the birth and development of democratic institutions within states. They can serve as vigilant monitors, helping to guarantee respect for democracy throughout the world.

Today we are all searching for an international order that is acceptable to all. Nevertheless, we also know how profoundly ambiguous the very notion of an international order is. For the concept of an international order—if there is one at all—fulfills various functions in the lives of states and peoples. It has a political and an ideological dimension, as well as an economic and a cultural one. It can be used by the powerful to buttress a legal argument, and it can also be used by the weak in support of a militant speech. In short, what we call the international order is both the expression of the present-day balance of power and an idealization of a society in evolution.

In order for every woman and every man in the world to perceive a true stake in the great ideals of the world organization, it is necessary to continue to build nongovernmental organizations and to understand their contribution to global governance. It is also essential to pursue first-rate research and analysis, like that in this volume, to understand the complex interactions among states, non-states, and the United Nations.

Only thus shall we be faithful to the urgent exhortation with which the preamble of the Charter begins: "We the peoples of the United Nations"!

Preface

I owe a profound debt of gratitude to many for making this book possible.

Chapters 1–11 first appeared as a special issue of the *Third World Quarterly* (volume 16, number 3), published in Great Britain in September 1995. The present and expanded version includes a foreword from UN Secretary-General Boutros Boutros-Ghali and an annotated bibliography to guide further reading, but the text reflects the thoughtful guidance of Shahid Qadir, the editor of the *Third World Quarterly*.

The John D. and Catherine T. MacArthur Foundation made it possible for the Academic Council on the United Nations System (ACUNS) to commission the writing of original essays for this undertaking. As part of a three-year research effort to analyze critically important issues for the future of the United Nations, ACUNS hopes that this analysis of the interface between nongovernmental organizations and the world organization will be useful to scholars and to staff members of both NGOs and international secretariats. On behalf of the board of directors, I would like to express our gratitude to the MacArthur Foundation for its generous support.

I would like to record my debt—not only for this volume but also for much of my own professional and personal growth—to my coeditor, Leon Gordenker. Our relationship has evolved from that of a green graduate student and his professor to one of collegiality and friendship. I learned much during our planning efforts for this project, and especially during the drafting of our two chapters in this book. I have enjoyed our conversations and jousting over the last twenty-five years. Every student should have such a mentor.

Melissa Phillips, the program coordinator of ACUNS, manages to keep body and soul together, notwithstanding my best efforts to make her life difficult. The smooth functioning of this program, including the record-setting production of the present volume, owes much to her organizational skills and good humor. Two able Brown University undergraduates worked in the ACUNS office and facilitated my research: I thank Carrie Murphy '96 for her help in the preparation of the first two chapters, and Minh Vo '95 for her assistance in the compilation of the annotated bibliography.

The authors of individual chapters and I profited substantially from numerous reflections from participants who gathered with us in Toronto in April 1995 to comment on drafts. We would like to acknowledge them: Howard Adelman, Chadwick F. Alger, Mary Anderson, Helmut Anheier, L. David Brown, Kenneth Bush, Cynthia Price Cohen, W. Andy Knight, Flora MacDonald, Rama Manai, Kevin McCort, Clement Nwankwo, Ian Smillie, Muriel Smith, Peter Spiro, and Sarah L. Timpson.

I also thank David B. Dewitt and his colleagues in Toronto at York University's Centre for International and Strategic Studies for having hosted the workshop. Canada has of course been a leader in the growth of both multilateralism and NGOs, and it was appropriate that our discussions occurred there.

As with previous books in the Emerging Global Issues series sponsored by Brown University's Thomas J. Watson Jr. Institute for International Studies, this one is interdisciplinary. It combines the thoughtful views of both scholars and practitioners who are in a position to scrutinize the actual performance of the UN system and nongovernmental organizations as they grope with changing world politics in the post–Cold War era. As always, I am indebted to those staff members at the Watson Institute who made possible the accurate and timely production of this book: Fred Fullerton, Mary Lhowe, Amy Langlais, and Jennifer Patrick.

—Thomas G. Weiss

■ Part 1 ■
Theoretical Framework

▪ 1 ▪

Pluralizing Global Governance: Analytical Approaches and Dimensions

LEON GORDENKER AND THOMAS G WEISS

Nongovernmental organisations (NGOs) have in increasing numbers injected unexpected voices into international discourse about numerous problems of global scope. Especially during the last 20 years, human rights advocates, gender activists, developmentalists, groups of indigenous peoples and representatives of other defined interests have become active in political work once reserved for representatives of states. Their numbers have enlarged the venerable, but hardly numerous, ranks of transnational organisations built around churches, labour unions and humanitarian aims.

The United Nations (UN) system provides a convenient, accessible vantage point to observe some of the most active, persuasive NGOs in the world. During the last 50 years, various UN organisations have felt the direct and indirect impact of NGOs. According to the Union of International Associations, the NGO universe includes well over 15 000 recognisable NGOs that operate in three or more countries and draw their finances from sources in more than one country; this number is growing all the time.[1] In their own ways, NGOs and intergovernmental organisations (IGOs) grope, sometimes cooperatively, sometimes competitively, sometimes in parallel towards a modicum of 'global governance'. We define global governance as efforts to bring more orderly and reliable responses to social and political issues that go beyond capacities of states to address individually. Like the NGO universe, global governance implies an absence of central authority, and the need for collaboration or cooperation among governments and others who seek to encourage common practices and goals in addressing global issues. The means to achieve global governance also include activities of the United Nations and other intergovernmental organisations and standing cooperative arrangements among states.

This introductory essay generally discusses the NGO phenomenon. It proposes a definition of NGOs to serve for the purpose of this issue, although much controversy remains about the concept and individual authors may offer refinements. It also provides a general backdrop of historical, legal and political factors for the study. It offers some analytical detail needed for deeper understanding of the phenomenon, and outlines a set of fundamental factors for studying NGOs. It does not assume that NGOs always or even usually succeed in reaching their goals or, if they do, that the result is beneficial for peace, social or personal welfare, or human rights.

The studies that follow all employ the United Nations as a central and reasonably transparent point of observation that has legal and historical underpinnings, and branching activities that reach to the social grass roots. Moreover, NGOs are omnipresent in many aspects of international relations, and they may have become crucial to the UN's future. It is significant that in its essay, 'Reforming the United Nations', the Commission on Global Governance—whose members are virtually all former governmental officials or international civil servants—examined NGOs and observed that 'in their wide variety they bring expertise, commitment, and grassroots perceptions that should be mobilized in the interests of better governance'.[2] NGOs assume centre stage for activities that once 'were irrelevant to the overall plot'.[3] The case studies, each written by an author who has directly observed or experienced NGO activities, examine NGO work on human rights, complex humanitarian emergencies, the United Nations relationship, the global environment, AIDS, the international women's movement, scaling up and scaling down, operational coalitions and state relations. The final essay draws on the specific studies to reach conclusions about the nature, function and prospects for NGOs in relation to the UN system.

The phenomenon

In spite of the growth of the NGO phenomenon, confusion or ignorance persists as to the definition of the participants and the nature of their relationships to the UN system and to one another. Theoretical explorations have tended to be few in number and specific to a particular sector of activity, especially aspects of economic and social development and of the environment. A considerable body of writing has a primarily legal character, which overlooks or understates the richness of NGO activity and politics. Definitional clarity connects closely with concepts of structure, organisation and institutionalisation.

The very site of NGO activity under examination here suggests paradoxes. IGOs join with governments in common undertakings. By definition, NGOs have no formal standing in this realm. Yet they have become exponentially more visible precisely in connection with governments. IGOs were intended to serve governments and to assist in cooperatively reaching goals on which both generally agree. Yet NGOs have now become an integral part of the process of setting agendas for cooperation and in carrying the results not only to governments but to other NGOs and individuals. This study seeks to analyse this process, which requires examining both broad and deep interorganisational relationships.

The term 'nongovernmental organisation' itself is challenged by a host of alternative usages. These include officials, independent sector, volunteer sector, civic society, grassroots organisations, private voluntary organisations, transnational social movement organisations, grassroots social change organisations and non-state actors. Some of these refer to highly specialised varieties and many are synonyms for each other. There seems no quarrel, however, with the notion that these organisations consist of durable, bounded, voluntary relationships among individuals to produce a particular product, using specific techniques. Like-minded organisations may analogously develop lasting relationships to one another and thus form meta-organisations.

Although the term 'non-state actors' may more closely resemble our inclusion of several varieties of meta-organisations that are engaged in transnational relationships, we maintain the term 'nongovernmental organisations' because of its common currency and because this is the term that appears in article 71 of the UN Charter. At the same time, 'non-state actors', according to a Lexis-Nexis search, connotes a host of transnational entities that we deliberately exclude from our inquiry. These include profit-making corporations and banks, criminal elements (both organised crime and terrorists), insurgents, churches in their strictly religious function, transnational political parties and the mass communication media.

A metaphor suggested by Marc Nerfin provides a starting point for locating NGOs in the political realm: the prince represents governmental power and the maintenance of public order; the merchant symbolises economic power and the production of goods and services; and the citizen stands for people's power.[4] As such, the growth of NGOs arises from demands by citizens for accountability from the prince and the merchant. In this perspective, NGOs compete and cooperate with the prince and the merchant for guidance in aspects of social life. They function to 'serve undeserved or neglected populations, to expand the freedom of or to empower people, to engage in advocacy for social change, and to provide services'.[5]

Such an approach contains much that is subjective. Citizens may believe themselves under-served by, or deprived of, rightful power, or they may seek more freedom and advocate change. Doing so implies reform or drastic changes in existing societies. Yet it is equally conceivable that citizens could demand preservation of the status quo as part of the accountability of merchants and princes. The objective point of such approaches, however, lies in the identification of organisation and activity beyond the conventional categories of state and business.

Questions can be raised about the accuracy of this metaphor. Although recognising the legitimacy of each sector of society, it tends to glorify NGOs at the expense of states and markets. NGO 'citizens' are portrayed as vanguards of the just society, as 'princes' and 'merchants' strive to dominate or to make profits. In a study of environmental NGOs in world politics, two authors concluded that the crucial function of NGOs was to create transnational links between state and non-state. NGOs, in this model, politicise the previously unpoliticised and connect the local and the global.[6]

Some NGOs do, in fact, politicise issues otherwise regarded by some as part of the nonpolitical realm, AIDS being a recent case in point. They also bring local experience to bear on international decision making. This may be the most important contribution NGOs have made to global governance. Once again, however, generalisation is dangerous because some NGOs continue to lead a more marginal existence, without links to international bodies. Most NGOs have not managed to break out of the local setting and become engaged in transnational activities.

If NGOs exist and operate above and beneath the level of government, they parallel the pattern of IGOs, particularly those of the UN system. These entities, too, are intended to operate to some degree beyond the states that form them. IGOs do not govern; they attempt to cope with and help manage complex interrelationships and global political, economic and social changes by arranging cooperation of other actors, especially governments. In doing so, they have also

extended their operations below the classical boundaries of governmental autonomy.

Distinctions between IGOs and NGOs rest on legal grounds and tend to
exaggerate the boundary between the two categories. In reality, there are great
variations within, and unclear borderlines between, the two categories. The sheer
number of different types of NGOs, ranging from community-based self-help
groups to international NGOs with staff and budgets surpassing those of many
IGOs, calls for conceptual differentiation and clarification.

Students of international relations have proposed alternative terminologies to
conceptualise transnational relations. James Rosenau, for instance, distinguishes
between sovereignty-bound and sovereignty-free actors.[7] While sociological
rather than legal, this dichotomy can also be misleading insofar as organisations
composed of governments are automatically assumed to be sovereignty-bound
and other actors sovereignty-free. Perhaps it would make more sense to speak of
sovereignty-bound and sovereignty-free behaviour.[8] Regardless of their legal
status, organisations may engage in behaviour that is guided by, or pays heed to,
state sovereignty to varying degrees. Loyalties do not always follow state
borders, and secretariats of IGOs are not necessarily more dominated than
secretariats of big NGOs.

This essay and this journal issue retain the traditional IGO–NGO distinction for
lack of better alternatives, while remaining attentive to sovereignty-bound and
sovereignty-free behaviour by IGOs and NGOs alike. The important puzzle is what
specific roles NGOs may play in transnational networks as intermediary organisations that provide links between state and market, between local and global
levels.

The challenges to sovereignty, according to a recent analytical study, include
four categories of interdependence—trade and finance, security, technology and
ecological problems—and 'the emergence of new social movements with both
local and transnational consciousness'.[9] Both NGOs and IGOs, then, busy themselves with the paradox of global economic and technological integration with
local fragmentation of identities.

 Apart from the function of representing people acting of their own volition,
rather than by some institutional *fiat*, NGOs have other defining characteristics.
They are formal organisations that are intended to continue in existence; they are
thus not *ad hoc* entities. They are or aspire to be self-governing on the basis of
their own constitutional arrangements. They are private in that they are separate
from governments and have no ability to direct societies or to require support
from them. They are not in the business of making or distributing profits. The
NGOs of interest here have transnational goals, operations or connections, and
have active contacts with the UN system.

Not every organisation that claims to be an NGO exactly fits this definition of
a private citizens' organisation, separate from government but active on social
issues, not profit making, and with transnational scope. At least three significant
deviations from these specifications can be identified. The first of these is a
GONGO—government-organised nongovernmental organisation. They achieved
notoriety during the Cold War because many so-called NGOs owed their very
existence and entire financial support to communist governments in the Soviet

bloc or authoritarian ones in the Third World. There were also a few such 'NGOS' in the West, particularly in the USA, where they were often a front for administration activities. Although the Western species may have been more nongovernmental than their Soviet or Third World counterparts, they were not created for the classic purposes of NGOs. Thus, GONGOS can be treated as only tangential to our examination.

The second special type of NGO is QUANGOS (quasi-nongovernmental organisations). For example, many Nordic and Canadian NGOs, a handful of US ones, and the International Committee of the Red Cross (ICRC) receive the bulk of their resources from public coffers. The staffs of such organisations usually assert that as long as their financial support is without strings attached and their own priorities rather than those of donor governments dominate, there is no genuine problem. This is clearly a subjective judgment, but most of these NGOs are relevant for our discussion. Their services aim at internationally-endorsed objectives and their operations are distinct from those of governments, even if their funding is public.

We are at an early stage in understanding how NGOs adapt to changing external and internal environments. In examining recent trends at the domestic level in the USA and Britain, one analyst has gone so far as to call into question voluntary agencies as a 'shadow state'.[10] With more governmental and intergovernmental resources being channelled through international NGOs, the issue of independence—or a willingness to bite the hand that feeds in order to make autonomous programmatic decisions in spite of donor pressures—assumes greater salience. 'One of the real issues for NGOs is how much money can they take from the government while still carrying out advocacy activities that may involve criticizing the source of those funds'.[11]

The third mutant type—the donor-organised NGO (DONGO)—is also distinguished by its source of funds. 'As donors become more interested in NGOs, they also find themselves tempted to create NGOs suited to their perceived needs'.[12] Both governments and the UN system have 'their' NGOs for particular operations and purposes. The United Nations Development Program (UNDP) has been involved in fostering their growth for a decade. The UN itself created local NGOs that contributed to mobilising the population for elections in Cambodia[13] and to de-mining in Afghanistan.[14]

QUANGOS and DONGOS fit well enough in the general definition to warrant inclusion in this study. They aim at internationally-endorsed purposes and have a private status, even if their funding is public. They offer services that clearly fall within the usual range of NGO operations.

Relationship to the UN

A conventional, legally-based way of describing NGOs and their relationship to the United Nations begins with the formal structure that derives from UN Charter article 71.[15] It empowers the Economic and Social Council (ESOSOC) to 'make suitable arrangements for consultation with non-governmental organizations which are concerned with matters within its competence'. It is the only mention of NGOs in the Charter, largely an afterthought stimulated by the Soviet

Union's attempt to put a GONGO on a par with the International Labour Organisation (ILO), another IGO dating to the formation of the League of Nations that constitutionally included representation of labour and management in its governing structure.[16] Early attempts to give meaning to article 71 were heavily coloured by cold-war manoeuvers, but a growing list of organisations with consultative status developed around fairly restricted practices laid down by ESOSOC.[17] Historically speaking, the UN Charter formalises the relationship between NGOs and the world organisation in a significantly different way from the previous experience with international organisation. For example, NGOs were completely excluded from the Hague Conferences in 1899 and 1907. At the League of Nations, NGOs achieved only an informal consultative arrangement that had some effect, however, on proceedings there.[18]

The present legal framework dates from 1968 in the form of the elaborate ESOSOC Resolution 1296 (XLIV). It is now undergoing reexamination in a stately process whose diplomatic tone is heavily coloured by NGO participation. Resolution 1296 retains but refines the earlier UN principle that any international organisation not established by intergovernmental agreement falls into the NGO category. In 11 paragraphs of principles, the text emphasises that NGOs that seek consultative status must have goals within the UN economic and social ambit. These NGOs must also have a representative and international character, and authorisation to speak for members who are supposed to participate in a democratic fashion. The text requires submission of data from organisations on their budgets and the sources of their financing. It also promotes a vague hierarchy by encouraging the formation of umbrella organisations composed of organisations with similar purposes that pool their advice to the council and transmit results of consultations from national organisations. The process of admission to consultative status is supervised by the Committee on Non-Governmental Organizations, elected each year by ESOSOC from among its member governments, 19 of which provide the actual personnel.

Consultations remain largely under ESOSOC control, in contrast to the fuller rights of participation available to IGOs in the UN system. NGOs can be granted status in one of three categories, designated as 'I', 'II', and 'the roster'. Those in category I are supposed to have broad economic and social interests and geographical scope; those in category II have more specialised interests. The remainder of accepted applicants are listed in a roster for organisations that may make occasional contributions. Category I organisations have the broadest access to the council. They may propose ESOSOC agenda items to the Committee on Non-Governmental Organizations, which in turn can ask the secretary-general to include their suggestions on the provisional list. This is far from a right to submit agenda items. Like category II NGOs, category I organisations may send observers to all meetings and may submit brief written statements on their subject matter. The council has the right to ask for written statements from any of the consultative NGOs, and it may invite category I and II organisations to hearings, which, in fact, are rare. Other rules set out limitations on NGOs in dealing with ESOSOC subsidiaries and international conferences summoned by it.

The UN Department of Public Information simultaneously developed a parallel set of relationships with NGOs under its own legislative authority.[19] This emphasises the information-disseminating function of NGOs, rather than any input in policy formation. It includes briefings, mailings, access to documentation and an NGO Resources Center in New York.[20]

Both of these consultative arrangements gave birth to meta-organisations representing NGOs. Some of those in contact with ESOSOC soon formed a Conference of Non-Governmental Organizations in Consultative Status, which adopted the acronym CONGO. It takes no substantive positions, but concentrates on procedural matters and the promotion of better understanding of the ESOSOC agenda. For the organisations in the public information orbit, an NGO/Department of Public Information (DPI) Executive Committee serves as liaison.[21]

These consultative arrangements signal the presence of two trends. One of them indicates the almost unprecedented establishment of 'formal relations between "interest" groups and an intergovernmental body'.[22] Even though this relationship was conditioned by the Cold War, both in the formation of the list of accredited organisations and the attention given them by the largely diplomatic ESOSOC, it offered some access to the UN system by NGOs. The fact that this access was seen as worthwhile by NGOs may be inferred from the growth in category I listings from seven in 1948 to 41 in 1991, and in category II organisations from 32 to 354 during the same period, while an even faster expansion took place on the roster.[23]

The other trend looks towards the vast broadening of scope and reach of the programmes reviewed in ESOSOC. Although this organ by itself has never achieved the influence implied by its place in the UN Charter,[24] reports submitted from elsewhere in the system make it a central source of documentation and information. Senior officers of other IGOs also appear as authors, and those related to ESOSOC in the UN system make statements. The subject matter covers not only old-style international cooperation, but also takes in new subjects such as the environment, an enlarged operation to succour refugees and disaster victims, and a variegated web of economic and social development projects.[25]

Furthermore, the ESOSOC machinery and the international secretariats that serve it are intimately involved in the organisation of large-scale international conferences on special themes, such as population, the status of women and the environment. Such gatherings, in which governments are represented by senior officials, attract heavy NGO interest. The UN Conference on the Environment and Development in Rio de Janeiro in 1992, for example, registered 1 400 NGO representatives who formally participated in a Global Forum and informally did their best as lobbyists. Only a minority of these NGOs had official consultative status with ESOSOC.

Consequently, over the years ever more officials and members of NGOs have come into contact with UN affairs or see some reason to seek such connections. In addition, the formation of NGO alliances and coalitions among them—the UN has picked up social science jargon and calls them 'networks'—has become a routine response to activities in the UN system.[26]

A salient phenomenon

Evidence of an NGO presence around the IGOs of the UN system alone hardly demonstrates what the Club of Rome has called 'the barefoot revolution' and the Worldwatch Institute has called 'people power'.[27] Instead, both external and internal factors can be cited in what has become a salient phenomenon in international policy making and execution.

End of the Cold War

The first and perhaps most important explanation of NGO expansion is the end of the Cold War. With the breakdown of ideological and social orthodoxy, the reluctance of many, perhaps most, diplomats and UN practitioners to interact with nongovernmental staff evaporated. This has opened new possibilities of communication and cooperation within decision-making processes. With the waning of East–West tensions, the United Nations has become a better forum for the reconciliation of views among governments on the old geopolitical compass of North-South-East-West. The UN also has become an obvious forum for discussions between governments and NGOs. 'Before it was not possible to have any contact with nongovernmental organizations in the Soviet Union, for example, because this would be seen as neo-imperialist intervention', said UN Secretary-General Boutros Boutros-Ghali. 'On the other side, it was called communist intervention'.[28]

The explanation goes beyond procedures. Issues recognised in the revealing light of the post-Cold War world as extending beyond and below state borders also needed and demanded the strengths of NGOs. As part of a major reappraisal of the role of the state and of alternative ways to solve problems, NGOs are emerging as a special set of organisations that are private in their form but public in their purpose.[29] The environment, grassroots development, more equitable trade relations, human rights and women's issues had been on NGO agendas throughout the last two or three decades. But now they have assumed new vitality. Additional pressures for NGO involvement grew around such new issues as investment needs of the erstwhile socialist bloc and ethnonationalism, with its accompanying flood of refugees and internally displaced persons. These issues simply could not be addressed solely through intergovernmental operations and recommendations characteristic of the United Nations.[30]

Moreover, when high politics and security, particularly over nuclear issues, dominated the international agenda, NGOs were at a comparative disadvantage. They obviously had no weapons and only limited access to people wielding decision-making power. As low politics rose on the international agenda, NGOs that had promoted relevant policies and actions energetically exploited or expanded direct access to policymakers. For example, NGOs not only have a capacity for direct action but they may also bring advanced knowledge to bear on such issues as gender, the environment, AIDS, relief assistance, human rights and community development.

Technological developments →powers

Technological developments represent a second explanation for the increasing salience of NGOs in UN activity. '[New] technologies increasingly render information barriers either ineffective or economically infeasible'.[31] Governments that are hostile to NGOs fail in their sometimes zealous efforts to prevent information flows, interaction and networking through the Internet and fax communications. Electronic means have literally made it possible to ignore borders and to create the kinds of communities based on common values and objectives that were once almost the exclusive prerogative of nationalism.[32]

Modern communications technology is independent of territory. 'By providing institutional homes in the same way that states have accommodated nationalism', one observer suggests, 'NGOs are the inevitable beneficiaries of the emergence of the new global communities'.[33] Consequently, global social change organisations (GSCOs), another study claims, 'may represent a unique social invention of the postmodern, postindustrial, ie information-rich and service-focused, globally-linked world system'.[34]

Growing resources →

A third explanatory factor can be found in the growing resources and professionalism of NGOs. Both indigenous and transnational NGOs have recently attracted additional resources from individual donors, governments and the UN system. In 1994 over 10% of public development aid ($8 billion) was channelled through NGOs, surpassing the volume of the combined UN system ($6 billion) without the Washington-based financial institutions. About 25% of US assistance is channelled through NGOs; at the Social Summit in Copenhagen, Vice-President Al Gore committed Washington to increasing this figure to 50% by the turn of the century.[35] Western governments have increasingly turned towards NGO projects on the basis of a reputation for cost-effectiveness.

This trend fits well with the progressively declining funds for foreign assistance and generally with domestic pressures in donor countries to cut back on overseas commitments. In fact, two prominent analysts have recently written: 'The increase of donor-funded NGO relief operations and Western disengagement from poor countries are two sides of the same coin'.[36]

Interorganisational relations in the NGO realm

Networking is perhaps a cliché in the lexicon of transnational organisation, but it aptly points to a key function of many NGOs: the process of creating bonds, sometimes formal but primarily informal, among like-minded individuals and groups across state boundaries. New communications technologies are helping to foster the kinds of interaction and relationships that were once unthinkable except through expensive air travel. Scaling up certain kinds of transnational efforts from neighbourhoods and regions to the global level and scaling down to involve grassroots organisations are no longer logistic impossibilities, but may be treated as institutional imperatives.

Claims about NGOs' eclipsing the role of the state are exaggerated, but significant change is nonetheless taking place regarding their weight in world politics. NGOs may 'create conditions that facilitate the formation of international institutions' and 'reinforce the norms promoted by these institutions through public education as well as through organized attempts to hold states accountable to these, and enhance institutional effectiveness by reducing the implementation costs associated with international institutions'. Moreover, the potential for enhanced networking increases the 'capacity to monitor states' compliance with international agreements, promote institutional adaptation and innovation, and challenge failed institutions'.[37]

NGOs that have relations with IGOs go far beyond the officially-sanctioned diplomatic networks and the narrowly-defined contacts implied by a legalistic approach. NGOs are based upon interpersonal ties and relationships among people with similar convictions, goals and interests. The result is a web of personal connections that do not fit within a formal, legal framework.

NGOs employ a variety of devices to increase the persuasiveness and efficiency of their work in conjunction with IGOs. Some of these have formal structures, while others rely primarily on interpersonal relationships. Some are constructed for service with only one UN organisation, while others have a more general scope across the UN system. Four types of interorganisational devices that involve NGOs—formal bridging groups, federations, UN coordinating bureaus and connections to governments—can be identified. Aside from these fairly defined structures, many NGOs coordinate their activities with others for a specific issue or within a particular geographical area. These occurrences may be formal but are probably usually informal and may last only briefly. There is a variety of mechanisms for NGOs to relate collectively to the UN system. Probably the best known coordination mechanisms are represented by the World Bank within its own investment or aid projects, or by the United Nations Development Program within a country-wide framework. Many NGOs coordinate their own activities for a specific issue or within a particular geographical area through formal coalitions and these, too, should be considered in understanding NGOs and the United Nations.

Some NGOs have a long institutional history or are part of federations of the organisations that they represent. Others get together only for particular issues for short periods. In either form, NGO coalitions seek to represent the views of their constituent members and to pursue shared goals. Examples would be the International Council of Voluntary Agencies (ICVA) in Geneva, originally for European NGOs but now composed primarily of Third World ones; Inter-Action in Washington, DC for US-based NGOs; or a gathering of the various Oxfams or country chapters of Médecins Sans Frontières (MSF). Within a recipient country where UN organisations operate, there sometimes exist umbrella groups for indigenous NGOs—for example, Coordinación in Guatemala facilitates contacts between external donors and local groups working with uprooted populations. Within a region there can also exist a similar pooling of efforts—for example, Concertación links development NGOs in five Central American countries.

Formal coalitions of NGOS

A main function of formal coalitions of NGOs is to develop as far as possible or to harmonise common positions for issues. Some examples are the lobbying efforts within the United States for the extension of Public Law 480, the source of foodstuffs for relief and development; or the search for a common stance by women's groups for international conferences on human rights in Vienna and on population in Cairo. Concrete examples include an invitation to ICVA to address the Executive Committee of the UN High Commissioner for Refugees (UNHCR), and a request to EarthAction (one of the largest global NGO networks with over 700 member associations in about 125 countries) to put forward views to the Commission on Global Governance.

These formal coalitions may attempt headquarters-level coordination of activities within a certain region or in relationship to a specific crisis, as for example, Somalia and Rwanda. Member NGOs of formal groups are not, however, bound by organisational decisions, and dissenters are free to follow their own counsel or take individual positions on policies of IGOs.

'Bridging organisations', created for service in developing countries, seek on one hand to create both horizontal links across economic and social sectors and vertical links between grassroots organisations and governments. On the other hand, they try to form similar links to external donors, whether governmental, intergovernmental or nongovernmental.

Constituent NGOs working in different sectors can interact in these bridging organisations that furnish what otherwise would be absent—a forum for discussion and cooperation. As a consequence, grassroots groups get a voice and attempt to influence policy-making. Bridging organisations function as a conduit for ideas and innovations, a source of information, a broker of resources, a negotiator of deals, a conceptualiser of strategies and a mediator of conflicts. Such organisation, it is argued, helps lead to sustainable development.[38] Examples of such bridging organisations include the Asian NGO Coalition for Agrarian Reform and Rural Development (ANGOC Asia), the Society for Participatory Research in Asia (PRIA), Savings Development Movement (SDM, Zimbabwe), and the Urban Popular Movement and the Coalition of Earthquake Victims (MUP and CUD, Mexico City).

Relief operations, and to a lesser extent development efforts, have drawn together in-country consortia of local and international NGOs with the support of donors. These groupings are often shaped to accommodate a division of labour for a geographical region or for a function like transport.[39] The Khartoum-based Emergency Relief Desk, for example, was backed by a number of European religious NGOs and then reorganised and adapted to help crossborder operations into Eritrea and Tigray.[40] In the southern Sudan, the combined Agency Relief Team was established in the mid-1980s as a relief transport consortium.[41]

Transnational federations of NGOS

Save the Children, Oxfam, Amnesty International, MSF, the International Federation of Red Cross and Red Crescent Societies (IFRC) and CARE are examples of large NGOs with a global scope and autonomous chapters in individual countries. Organisational members of a federation share an overall image and ideology. For example, Oxfam's ideology sets out a grassroots development orientation that all its national affiliates employ. But the national groups are responsible for their own fundraising and projects. Although members of such federations meet periodically at both the management and working levels to discuss common problems, each national member maintains autonomy.

Federations of NGOs try to, and frequently do, present a united front on the policies that they advocate in IGOs and in their field operations. Yet this is not always possible because of differences in view and leadership styles, and the needs in respective country branch offices and headquarters. Federations differ in how much control they can exert over their branches and how much branch activity can be coordinated with worldwide partners as well as how they finance administrative costs for common activities.

For example, Save the Children US has limited coordination with its European partners, and there is little consensus about how to address this rift. Save the Children UK does not necessarily wish to increase coordination, but the US headquarters seeks to increase interaction to improve cost-effectiveness. Also, some Save the Children branches and projects have different emphases and agendas. For example, Save the Children Sweden acts as a sort of amnesty international for children, focusing on child abuse and child advocacy to a greater extent than other chapters do.

Large federations with headquarters and many branches face the tension of accountability versus autonomy and independent action by their many satellites. Friction rises when branch offices stray from a supposedly common vision of a federation or engage in controversial or unprofessional activities. These could have negative repercussions for other chapters. At the same time, imposing constraints on branch offices may be impossible and may risk sacrificing independent and innovative thinking and acting.

UN coordination of NGOs

In contrast to the conventional Roman wisdom of divide and conquer, UN officials concerned about the proliferation of nongovernmental entities have responded with the attitude: 'If you can't beat 'em, organize 'em'. The efforts by the World Bank, UNHCR and the UNDP to structure project relationships are probably the best known.[42] UN organisations vary not only in how they coordinate their activities with NGOs but also in the extent to which they work with NGOs in the first place. When no formal structures for coordination exist, cooperation often proceeds on a case-by-case basis. Even with the existence of formal mechanisms, coordination is often *ad hoc*, based on individual relationships. Especially in crises, coordination may occur spontaneously. Nevertheless, NGOs are notorious for their independence; coordinating NGOs is 'like herding cats', according to one UN official.

Cooperation is not cost-free for NGOs. From a logical management perspective, for example, the current systems for development cooperation or humanitarian action have too many moving parts.[43] Greater collaboration among the various agencies would appear at first glance to be helpful in limiting random activity, overlap and duplication. Yet, assuming it could be arranged, even improved coordination may involve significant opportunity costs for NGOs in terms of use of personnel, resources or even diminished credibility because of their association with the United Nations. There is no guarantee of greater effectiveness or savings. As James Ingram, the former executive director of the World Food Programme (WFP), has written: 'The appearance of improved coordination at the center is not necessarily a factor in more effective and timely interventions in the field'.[44] Hence, formal UN-led efforts at coordination, comprehensive or not, are not viewed by NGO leaders as always desirable.

Such coordinating bodies in fact have a mixed record for viability and effectiveness. They have often struggled to find funding, a task that is more than a mere forum for endless NGO meetings.[45] If the main concern is effectiveness, then both formal and informal coordinating should be able to increase contact and collaboration among NGOs (exchange ideas and information); provide genuine services to members; improve liaison with governments and the UN system; and increase resources available for NGOs.

An intriguing question arises as to why certain operational IGOs—observers point to UNICEF and UNHCR—cooperate easily with NGOs while others experience considerably more difficulty. The structures, charters and goals of these UN organisations play a part, but more intangible elements such as organisational culture are among the plausible explanations.

A significant number of staff in both UNICEF and UNHCR have themselves worked in NGOs and appreciate their strengths and weaknesses. The rough-and-ready, roll-up-the-sleeves approach to disasters also makes cooperation seem more necessary and sensible than in other contexts, where the lack of an emergency permits more time and leisure for turf battles.

On a more political level, one possible explanation for easy cooperation is complementary tasks. For example, in election monitoring within UN-orchestrated operations in El Salvador and Cambodia, NGOs could more easily make public pronouncements about irregularities than could the civilian or military staff of the UN Observer Mission in El Salvador (ONUSAL) and the UN Transition Authority in Cambodia (UNTAC). In such circumstances, rather than rivalry, a sensible division of labour appeared between NGOs and IGOs. For some of the same reasons, discernible complementarity has developed between Amnesty International or Human Rights Watch and the United Nations. Because NGOs can push harder and more openly for more drastic changes, which can then be codified over time by the UN, a 'symbiotic' relationship has developed in the context of establishing new human rights standards and implementing existing ones.[46]

Some participants view the coordination effort launched in the early 1990s by UNHCR and ICVA as promising. It is titled PAR in AC (Partners in Action) and is intended to 'enhance dialogue and understanding between UNHCR; to facilitate closer collaboration and increase the combined capacity to respond to the global refugee problem and … the problem of internal displacement'. PAR in AC aims to 'enhance and improve future NGO/UNHCR collaboration', and is motivated by UNHCR's belief that NGOs have a 'community-based approach [that] is an asset in bridging the gap between relief and development'.[47] Behind the official language lies the intense field experience of Bosnia and elsewhere in the former Yugoslavia and northern Iraq as well as the belief among some leading participants that earlier contact mechanisms delivered less than was hoped.

NGOs and governments

The relationships between governments and NGOs take several forms. Some of these are adversarial, as certain NGOs criticise and hope to change governmental policies. Other relationships are cooperative and businesslike. Host governments regulate activities by NGOs through domestic legislation and activities of international NGOs by administrative procedures (for example, visas and foreign exchange procedures). Donor governments hire NGOs to implement projects and sign contracts subject to national legislation. NGOs may lobby governments for altruistic reasons, such as new international agreements and policies, and for more self-serving reasons, such as increased budgetary allocations for their own work. In the process, they must abide by national regulations governing such activity. In some extraordinary situations, NGOs have provided services to citizens that are normally expected from governments. For example, the primary education system in the north of Sri Lanka was coordinated largely by NGOs after the government system collapsed following the onset of civil war in 1987; and the Bangladesh Rural Action Committee (BRAC) is responsible for 35 000 schools.

In general, throughout much of the Third and former Second World, the decline of oppressive regimes and the rise of democracy mainly since the end of the Cold War has tempered the former automatic hostility by governments toward the activities of local and international NGOs. Previously, NGO–government relationships were often ones of benign neglect at best, or of suspicion and outright hostility at worst.

A significant experiment

One noteworthy international experiment in combining intergovernmental and nongovernmental action in a coordinated policy and resource mobilisation for refugees and internally displaced populations took place in the early 1990s when the International Conference on Refugees in Central America (CIREFCA) brought together UN organisations and the NGO community.[48] With UNHCR in the lead, such organisations as UNDP and WFP were brought into greater contact with external and local NGOs.

Actual and potential beneficiaries were involved from the outset in project design, implementation, and monitoring. The process induced governmental, intergovernmental and nongovernmental organisations to forge new relationships with one another as well as with dissident and insurgent groups outside internationally recognised governments. This wider orchestration also took into consideration the activities of the various UN peacekeeping and peacemaking operations.

Finances, size and independence

The relationship between governments and NGOs includes many complexities and rapid changes that sometimes run parallel to the pluralism permitted by governments. Most governments that decide to do so have little difficulty in crippling NGO activities or favouring those that increase governmental capacity either to do harm or to provide popular benefits. Foreign-based NGOs may be particularly vulnerable to host government pressure since they need permission to bring in personnel and goods, such as automobiles and communications equipment. Relief NGOs that must import large quantities of supplies, as was repeatedly demonstrated in the Horn of Africa during the two decades beginning in the 1970s, can encounter direct limitations emanating from political authorities, either in the host government or in insurgent territory.

At the same time, some NGOs operating outside of their base countries have reached formidable proportions. Agencies such as CARE or Oxfam have enough prestige not to be easily or silently dismissed with the wave of an authoritative hand. Some have programmes that, once begun, burrow deep into the social fabric. To liquidate such activities can cost a government popularity and even stimulate resistance. Moreover, development NGOs may have close working relationships and direct support from IGOs, thereby raising the potential that a local incident of interference can become a matter of unpleasant discussion in an international forum. In addition, other NGOs have impressive bases of popular support. Repressive governments, for instance, intensely dislike the activities of human rights monitoring groups and try to inhibit them. Yet such interference is also restrained by the sure knowledge that these groups have developed the ability to persuade powerful governments in Western countries. Thus, a government or an insurgent group that acts in an unrestrained manner against human rights monitors may soon be faced with formal protests and action through bilateral or intergovernmental channels.

The vigour of NGO activities may ultimately be determined by the levels and sources of their finances. Some of the largest NGOs, such as the International Committee of the Red Cross and CARE, rely on contributions from governments of rich countries for most of their operating funds. As much as 90% of financing emanates from governments. The World Bank has entered into numerous partnerships with DONGOs that execute projects financed by the International Bank for Reconstruction and Development (IBRD). In 1993, for example, 30% of Bank projects had provisions for NGO participation.[49] The UNDP has changed policy over the last decade so that local NGOs are receiving allocations in the Indicative Planning Figures (IPFs) that used to be exclusively reserved for governments. The depth of such relationships, however, may vary from formal to close collaboration in phases from planning to execution.

Many organisations of the UN system routinely rely upon both international and indigenous NGOs for the delivery of relief and development assistance. For instance, in northern Iraq since the April 1991 Kurdish crisis, NGOs (including the Red Cross) have been responsible for 40% of refugees, whereas the UN system has been responsible for about 30%.[50]

Putting an exact dollar value on these resources is not easy. It would be hard to prove the contention that '[i]n net terms, NGOs now collectively transfer more resources to the South than the World Bank'.[51] Over time, however, shifts of a significant magnitude have taken place. During the last two decades, private grants from the 21 Western countries of the Development Assistance Committee (DAC) to DAC-country NGOs for use in developing countries have grown dramatically. NGO activities represent well over 10% (perhaps even 13%) of official development assistance (ODA) in comparison with only 0.2% in 1970.[52] Particularly over the last decade, when ODA has stagnated, NGOs have positioned themselves for a greater proportional share of total resources. Moreover, the visibility and credibility of such efforts have increased dramatically.

From another direction, private foundations have increasingly stimulated the growth of NGOs and added to the knowledge base for their work.[53] Favourable tax laws and a tradition of voluntarism have made this influence particularly important in the USA, where the family names of Ford, Rockefeller, MacArthur and Pew are familiar philanthropic entities. In fact, 5500 independent foundations, not including those from corporations, have assets in excess of $2 million or give grants of at least $200 000 per year.[54] Such institutions as the Volkswagen Foundation attest to the significance of this type of source in other parts of the Western world as well. Although the exact numbers are difficult to gauge, many directly finance operational activities, institution-building and research by NGOs at home and in connection with partners in other countries.

All NGOs and foundation donors operate under some governmental, donor-imposed or doctrinal restrictions. Especially in the USA, foundations owe their prosperity to provisions of tax laws that could be changed. They are also forbidden to act in electoral and other political spheres, and may not lobby in the way that special interest groups do. As for NGOs receiving outside governmental or IGO financing, these set out in programme proposals their plans for using funds. Proposals for programmes that ran counter to donor policies would hardly be likely to succeed.

Conversely, NGOs dispose of some persuasiveness in relations with donors, whether official or private. No donor would wish to invest in a programme that was foredoomed to failure. NGOs can thus signal their estimate of the practicality of policies. Moreover, once embarked on the execution of an agreed project, the NGO is in a good position to suggest policy and methodological changes, if only because the donors prefer their funds to be used in ways that can be defended against criticism.

Theories of international cooperation

Despite the rapidly rising curve of NGO numbers and activity in the context of the UN system, a firm consensus about their nature and function remains elusive. Consequently, some generalising about NGOs that operate in the international environment is necessary for a better understanding of NGO roles, but it is larded with uncertainty. The rest of this essay takes up some of the theoretical approaches that pertain to NGOs and sets out a set of dimensions that may be useful in drawing conclusions.

In general, theoretical approaches to explain international cooperation provide little specific insight into the nature and function of NGOs. Most are based on the state as the only noteworthy entity in international cooperation, and provide no category for considering the possibility that NGOs are significant actors in their own right.

States as actors

The dominant approaches employed by governmental representatives, international officials and academic scholars to transnational cooperation emphasise states as the basic units of analysis.[55] Officials usually leave this assumption in implicit form, although international civil servants constantly underline the role of member states in their organisations. Academic scholars of this persuasion quite explicitly use the state as the basic counter, although biodiversity is increasingly obvious for a category that cannot be captured by narrow nations.[56]

Since the state stands by definition, not to speak of ideology, as an autonomous organisation in a universe where only consensual limits to action are accepted as binding, an explanation is needed as to why they sometimes cooperate. Two main possibilities, both based on promotion of national interest, emerge.

The first is that cooperation among states is actually induced by the use of persuasion or coercion by one state over another.[57] This line of argument accords with analyses that set out mainly military power as the final arbiter of international relations. No state finds it in its interest to be expunged or defeated militarily, and therefore it eventually bows to superior force, whether it is latent or applied. Thus, a hierarchy based on military calculation in fact reigns among nominally equal states. This approach, incidentally, accords with much of the rhetoric of diplomats and foreign policy specialists.

The second explanation relies implicitly or explicitly on a market rather than a military calculation.[58] States cooperate in the search for material advantages. Thus, they reckon whether there is more to gain from cooperation than from withdrawal or conflict. If they do not cooperate, in all but a few instances coercion to do so is absent.

This line of reasoning is the basis for the extensive academic theorising about international regimes.[59] These institutions for international governance, based on the voluntary acceptance of rules of state conduct in regard to specific issues, do not require explicit international organisations or even formal international accords, but they continue over extended periods of time as the actual guides to state policy. Thus, international regimes do not necessarily always have much relationship to the organisations of the UN system, even though their concerns may overlap.

Paralleling these approaches is the conventional legal approach to NGOs.[60] This depends on the exercise of authority by states, on the consent of states as the basis of application of rules, and on the notion of some type of self-interest as the underlying reason for acceding to cooperative arrangements. International organisations are treated ultimately as creatures of national self-interest, however and by whomever that is defined. NGOs fit into this scheme of thinking as entities whose activities have to be regulated to conform to the broader undertakings of states.

Even if it is accepted that the state is the primary unit of international relations, the political and legal explanations based on self-interest leave little room for autonomous NGO activity. If such theoretical approaches are made more sophisticated by incorporating considerations of domestic political processes as the determinant of national interest, a focus on transnational NGO activity in shaping decisions is usually left distant or obscured. Moreover, the national self-interest approaches imply a crisp consensus within governments as to the degree of international cooperation and its desired outcome. Whether this can be demonstrated empirically is subject to doubt. Finally, the implicit emphasis of rational decision making on the basis of national interest draws attention away from the social bases of the state. The state is an abstraction. Governments, not states, actually make decisions to cooperate or not. Governments consist of people, a point that NGOs obviously do not neglect.

Social approach

A different and less widely accepted approach to international cooperation emphasises the social bases of politics.[61] It begins with the proposition that governments are social organs made up of people who have complex relationships with other parts of their own and other societies. It is presumed that these relationships may have a bearing on the decisions taken by governments as the vital representation of states to involve themselves in international cooperation.

Among such approaches, organisation theory has general application but has been infrequently used as the basis for research on international cooperation.[62] This theory abandons the traditional view of organisations as formal and self-contained units. It is concerned with relations between formally autonomous organisations with diffuse accountability and division of responsibility, whether in the national or international arenas. Such relations typically involve inter-organisational bargaining where informal organisation is of the essence.

Organisation theory posits that organisations are made up of people who work together to produce a particular product by means of a relevant technique. From this base, propositions can be developed to analyse at least subgovernmental units, if not governments as a whole, as well as international agencies and NGOs. It asks what people are involved, what joint work they perform, what methods they use, and what emerges from their work. Such analyses can also trace changes taking place in organisations and their products.

Organisations, moreover, can be bound together to form new organisations, or what could be termed meta-organisations. International organisations such as the UN system, for instance, can be viewed as such meta-organisations, as can federations of NGOs. This notion necessarily involves interorganisational relationships that have great importance at the international level and in particular in connection with NGOs. But these relationships are carried on by people, rather than by abstractions, just as is the case within organisations made up only of individuals.

A commonplace of organisational analysis holds that informal links among organisational participants congeal alongside formal structures. This is a phenomenon that every diplomat and political leader acknowledges by seeking personal contacts with people who have ability to persuade within their own circles. Informal links often prove to be essential to organisational work, adaptation to changing conditions and continued existence. In transnational organisational relationships, which include those formed by NGOs, it is natural that a web of informal links develops to confront issues defined in the formal structures.

This points in the direction of network analysis, which focuses on the links between interdependent actors. Formal organisations—private and public, national and international—form the foundation of transnational networks. However, participants in networks are not organisations in their entirety but certain individuals in the constituent organisations. The interface between organisations consists primarily of boundary-role occupants. As 'activist brokers' between their organisation and its environment, boundary-role occupants must represent the organisation to its environment, and also represent the environment to their constituents.[63]

Students of networks have pointed to the centrality of so-called linking-pin organisations, which occupy central positions in terms of being reachable from and being able to reach most other organisations in the network. Serving as brokers and communication channels between organisations in the networks, linking-pin organisations are the 'nodes through which a network is loosely joined'.[64] One research question is to what extent NGOs have been able to assume linking-pin positions in transnational networks.

The sophisticated conceptual device of the social network has found little use in research on international cooperation. What exactly are the durable sets of relationships among individuals who are in a position to exchange information, resources and prestige? Individuals in this position in interorganisational relationships can usually be described as occupying boundary roles. In that role, they can easily be engaged in the activities characterised as a social network, which affect their own organisations as well. Thus, a transnational social network would depend on persons from different countries and organisations who engage in their relationships over a considerable period. The network, then, is defined by what it does, not by an organisational form, defined structure or material appurtenances.

In brief, networks represent flat or horizontal organisational forms in contrast to vertical ones based on hierarchical authority. Networks, in other words, rest on the coexistence of autonomy and interdependence. Whereas hierarchy is the natural organising principle of states, and markets are the natural organising principle of business organisations, networks are readily associated with NGOs.[65] By positioning themselves centrally in informal networks, NGOs can exert an influence above and beyond their weak formal status. In the international arena, these possibilities are enhanced because effective cooperation among states operating in an anarchic environment often implies precisely the kind of informality and network-building that work well for NGOs. Although network analysis requires the assembly of detailed data and sometimes lengthy observation, it would seem a most promising technique for analysing the function of transnational NGOs.

Another socially-oriented analytical concept that has been applied to international cooperation is that of the epistemic community.[66] This notion seeks to explain changes in the programs and doctrines of international organisations through the operation of transnational sets of experts. Their common vision on the proper outlook on a set of issues—protection of the environment has featured most prominently—underlies their efforts to capture existing organisations and redirect their work. Their persuasiveness derives from consensual knowledge growing from advanced technological competence. It eventually convinces other leaders and organisational managers. This concept, too, would appear to be relevant to a better understanding of NGOs, although its emphasis on technological expertness may limit its appropriateness to a narrow range of issues.

An even less formally organized type of participant in international policy and administrative processes is composed of prominent persons who, by dint of expertise, experience, office or other distinguishing characteristic, earn deference. They may be asked to serve on honorific official commissions and as highly expert technical consultants on defined issues. Many have high visibility and credibility from their previous tenure in senior positions in governments and parliaments, or from their reputations as insightful intellectuals. Some work on their own accounts, others for governments, corporations, universities and specialist firms. Some of the assignments are ongoing, some are for a fixed period. Their tasks are sometimes performed for immediate consumption by UN organisations but also with an eye on other consumers in a broader public. Examples are the members of the UN Advisory Committee on the Peaceful Uses of Atomic Energy (appointed by Dag Hammarskjöld) or Max van der Stoel, former foreign minister of the Netherlands, who was appointed by the Commission on Human Rights as Rapporteur on Human Rights in Iraq. Such 'influentials', with or without official appointments, are often consulted informally by opinion leaders and national and international officials.

An increasingly common practice has been to ask such prominent individuals to serve as members of high-visibility *ad hoc* commissions—those headed by Willy Brandt, Olaf Palme, Gro Harlem-Brundtland, Sadruddin Aga Khan, Julius Nyerere and, most recently, by Ingmar Carlsson and Sonny Ramphal are perhaps the best known.[67] They constitute visible groups that come together for short-term specialised advisory assignments. Their work has much in common with the efforts of educational NGOs. Other groups of less prominent professionals—not just Médecins Sans Frontières but also, for instance, architects and physicists without borders—attempt to make their collective views known in international policy circles and among broader publics. Parliamentarians for Global Action (PGA) is one such pooling of politicians who have a primary interest in global problem-solving and in the United Nations.

Broad roles for NGOs

These theoretical approaches to international cooperation could aid in analysing NGO activity and in reaching conclusions, but none of them appears fully apt for an investigation that emphasises concrete activities and observation born of participation. Rather, it might be better to base such an examination on a close scrutiny of goals, relationships among various organisations and operating methods. This may eventually lead to more general conclusions about the weight and scope of NGO participation in international cooperation. An initial sorting, suggested to the authors of the case studies that follow in this issue, sets out two general roles that reflect both goals and operating methods. Few if any NGOs are likely at all times to set out goals and use methods that are confined exclusively to these discrete categories, but this broad typology can help point out their main thrust.

Operational roles

At least part of the activities of most NGOs falls into the category of operations. Operational NGOs are the most numerous and have the easiest fundraising task. They are more and more central to international responses in the post-cold war world. Most NGOs provide some services, if only to their members, while others concentrate on providing them to other organisations and individuals. The delivery of services is the mainstay of most NGO budgets and the basis for enthusiastic support from a wide range of donors. Such services include intangible technical advice as well as more tangible resources for relief, development and other purposes. Many NGOs operate development programmes; they have become increasingly active in migration and disaster relief, which may now be their most important operational or advisory activities in total financial terms.

Bilateral and multilateral government organisations are relying upon NGOs more and more as project subcontractors. Some of these contractors, known as DONGOs, could be dedicated organisations and even disappear after the conclusion of a project. Others have long histories as contractors. NGOs recover their staff costs and overheads in addition to the direct costs of the products that they deliver but, unlike private contractors, they do not make a profit to redistribute since there are no shareholders. Some NGO managers are delighted with this trend since it expands the scope of their activities with increased resources. Others, however, are troubled about being exploited by governments or intergovernmental organisations rather than remaining institutions with their own unique purposes and independent wherewithal.

Such contractual relationships on the one hand offer opportunities to NGOs to persuade donors to adopt their approaches; but on the other hand they include powerful incentives in the form of financial support to accede to the views of donor organisations. The key to operational integrity is being a partner and not simply a contractor. The former term connotes authentic collaboration and mutual respect, and it accepts the autonomy and pluralism of NGOs. Such relationships are rare, more an aspiration than a reality.[68] It is difficult to imagine NGOs enjoying authentic collaboration and genuine partnership with large and powerful agencies. However, in certain circumstances and as mentioned earlier, there seems to be a greater possibility with more sympathetic funders like UNICEF and UNHCR.[69]

Educational and advocacy roles

The targets of operational NGOs are beneficiaries (or victims in emergencies), whereas those for educational and advocacy NGOs are their own contributors, the public and decision makers. Educational NGOs seek primarily to influence citizens, whose voices are then registered through public opinion and bear fruit in the form of additional resources for their activities as well as new policies, better decisions and enhanced international regimes. They often play a leading role in promoting the various dedication of 'days', 'years', and 'decades' that the UN system regularly proclaims. NGOs can help to reinforce various norms promoted by intergovernmental organisations through public education campaigns. This heightened awareness among public audiences can then help hold states accountable for their international commitments.[70]

Western operational NGOs are under growing pressure from their Third World partners to educate contributors and Western publics about the root causes of poverty and violence. This logic is driving some organisations to adapt to such harsh criticism as the following: 'Conventional NGO project activities are manifestly "finger-in-the-dike" responses to problems that require nothing short of worldwide and whole-hearted governmental commitment to combat'.[71] Hand-in-hand with operational activities is the need to educate populations and mobilise public opinion about the requirements for fundamental alterations in the global order.

Educational NGOs direct activities towards a broad public or towards specifically differentiated publics in order to persuade them to voice opinions on governmental policies in international organisations. The primary tool of the educational and advocacy NGO is collecting and disseminating information, which sometimes incorporates a high degree of expertness and sometimes consists of mainly emotional appeals.

Educational as well as other varieties of NGOs can be distinguished from social movements,[72] even if the aims and methods are sometimes similar. The former are organisations with visible structures, are generally tolerated as parts of the polity and can make sure that their interests are represented in decision processes. Social movements, in contrast, have loose or skimpy structures to give effect to a rather spontaneous coming together of people who seek to achieve a social goal that may include changing or preserving aspects of society. One or more NGOs may be associated with social movements but do not define or direct them.

Linked to education are the related concerns of NGOs working primarily in the corridors of governments and intergovernmental organisations. Using a distinctive venue for advocacy, these organisations aim at contributing to international agenda-setting, the design of programmes and overall supervision of international organisation activities. They do so by seeking discussions with national delegates and staff members of international secretariats. Under some circumstances they can make formal statements before UN deliberative organs, and they frequently submit documentation for use by government representatives. In the corridors of UN organisations, they offer expertise, research, drafting and even mediation to governmental representatives and organisational staff. In doing so, the NGO representatives hope to promote acceptance of their positions, which involve adjustment or change of policies.

These advocates pursue discussions with national delegates and staff members of international secretariats in order to influence international public policy. Calling this activity 'lobbying' is perhaps an accurate image but an inaccurate description according to dictionary definitions. In seeking to alter the policies of governments as well as of governmental, intergovernmental and nongovernmental agencies, these NGOs seek to influence all policy makers, not only legislators.

Rather than aiming at beneficiaries or the general public, as is the case for the operational and educational types, advocacy NGOs target key decision makers in parliaments as well as in governments and intergovernmental secretariats. Because they have a direct impact on international responses, advocacy NGOs have the most difficulty raising funds.

NGO advocacy may be generally described as unofficial participation by internal and external modes.[73] Internal modes can be observed in capitals and domestic arenas. They include such things as pressure on a government to participate in a treaty-making effort; formation of domestic coalitions and the mobilisation of public opinion to influence the positions a state takes during treaty negotiations; public pressure on a government to sign a treaty; and using the strengths and weaknesses of a country's domestic system to challenge governments, companies and others to comply.

External modes consist of urging the United Nations or one of its associated agencies to add an issue to the agenda; gathering data to help frame or define a problem or a threat in ways that influence the work of official UN-sanctioned conferences; and contributing to the implementation of treaties by assisting countries without expertise to meet their obligations. Through formal statements in UN forums and through informal negotiations with international civil servants and members of national delegations, advocacy NGOs seek to ensure that their positions, and those of their constituencies, find their way into international texts and decisions. They sometimes offer their research and drafting skills, and they provide scientific or polling data to support their positions.[74] Also, first-hand reports and testimony from field staff can be powerful tools before parliamentary committees.

External functions generally require mobilisation across state boundaries. Independent researchers and scholars, usually as part of transnational networks, contribute theoretical arguments or empirical evidence in favour of a particular response. This information is used by NGOs and helps build coalitions of individuals and groups that otherwise would not join forces.

A great deal of past NGO advocacy has been directed against government and UN policy. An important evolution is that a growing number of NGOs are eager to institutionalise a 'full-fledged partnership with the governmental members of the United Nations'.[75] Historically NGOs have had some responsibility for treaty implementation, but they may aspire to a more direct involvement in treaty-making. Some NGOs have contributed substantially to international agenda-setting, as at the San Francisco Conference in April 1945, where NGOs played a pivotal role in securing the inclusion of human rights language in the final draft of the UN

Charter. In fact, they have spurred action since the middle of the 19th century at each stage in the evolution of international protection for human rights.[76]

As with the venerable debate over the impact of the media on foreign policy, there is disagreement about NGO influence on governmental responses. However, NGOs that seek government policy change can be crucial for the timing and nature of international responses, even in such controversial arenas as civil wars. NGOs in the USA, for example, failed to get the Clinton Administration to acknowledge genocide and to take action in Rwanda in April and May 1994, but eventually they were more successful in getting the Pentagon to help in Zaire and Tanzania. For three years, many US NGOs encouraged a robust enough military invasion to restore the elected government of the Rev Jean-Bertrand Aristide in Haiti. In France, NGOs have been successful in launching and sustaining an activist humanitarian policy, *le droit d'ingérence*, which became the official policy of the Mitterrand government and its visible Minister Bernard Kouchner, and which survives both of their departures.[77]

NGOs that focus exclusively on education or advocacy in their own countries without overseas activities are not numerous, but they exist. For example, the Refugee Policy Group, Refugees International, and the US Committee for Refugees all focus on research with a view towards informing the public and altering public policy on people displaced by war. However, many of the most effective educators and advocates are those with the credibility, knowledge and convictions resulting from substantial operational activities.

Many NGOs that started their work at a project level mitigating the symptoms of problems have moved into attacking the structural roots of those problems. As such, they draw away from an exclusive concern with projects and move towards preventing the need for the assistance in the first place. Projects alone cannot promote structural change and prevention. The logic of the shift towards educating the public about the necessity for systemic change moves away from a preoccupation with relief, and is summed up by two observers: 'Many of the causes of underdevelopment lie in the political and economic structures of an unequal world ... and in the misguided policies of governments and the multilateral institutions (such as the World Bank and IMF) which they control. It is extremely difficult, if not impossible, to address these issues in the context of the traditional NGO project.'[78] In these efforts to target officials within governmental and intergovernmental institutions, NGOs can be loud and theatrical, like Médecins Sans Frontières and Greenpeace, or discreet and more subtle, like the International Committee of the Red Cross.

Advocacy is an essential and growing activity. As such, the debate about possible modifications of consultative status in UN forums is important at least for some NGOs. Consultative status provides additional access to and enhanced authority in the eyes of many governments and UN officials.

Political levels and constraints

A complementary or alternative approach to NGO roles depends on identifying relationships among them and their governmental levels of activity.[79] Primary associations are those serving members at the community level; these may be called people's organisations. As their base, scope of operations and methods are circumscribed, they can be excluded from the group of transnational NGOs with direct relevance to the UN system. Secondary organisations include public-serving groups that operate at the community level as well as federations of member-serving primary associations. Tertiary organisations are those that do not operate at the community level and also comprise federations of secondary organisations. Thus, only public-serving organisations and meta-organisations that they form may be considered as NGOs with transnational significance.

Further distinctions can be drawn between organisations that work at the community level and those that do not. National NGOs that work only within the boundaries of one developing country can be distinguished from international NGOs that are based in developed countries. Refining classificatory factors include constituency, primary functions and activities, ideology/philosophy, scale and coverage or organisational structure.

NGO interactions may be constrained or facilitated according to the consensus surrounding the issues that they address. Environmental NGOs, for instance, work within an overall and seemingly expanding agreement about protecting the biosphere. Development NGOs, in contrast, are partly sustained by a consensus about the necessity for growth, even though they often encounter significant discord when they begin to threaten elites. Human rights NGOs, however, pursue agendas in which governments, intergovernmental organisations and NGOs disagree profoundly about goals, ideas, the nature of violations and appropriate forms of redress. Therefore, NGOs working on the front lines where ethnic cleansing takes place, lobbying for human rights changes, or doing education and advocacy work face different constraints from NGOs struggling to save rain forests or to advance development.

Separate microsystems of issues have their own attributes and exigencies that condition the existence of NGOs. Within each microsystem, the potential for collaboration or conflict by NGOs and the UN is distinct.[80] Moreover, the varied aims and methods of NGOs range from constructive dialogue, that is incrementalism or reform from within, to shouting from the sidelines for revolution, rejection and nihilism.

Dimensions for analysing NGOs

A search for identities within the explorations in the specific case studies in this volume offer data on which further research could be based and would provide tests of the appropriateness of typologies and theoretical approaches. Accordingly, four sets of dimensions—organisation, governance, strategies and output—were suggested to the authors of subsequent essays. These dimensions are displayed in Table 1 and discussed in the succeeding paragraphs; they also provide a structure for the concluding essay.

The dimensions are divided into four categories. The first two, organisation and governance, have special relevance to locating the site of activities within governing structures and understanding the structures and aims of NGOs. The second two, strategic and output, have to with the techniques and products of NGOs.

TABLE 1
NGO dimensions

Organisational dimensions	Governance dimensions	Strategic dimensions	Output dimensions
Geographic range	*Governmental contact*	*Goal definition*	Information
Community	Intergovernmental	Single issue	Expert advice
Subnational	International conferences	Multisectoral	Financing
National	Regional	Broad social	Material goods and services
Regional	National	Church related	Support for policies
Transnational	Subnational	Social ideology	Mobilisation of opinion
	Community	Revolutionary/rejectionist	(leaders and followers)
Support base	Informal transnational		Maintenance of
Personal memberships		*Tactical modes*	interorganisational relations
Other organisations	*Range of concern*	Monitoring	Political feedback among
Quasi-governmental	Norm setting	Advocacy/lobbying	governmental units
Mixture of above	Policy setting	Mass propaganda	Encouragement of networks
	Policy execution	Mass demonstration	Education of specific publics
Personnel	Contractor		
Managerial	Mediation between levels		
Basic research			
Expert and professional (applied)			
Undifferentiated			
(popular, voluntary)			
Financing			
Membership dues			
Contributions			
Endowment income			
Compensation			
Legal relationships			
General rules			
Regulations			
Ad hoc guidelines			

Organisational dimensions

These dimensions are intended to make clear two aspects of NGO existence and operation. The first is where they fit in an organisational framework that extends from the village to the globe, and who supports them. The second aspect concerns their internal arrangements and participation, their resource bases, and their legal status. Membership and financial information make possible comparisons relating to the size of NGOs. Since the legal dimensions of NGOs have had a great deal of attention, they are touched on only briefly in the case studies.

Governance dimensions

These dimensions comprise information about the instruments of governmental policy and programme administration with which NGOs come into contact. The subcategory, 'Range of Concern', helps distinguish among the characters of the arrangements for governance in which NGOs may participate. For example, a substantial difference in governance may be presumed between a situation in which an NGO simply works as a contractor for a regional intergovernmental agency from one that is involved in the discussion of a new global law-making treaty.

Strategic dimensions

These dimensions set out what NGOs hope to achieve within the organisational and governance dimensions. The emphasis here is on relationships directed inwards, ie, how NGOs choose to relate to IGOs and governments on policy issues and design of projects. They include both the normative basis for action and, under tactical modes, the methods employed for reaching the goals. A wide range of data can be expected by searching out the effects of these dimensions. Along their lines, NGOs differentiate themselves from each other and reinforce their support bases. The tactical modes, however, have primary significance in the relation to the UN system.

Output dimensions

These dimensions are framed to make evident the results of NGO activity within the framework of the UN system. They are highly significant in determining whether NGOs can reach their goals. They include a set of products of organisational work that bear on how the UN system reacts and also on how NGOs maintain relationships with one other in reaching their goals. The outputs relate to services delivered to organisational membership as well as to external persons and organisations.

Conclusion

NGOs are omnipresent in the policy and administrative process of UN organisations; the extent of their participation has progressively deepened. The turbulent pluralism of the NGO realm has clearly brought new and unanticipated groups into the process. Without attributing either a positive or negative value to NGO activity, it can nevertheless be recognised as a factor in global governance. Yet this phenomenon, contrary to the conventional assumptions about the virtually exclusive role of governments in international politics, has not been fully described nor adequately encompassed in theoretical approaches.

Defining categories of NGO tasks, their transnational relationships and the impact of their efforts marks an initial step towards understanding the variety of nongovernmental interactions with the UN system. They form part of a larger set of analytical challenges as the international community gropes and copes with changing world politics and trends towards the decentralisation and democratisation of global governance. These include a vast variety of cooperative structures and practices that have emerged in and around the United Nations and its associated organisations.

There is an obvioûs hypothesis: NGOs have been essential in this evolution. Because NGOs, both local and international, increasingly affect world politics, theoretical and practical understandings of NGO activities are intrinsically important. Moreover, they are crucial for comprehending the problems and prospects of the UN system more generally. It is to an examination of cases of NGOs in action that this volume now turns.

Notes

The authors acknowledge the assistance of Carrie Murphy and Minh Vo in the preparation of this article.
[1] *Yearbook of International Associations*, Brussels: Union of International Associations, 1993/94. The actual figure is 16 142 but it is increasing constantly. In fact, the figure more than doubled from 1991. The OECD *Directory of NGOs* (Paris: Organisation for Economic Cooperation and Development, 1991) estimates some 2500 INGOs in OECD countries in 1990, up from 1600 a decade earlier. They also estimate some 20 000 local NGOs in developing countries, although the UNDP's *Human Development Report 1994* (New York: Oxford University Press, 1994) estimates that the number is considerably higher, at about 50 000.
[2] Commission on Global Governance, *Our Global Neighbourhood*, Oxford: Oxford University Press, 1995, p 254.
[3] John Clark, *Democratizing Development: The Role of Voluntary Organizations*, Hartford, CT: Kumarian Press, 1991, p 3.
[4] Marc Nerfin, 'Neither prince nor merchant: citizen—an introduction to the third system', *IFDA Dossier*, 56, November/December 1986, pp 3–29. See also David C Korten, *Getting to the 21st Century: Voluntary Action and The Global Agenda*, Hartford, CT: Kumarian Press, 1990, pp 95–112.
[5] Kathleen D McCarthy, Virginia Hodgkinson, Russy Sumariwalla *et al.*, *The Nonprofit Sector in the United States*, San Francisco, CA: Jossey-Bass, 1992, p 3.
[6] Thomas Princen & Matthias Finger, *Environmental NGOs in World Politics*, London: Routledge, 1994.
[7] James N Rosenau, *Turbulence in World Politics: A Theory of Continuity and Change*, Princeton, NJ: Princeton University Press, 1990 and *The United Nations in a Turbulent World*, Boulder, CO: Lynne Rienner, 1992.
[8] The authors are grateful to Christer Jönsson and Peter Söderholm for their formulations.
[9] Joseph A Camilleri & Jim Falk, *The End of Sovereignty? The Politics of a Shrinking and Fragmenting World*, Aldershot, UK: Edward Elgar, 1992, p 3.
[10] Jennifer Wolch, *The Shadow State: Government and Voluntary Sector in Transition*, New York: The Foundation Center, 1990.
[11] Brad Smith, President of the Inter-American Foundation, quoted by Mary Morgan, 'Stretching the development dollar: the potential for scaling-up', *Grassroots Development*, 14 (1), 1990, p 7.
[12] David L Brown & David Korten, *Understanding Voluntary Organizations: Guidelines for Donors*, Working Papers No 258 (Washington, DC: Country Economics Department, World Bank, September 1989), p 22.
[13] *UNIFEM Annual Report 1993*, New York: United Nations Development Fund for Women, 1993, p 9. See also

Stephen P Marks, 'Forgetting "the policies and practices of the past": impunity in Cambodia', *The Fletcher Forum of World Affairs*, 18 (2), 1994, pp 17–43; and Jarat Chopra, *United Nations Authority in Cambodia, Occasional Paper #15*, Providence, RI: Watson Institute, 1994.

[14] Antonio Donini, 'Missions impossibles', *Le monde des débats*, July-August 1994, p 4.

[15] For a useful discussion of the literature about NGOs in the context of teaching international relations, international law and international organisation, see Lawrence T Woods, 'Nongovernmental organizations and the United Nations system: reflecting upon the Earth Summit experience', *Research Note*, 18 (1), 1993, pp 9–15.

[16] Leland M Goodrich, Edvard Hambro & Anne Patricia Simons, *Charter of the United Nations*, New York: Columbia University Press, 1969, pp 443–446.

[17] See United Nations, Economic and Social Council Resolutions 3 (II) (1946) and 288 B (X) (1950).

[18] Chiang Pei-Heng, *Non-Governmental Organizations at the United Nations: Identity, Role and Function*, New York: Praeger, 1981, pp 19–57. For historical discussions, see also J Joseph Lador-Lederer, *International Non-governmental Organizations and Economic Entities: A Study in Autonomous Organization and Ius Gentium*, Leiden: Sythoff, 1963, Borko Stosic, *Les Organisations non Gouvernementales et les Nations Unies*, Geneva: Librarie Droz, 1964; and Lyman C White, *International Non-Governmental Organizations: Their Purposes, Methods, and Accomplishments*, New Brunswick, NJ: Rutgers University Press, 1951.

[19] UN, General Assembly Resolution 13 (1), Annex I (1946); and ECOSOC Resolution 1297 (XLIV).

[20] UN, Economic and Social Council, Open-Ended Group on the Review of Arrangements for Consultations with Non-Governmental Organizations, 'General review of arrangements for consultations with non-governmental organizations', UN Doc. E/AC.70/1994/5 (26 May 1994), p 18. Hereafter cited by document number. The ILO tri-partite structure was an earlier precedent.

[21] Ibid, pp 17–18.

[22] Ibid, p 11.

[23] Ibid, p 17.

[24] Johan Kaufmann & Nico Schrijver, *Changing Global Needs: Expanding Roles of the United Nations System*, Hanover, NH: Academic Council on the United Nations System, 1990, pp 40–45.

[25] See Francesco Mezzalama & Siegfried Schumm, *Working with NGOs: Operational Activities of the United Nations System with Non-governmental Organizations and Governments at the Grassroots and National Levels*, Geneva: Joint Inspection Unit, 1993, document Jiu/REP/93/1.

[26] UN Doc. E/AC.70/1994/5, p 8.

[27] Bertrand Schneider, *The Barefoot Revolution*, London: IT Publishers, 1988; and Alan Durning, 'People power and development', *Foreign Policy*, 76, Fall 1989, pp 66–82.

[28] Barbara Crossette, 'UN Leader to Call for Changes in Peacekeeping', *New York Times*, 3 January 1995, A3.

[29] For a theoretical and empirical investigation, see Lester M Salamon & Helmut K Anheier, *The Emerging Sector: An Overview*, Baltimore, MD: Johns Hopkins University Institute for Policy Studies, 1994.

[30] See Jackie Smith, Ron Pagnucco & Winnie Romeril, 'Transnational social movement organizations in the global political arena', *Voluntas*, 5 (2), 1994, pp 121–154.

[31] Maria Garner, 'Transnational alignment of nongovernmental organizations for global environmental action', *Vanderbilt Journal of Transnational Law*, 23 (5), 1991, p 1077.

[32] See Benedict Anderson, *Imagined Communities: Reflections on the Origins and Spread of Nationalism*, London: Verso, 1991.

[33] Peter Spiro, 'New global communities: nongovernmental organizations in international decision making institutions', *Washington Quarterly*, 18 (1) 1995, p 48.

[34] David Cooperrider & William Pasmore, 'The organization dimension of global change', *Human Relations*, 44, (8), 1991, p 764.

[35] 'NGOs and conflict: three views', *Humanitarian Monitor*, 2, February 1995, pp 32–33.

[36] Rakiya Omaar & Alex de Waal, *Humanitarianism Unbound?* Discussion Paper No 5, London: African Rights, November 1994, p 6.

[37] Janie Leatherman, Ron Pagnucco & Jackie Smith, *International Institutions and Transnational Social Movement Organizations: Challenging the State in a Three-level Game of Global Transformation*, Working Paper Series, South Bend, IN.: Kroc Institute, October 1993, p 4.

[38] L David Brown, 'Bridging organizations and sustainable development', *Human Relations*, 44 (8), 1991, pp 807–831. Brown argues that 'development sustainability depends in part on institutional factors—effective local organizations, horizontal linkages that enable intersectoral cooperation, and vertical linkages that enable grassroots influence on policy-making—that can be influenced by bridging organizations'. Ibid, p 825.

[39] See Mark Duffield, 'Sudan at the cross roads: from emergency preparedness to social security', *IDS Discussion Paper #275*, Brighton: Institute for Development Studies, 1990.

[40] Barbara Hendrie, 'Cross border operations in Eritrea and Tigray', *Disasters*, 13 (4), 1990, pp 351–360.

[41] R Graham & J Borton, *A Preliminary Review of the Combined Agencies Relief Team (CART), Juba 1986–1991*, London: Overseas Development Institute, 1992.

[42] UN Doc. E/AC.70/1994/5, pp 67–71.

[43] For a discussion in relationship to the UN, see Erskine Childers with Brian Urquhart, *Renewing the United Nations System*, Uppsala: Dag Hammarskjöld Foundation, 1994.

[44] James O Ingram, 'The future architecture for international humanitarian assistance', in Thomas G Weiss & Larry Minear (eds), *Humanitarianism Across Borders: Sustaining Civilians in Times of War*, Boulder, CO: Lynne Rienner, 1993, p 181.

[45] Carolyn Stremlau, 'NGO coordinating bodies in Africa, Asia and Latin America', *World Development*, 15, Supplement, 1987, pp 213–225.

[46] Ramesh Thakur, 'Human rights: Amnesty International and the United Nations', *Journal of Peace Research*, 31 (2), 1994, pp 143–160.

[47] Sadako Ogata, UNHCR High Commissioner, 'Opening statement to the 44th Session of the Executive Committee of the High Commissioner's Programme', PARinAC Information Note and Update No 1, Geneva: UNHCR and ICVA, 1993, p 1.

[48] See Adolpho Aguilar Zinzer, *CIREFCA: The Promises and Reality of the International Conference on Central American Refugees*, Washington, DC: CIPRA, 1991; and Cristina Eguizábal, David Lewis, Larry Minear, Peter Sollis & Thomas G Weiss, *Humanitarian Challenges in Central America: Learning the Lessons of Recent Armed Conflicts*, Occasional Paper #14, Providence, RI: Watson Institute, 1993.

[49] World Bank, *Cooperation Between the World Bank and NGOs: 1993 Progress Report*, Washington, World Bank, 1993, p 7. Some NGOs would contest that 'participation' is not as meaningful as these statistics might imply.

[50] Judith Randel, 'Aid, the military and humanitarian assistance: an attempt to identify recent trends', *Journal of International Development*, 6 (3), 1994, p 336.

[51] Mark Duffield, 'NGOs, disaster relief and asset transfer in the Horn: political survival in a permanent emergency', *Development and Change*, 24, 1993, p 140.

[52] UN Doc. E/AC.70/1994/5, Annexes IV and V.

[53] See James G McGann, *The Competition for Dollars, Scholars and Influence in the Public Policy Research Industry*, Lantham MD: University Press of America, 1995.

[54] Margaret M Feczko (ed), *The Foundation Directory*, New York: The Foundation Center, 1984, p vii.

[55] See, for example, Hans J Morgenthau, *Politics Among Nations*, New York: Knopf, 1973; and Kenneth N Waltz, *Theory of International Politics*, Reading, MA: Addison-Wesley, 1979. See also Robert O Keohane, *Neorealism and Its Critics*, New York: Columbia University Press, 1986.

[56] See Stephen J Del Rosso, Jr, 'The insecure state: reflections on "the state" and "security" in a changing world', *Daedulus*, 124 (2), 1995, pp 175–204.

[57] Robert Gilpin, *The Political Economy of International Relations*, Princeton, NJ: Princeton University Press, 1987.

[58] See for example, Joseph S Nye, Jr, *Bound To Lead: The Changing Nature of American Power*, New York: Basic Books, 1990, which makes a case for the validity of 'soft power'. See also Hedley Bull, *The Anarchical Society*, New York: Oxford University Press, 1977.

[59] See, for example, Stephen D Krasner (ed), *International Regimes*, Ithaca, NY: Cornell University Press, 1983; and Robert O Keohane, *After Hegemony: Cooperation and Discord in the World Political Economy*, Princeton, NJ: Princeton University Press, 1984.

[60] See Henry G Schermers, *International Institutional Law*, Alphen aan den Rijn, Netherlands: Sijthoff & Noordhoff, 1980, pp 15–18, 164–75. Much legal commentary relates to specific subject matter, eg the UN Conventions on Human Rights, the UN Convention on the Status of Refugees and a host of other legal documents in force or in the developmental stage.

[61] An overview of this approach is found in Leon Gordenker, Christer Jönsson, Roger A Coate & Peter Söderholm, *International Responses to AIDS*, London: Pinter, forthcoming 1995.

[62] Gail D Ness & Steven B Brachin, 'Bridging the gap: international organizations as organizations', *International Organization*, 42 (2), 1988, pp 245–274.

[63] Dennis W Organ, 'Linking pins between organizations and environment', *Business Horizons*, 14, 1971, pp 73–80.

[64] Howard Aldrich and David A Whetten, 'Organization-sets, action-sets, and networks: making the most of simplicity', in Paul C Nystrom & William H Starbuck (eds), *Handbook of Organizational Design*, Vol 1, New York, Oxford University Press, 1981.

[65] Grahame Thompson, Jennifer Frances, Rosalind Levacic & Jeremy Mitchell (eds), *Markets, Hierarchies and Networks: The Coordination of Social Life*, London: Sage, 1991.

[66] Ernst B Haas, *When Knowledge Is Power: Three Models of Change in International Organizations*, Berkeley, CA: University of California Press, 1990; and Peter M Haas, 'Introduction: epistemic communities and international policy coordination, *International Organization*, 46 (1), 1992, pp 1–35, and 'Do regimes matter? Epistemic communities and Mediterranean pollution control', *International Organization*, 43 (3), 1989, pp 377–403.

[67] Independent Commission on International Development Issues, *North–South: A Programme for Survival*,

London: Pan, 1980; Independent Commission on Disarmament and Security Issues, *Common Security: A Blueprint for Survival*, New York: Touchstone, 1982; World Commission on Environment and Development, *Our Common Future*, New York: Oxford University Press, 1987; Independent Commission on International Humanitarian Issues, *Winning the Human Race?*, London: Zed, 1988; South Commission, *The Challenge to the South*, Oxford: Oxford University Press, 1990; and Commission on Global Governance, *Our Global Neighbourhood*.

[68] See International Council of Voluntary Agencies, NGO Working Group on the World Bank, 'Brief history of the NGO Working Group on the World Bank', informal document dated December 1993.

[69] Part of the explanation may be that many UN staff members in these institutions have actually worked in NGOs or are at least very sympathetic towards goals and styles of operation. For example, see the UNHCR's special issue of *Refugees*, 97, March 1994, entitled 'Focus: NGOS & UNHCR'.

[70] See Leatherman *et al.*, *International Institutions*.

[71] John Clark 'Policy influence, lobbying and advocacy', in Michael Edwards & David Hulme (eds), *Making a Difference: NGOs and Development in a Changing World*, London: Earthscan, 1992, p 199.

[72] Dennis R Young, 'The structural imperatives of international advocacy association', *Human Relations*, 44 (9), 1991, p 925. See also M N Zald & J D McCarthy (eds), *Social Movements in an Organizational Society*, New Brunswick, NJ: Transaction Books, 1987.

[73] Lawrence Susskind, *Environmental Diplomacy: Negotiating More Effective Global Agreements*, New York: Oxford University Press, 1994, p 50.

[74] For discussions, see Cynthia Price Cohen, 'The role of nongovernmental organizations in the drafting of the convention on the rights of the child', *Human Rights Quarterly*, 12 (1), 1990, pp 137–147; Thakur, 'Human rights'; and Princen & Finger *Environmental NGOs in World Politics*.

[75] Susskind, *Environmental Diplomacy*, p 51.

[76] See David P Forsythe, *Human Rights and World Politics*, Lincoln, NB: University of Nebraska Press, 1989, pp 83–101, 127–59.

[77] See Bernard Kouchner & Mario Bettati, *Le devoir d'ingérence*, Paris: Denoël, 1987; Bernard Kouchner, *Le malheur des autres*, Paris: Odile Jacob, 1991; and Mario Bettati, 'Intervention, ingérence ou assistance?', *Revue Trimestrielle des Droits de l'Homme*, 19 July 1994, pp 308–358.

[78] Edwards & Hulme (eds), *Making a Difference*, p 20.

[79] The authors are grateful to Marty Chen for suggesting these categories.

[80] The authors are grateful to Charles MacCormack for having helped develop ideas along these lines during the July 1994 summer workshop organised by the Academic Council on the United Nations System.

■ Part 2 ■
NGOs in Action

■ 2 ■

Reality Check: Human Rights NGOs Confront Governments at the UN

FELICE D GAER

Official acknowledgement of the importance of nongovernmental organizations (NGOs) in the work of the United Nations (UN) human rights programmes remains a subject of intense controversy. Warm admiration for the full range of actions by human rights NGOs expressed in the draft text prepared for the 1993 World Conference on Human Rights in Vienna stands in stark contrast to the more cautious final text that was adopted.[1] Governments limited their appreciation to some but not all nongovernmental activities by notably excluding human rights monitoring from the list. Further, they declared, international human rights principles and national law protect only those NGOs 'genuinely involved in human rights'. The draft was prepared by members of the secretariat, and the final text was negotiated by government representatives from 171 countries. The differences between the two reveal the gap between, on the one hand, the dependency of UN expert human rights mechanisms on information supplied by human rights NGOs and, on the other hand, government resentment of NGO reports and activism. Many governments, especially those criticised by nongovernmental organizations, persistently labour to limit the formal access and participation of nongovernmental human rights organisations and to challenge the legitimacy of their findings.[2]

This seeming contradiction of maintaining both dependency and distance reflects certain fundamental characteristics associated with human rights NGOs themselves and the goals that they seek to advance through the United Nations and other international bodies. Yet human rights NGOs are the engine for virtually every advance made by the United Nations in the field of human rights since its founding.

NGOs put human rights into the UN Charter

That the United Nations addresses human rights issues at all is revolutionary. The initiative to turn the UN Charter into an instrument concerned with promoting respect for the human rights of individuals came from the 42 US organisations invited to be present as 'consultants' to the United States delegation at the founding conference in San Francisco in 1945. Their conviction that respect for human rights and the dignity of the individual was essential to peace and conflict prevention stemmed not merely from deep-seated American

values, but also reflected their realistic assessment of events—the failure of
interwar treaties to protect minorities and a world war stoked by the fires of
hatred, dehumanisation and genocide. They were convinced that only if the
rights of all people were protected would the rights of particular minority, ethnic
and religious groups be ensured and future conflicts avoided. The consultants—
led by Joseph Proskauer and Jacob Blaustein of the American Jewish Committee, together with Frederick Nolde of the Federal Council of the Churches of
Christ, Clark Eichelberger of the American Association for the UN and James
Shotwell of the Carnegie Endowment—persuaded the US delegation and to
make the world organisation different from its predecessor.

On 2 May 1945, upon being informed by a US delegate that human rights
would not appear in the Charter, Proskauer and his colleagues stayed up into the
night preparing a detailed memorandum, which argued that human rights are
essential not only to domestic life but also to international peace. The next day,
they rallied those organisations present in San Francisco to sign it, including the
groups named above and other civic groups such as the National Association of
Manufacturers, the Chamber of Commerce, the National Council of Farmer
Cooperatives, the American Bar Association, the National Association for the
Advancement of Colored People, and the League of Women Voters. The
organisations met US Secretary of State Edward Stettinius. Nolde summarised
the memorandum and Proskauer argued the political necessity of including
human rights in the Charter:

> I said that the voice of America was speaking in this room as it had never spoken
> before in any international gathering; that that voice was saying to the American
> delegation: "If you make a fight for these human rights proposals and win, there
> will be glory for all. If you make a fight for it and lose, we will back you up to the
> limit. If you fail to make a fight for it, you will have lost the support of American
> opinion—and justly lost it. In that event, you will never get the Charter ratified..."[3]

The Secretary of State declared that he was convinced; and within a day, all the
Big Four powers agreed. As a result, encouraging respect for human rights is one
of the four purposes of the United Nations set forth in the Charter, and a
Commission on Human Rights is called for by name.

Several consultant organisations had advocated an 'international bill of rights'
well before the San Francisco Conference. On 20 March 1945, the American
Jewish Committee presented this proposal to President Roosevelt and obtained
his support. A petition with 1300 prominent signatures appeared in the newspapers. This NGO coalition also decisively backed formal status of nongovernmental organisations in the United Nations Economic and Social Council (ECOSOC);
Article 71 established such status.[4]

Nevertheless, in a 1947 resolution, member states proclaimed that the UN
'had no power to take any action in regard to any complaints concerning human
rights'.[5] For years, this rendered the United Nations Human Rights Commission
largely a talking shop for talented lawyers. Undeterred, nongovernmental organisations provided expert advice on the human rights standards that the commission had begun to draft. In 1948 the Universal Declaration of Human Rights
was adopted, affirming civil and political rights and including freedom from

torture, rights to free speech, association, and religion, and such economic and social rights as the right to education, social security, and equal pay for equal work. As UN human rights programmes conducted studies and continued standard-setting (resulting in six human rights treaties), NGOs regularly offered theoretical insights, examples, draft language and other advice.

Creating UN machinery to respond to human rights abuses

Although mentioning specific countries or violations was long forbidden in UN chambers, human rights NGOs called for intergovernmental machinery to combat abuses. At first, they asked for an 'Attorney General' or 'High Commissioner for Human Rights'—a senior official able to investigate and take action to combat gross abuses. For a long time, this idea languished.[6] The mere mention by name of a country by an NGO in a speech at the Commission on Human Rights was cause enough for it to be ruled out of order, and such behaviour often led to threats of expulsion.[7]

Nongovernmental human rights organisations have shown that individuals are protected from abuses as a result of the 'mobilisation of shame'—heightened embarrassment of government officials over specific violations, directed against specific individuals, and not as a result of bland expressions of concern over generic rights standards. Reports issued by nongovernmental organisations about identifiable atrocities—torture, disappearances, political killings and massacres, among others—motivated governments to support new UN machinery to address specific violations. A confidential UN procedure begun in the late 1960s as a result of Resolution 1503 looked into documented complaints of human rights violations. Later, scrutiny took place in public sessions of the Commission on Human Rights (Resolution 1235).

For years, the choice of countries criticised publicly by the Commission on Human Rights reflected the politics of the United Nations and its member states more than independent or comparative judgments about the nature of abuses. Thus, the first special human rights teams investigating violations examined South Africa in 1967, Israel in 1968 and Chile in 1975. The Commission on Human Rights, composed of government representatives, continues to cite specific countries for their human rights abuses only when the votes can be gathered.[8]

Often, individuals (alternatively called 'expert', 'special representative' or 'special rapporteur') were charged with investigating the facts and reporting back. In virtually every instance—before the UN decided to appoint rapporteurs on Guatemala, Bolivia, El Salvador, Poland, Afghanistan, Iran, Cuba, Myanmar, Sweden, Zaire, and, following emergency sessions in 1992 and 1993, former Yugoslavia and Rwanda—NGOs stepped forward with documentary evidence of abuses, often detailed in plenary speeches at the Commission on Human Rights. Not surprisingly, violator countries themselves compete actively for election to the Commission and the ECOSOC NGO committee, both to protect themselves from a negative vote and to reply to and often intimidate the nongovernmental organisations.

Frustrated by the political obstacles to public criticism, NGOs and concerned governments advocated establishment of effective, independent and impartial UN human rights machinery to report on and stop violations. Nongovernmental organisations contribute decisively to this by providing the facts and specific case materials.

Creation of a regionally-balanced, five-person Working Group on Forced or Involuntary Disappearances—the first mechanism that could take action globally on individual cases on an emergency basis—was motivated largely by the horrific, detailed local and international NGO reports about 'disappearances', first in Chile and later in Argentina. In the words of one author, Amnesty International's (AI) 1977 fact-finding mission to Argentina was 'one of the most significant human rights missions ever undertaken by a nongovernmental organisation'. It energised those directly involved, turning supporters of the regime into critics, making the organisation a focal point for the families of victims and adding credibility and authenticity to Amnesty's reporting as a human rights NGO. Additionally, it mobilised AI and governments to develop the first issue-specific UN 'thematic' mechanism.[9]

In response to the reporting and speeches by human rights NGOs at the February 1977 session of the Commission, Argentina threatened to withdraw UN consultative status from the small group of human rights NGOs, including the International Commission of Jurists, Pax Romana, the International League for Human Rights, Amnesty International and the International Federation of Human Rights. Several of these nongovernmental organisations brought Argentinean 'witnesses' (victims, family members or human rights defenders) to Geneva to testify. Not only did the Argentine government question the witnesses' facts and motives, it also challenged their right to speak, on the grounds that they were not properly designated representatives, or members of the organisations under whose aegis they appeared.[10]

In 1980, when the proposal to establish a working group on disappearances formally came to the floor of the Commission on Human Rights, no government was ready to speak. Instead, the chair turned to the NGO speakers list. Amnesty International began to describe its efforts to document thousands of disappearances worldwide, citing Argentina, Afghanistan, Cambodia, Ethiopia, Nicaragua and Uganda.[11] When AI started to describe the experience of two Argentineans who had been tortured and imprisoned in a secret detention centre, Argentina's government delegate tried to stop this speech by questioning the right of a nongovernmental organisation to attack a government by name. Commission members Uruguay and Ethiopia backed Argentina, while Canada and the United States supported the right of NGOs to mention specific countries. In an important decision, the Jordanian chairman then ruled that nongovernmental organisations could not 'attack' governments but could 'provide information' about countries. The ability to confront governments at the United Nations with the facts was thus sustained. Next, the International Commission of Jurists and the International League for Human Rights each presented more information on disappearances.

The action soon shifted to behind-the-scenes diplomacy. It was another week until public debate on disappearances resumed, with intense manoeuvering aimed at creating a genuinely effective new mechanism. In the meantime, NGOs mobilised media and diplomatic pressure favouring quick-acting UN machinery.[12]

Because of too few votes to cite Argentina by name, the Commission on Human Rights created a UN expert body to examine 'disappearances' everywhere. This proved to be a strategically brilliant breakthrough. By 1995 about 10 similarly conceived 'thematic mechanisms' in human rights have been established: a five-person working group on arbitrary detentions and 'special rapporteurs' to conduct expert investigations on summary executions, torture, religious intolerance, freedom of expression, violence against women, sale of children, independence of the judiciary, internally displaced persons and contemporary forms of racism.

The NGO role: providing information to make the machinery work

The 'thematic mechanisms' capitalise on the UN's legitimacy as the premier global international institution and its ability to reach out or into virtually every society, and to establish universally applicable norms. They inquire into human rights violations affecting individuals, contact governments on an emergency basis, and report their findings and recommendations publicly. Mandates from the Commission on Human Rights, which are endorsed by the Economic and Social Council, authorise these mechanisms 'to *seek and receive* credible and reliable information from governments, the specialized agencies, and intergovernmental and *non-governmental organizations*' (emphasis added).

In fact, the mechanisms rely almost exclusively upon NGO information. Although there has been no detailed public accounting, some significant new indicators reveal how much NGOs fuel the special procedures of the Commission on Human Rights. At a June 1994 meeting of all special rapporteurs and experts serving on Working Groups of the Commission, the group appealed 'to non-governmental organizations whose work and information is crucial to human rights protection and to the effective discharge of our own mandates to continue providing us with relevant information and ideas ... '[13] The UN High Commissioner for Human Rights, José Ayala Lasso of Ecuador, informed those at the meeting that he had established a 'human rights hot line' to enable emergency information to be dealt with rapidly. He stated that 'this faxline ... is used exclusively ... by victims of human rights violations or relatives or informed NGOs ...'[14] Amnesty International sends more than 500 such communications, covering thousands of cases, to the UN special procedures branch every year.[15] Furthermore, the Working Group on Arbitrary Detentions reported in 1995 that 74% of the cases it took up in 1994 were brought by international NGOs, another 23% came from national NGOs, and 3% from families.[16] The Special Rapporteur on Arbitrary Executions acknowledges the 'important' role of nongovernmental organisations in alerting the international community about summary executions, and the Rapporteur on Freedom of Expression describes the NGO contribution as 'primordial'.[17]

The thematic mechanisms and country rapporteurs are joined by six committees of experts that review and comment upon compliance with UN human rights treaties. Normally, only states that have ratified the treaties may appear before the committee members to discuss their country reports on compliance.[18] But even in committees from which they had been barred and their information challenged, NGOs long ago developed an *ad hoc* role for themselves by providing treaty committee members with the facts about the human rights record of countries scheduled to present reports. Committee members eagerly look for NGO materials before each country review, because it helps make their questioning more precise, factual, and less abstract. Nongovernmental organisations essentially serve as unofficial researchers to committee members, rendering invaluable aid in place of the understaffed, poorly-financed secretariat.

Since the Cold War ended, these treaty supervisory committees have begun to acknowledge their dependency upon NGO information. In 1994 the fifth coordination meeting of chairpersons of all human rights treaty committees concluded:

> The chairpersons recommend that each treaty body examine the possibility of changing its working methods or amending its rules of procedure to allow non-governmental organisations to participate more fully in its activities. Nongovernmental organizations could be allowed, in particular, to make oral interventions and to transmit information relevant to the monitoring of human rights provisions through formally established and well-structured procedures. In order to facilitate the participation of non-governmental organisations, the chairpersons recommend that information about States parties' reporting be made available ... [and] advance information on the topic of proposed general comments should be made available to encourage non-governmental organizations to provide input to the drafts ... Attention should be given to securing a stronger, more effective and coordinated participation of national non-governmental organisations in the consideration of States parties' reports.[19]

Governments are not as friendly to NGOs as these experts. Repressive countries have made prodigious efforts to keep UN human rights bodies weak, inadequately financed, and substantively marginalised. Because intimidation and reprisals are often directed against those who submit information to the United Nations, the Commission on Human Rights installed a 'prompt intervention' procedure to protect those threatened. In 1995 the commission concluded that 'all the alleged victims were private individuals or members of nongovernmental organisations which were or had been sources of information about human rights violations for United Nations human rights bodies'. The 1995 UN report identifies harassment of local human rights defenders in Guatemala, Colombia, Mexico, Argentina, Honduras, Peru, Rwanda, Burma, Zaire and Iran.[20]

What are human rights NGOs?

Human rights organisations commonly identify their primary goals as monitoring and reporting of government behaviour on human rights, particularly violations, building pressure and creating international machinery to end the violations and to hold governments accountable. Other NGOs active on human rights issues may have considerably broader organisational goals such as religious organisations, trade unions, professional organisations, or groups concerned with refugees, children and others. But these nongovernmental organisations also devote substantial resources to human rights promotion and protection—sometimes exclusively for their members, but often for all persons. Human rights organisations aim to be independent both of government and of partisan groups seeking political power.[21]

The proliferation of human rights NGOs since the mid-1970s makes it almost impossible to categorize them. Human rights NGOs often pursue differing aims, depending on their formal mandates, geographical location and preferred means of action.

The difficulties that such nongovernmental organisations encounter commonly reflect the weaknesses of national and international enforcement of the norms established in UN human rights treaties. The most effective NGOs have concentrated on establishing and operating instrumentalities at home and abroad that can ensure protection of the specific rights for each group that is the focus of attention. Sometimes, however, there is no international agreement about the norms themselves, for example minority rights or the right to housing, or how to implement them. In such cases, NGOs focus on codifying new norms.

To exacerbate matters—and the hostility with which some human rights NGOs are treated by international agencies and diplomats—national human rights organisations often address volatile issues that directly attack fundamental power relationships in their own societies. In some instances these are issues of physical integrity of the person such as 'disappearances', political killings, and torture; in others, they address questions of societal distribution of wealth, services and power. Commonly, national human rights NGOs also challenge governments on the issue of popular participation in decision-making. Because of the breadth of issues on the human rights agenda—among them are political, civil, social, economic and cultural rights, indigenous rights, collective rights and the right to self-determination—nationally based groups will often be viewed and behave as opponents to the government. In many instances human rights groups will consist largely of, or be dependent primarily upon, political opponents and exiles from a particular country.

Many national human rights NGOs link with international human rights NGOs, either as 'affiliates' or as national members of other international organisations that sometimes work on human rights issues. Sometimes, national groups formally take action within the UN. Yet many representatives of national groups function in the UN on their own and only occasionally under the aegis of the international group.

'Dedicated' or 'exclusive' human rights NGOs, particularly at the international level, have found that their ability to reduce violations is often advanced because they can concentrate solely on international norms, treaties and specific legal obligations, rather than taking on the complex causes of political and economic inequality.

Tactics utilised by human rights NGOs commonly focus on protecting individual victims of abuse through several means:

1. By *exposing the abuses* and mobilising shame through public advocacy to end the abuses and ameliorate conditions. This is perhaps the most common tactic adopted by such groups, and requires information gathering.
2. By *communicating with decisionmakers* at both the national and international

level in a variety of ways, either specifically to the abuse and victim, or generally with regard to the establishment of human rights norms, and with gradations between the two. Armed with precise information and communicated persuasively, human rights NGOs often set the agendas of the international organisations to address the issues they present.

3. By *delivering services* such as legal aid, training in public advocacy skills and including broad educational services so that individuals and groups will 'know their rights' and how to act upon them.

Access and effectiveness depend on deliberate policy choices related to NGO goals; skills and professionalism of staff; resources devoted to UN matters; informal relationships developed with UN personnel, independent experts and diplomats; and, in turn, the successes of the organisation and other nongovernmental organisations in building new UN mechanisms to respond to the inputs from NGOs.

The World Conference on Human Rights

All these approaches to NGO activism came together at the two-week June 1993 World Conference on Human Rights in Vienna. Representatives of 171 governments met 'upstairs', and thousands of NGO representatives passed through the 'downstairs' meeting rooms. These representatives were made up of national and international, analytic and activist, North and South, 'exclusive' human rights groups, as well as single-issue and broader purpose organisations. NGO Forum organisers reported that 2721 representatives of 1529 organisations attended the three-day meetings. Of these, the largest group of 426 organisations were from Western Europe; next came 270 Asian groups and another 38 from Australia/ Oceania, 236 Latin American organisations, 202 African groups, 179 East and Central European groups and 178 North American organisations.[22] There had never been a human rights meeting of this size.

Under the expanded access rules for the conference, an additional 1004 non-ECOSOC human rights NGOs had been invited to the official proceedings. According to the United Nations, 3691 representatives of 841 organisations actually attended as NGO observers, but only 248 of those organisations had ECOSOC consultative status.[23] Few had ever attended a United Nations meeting before. Many grew impatient with the NGO Forum Planning Committee, which represented international human rights organisations with long experience at the world body. Not unexpectedly, clashes ensued between the new, national NGOs and traditional international NGOs; between nongovernmental organisations and government organisers; among governments that advocated a fuller role and presence of NGOs in the drafting committee of the conference, and those that opposed it. There was a fundamental disjuncture between governments that wanted to strengthen UN human rights procedures and governments that wanted to deal them a death blow. When a deal brokered by the US delegation to permit nongovernmental organisations in the drafting rooms was unexpectedly and summarily overruled by the Brazilian chairman, NGO representatives serving on some government delegations began to provide regular reports to the reconsti-tuted NGO caucuses, gaining their input and involvement in turn.

There could not have been a more vivid contrast than that of the 'down-stairs'—where a stream of NGO representatives put forward gruesome photos, horrifying videos and numerous reports—to the neat and clean 'upstairs', where the governments drafted a declaration. Despite the contradictions emerging within the NGO world, governments clearly understood that the groups had come to Vienna to demand action and challenge governments to do more than just debate.

Many issues were thrashed out at the conference and at its preparatory meetings. NGO ideas and priorities were well represented on two central ques-tions—universality of human rights and establishment of a High Commissioner for Human Rights—and NGO presence and proposals heavily influenced the outcome.

Universality

Just before the World Conference on Human Rights, debate intensified on whether human rights norms are universal in scope and applicability or whether regional differences or 'particularities'—such as culture, tradition, religion or history—render some of the concepts invalid for non-Western regions. At sessions of the Non-Aligned Movement and regional preparatory conferences for Vienna, Asian governments advanced arguments favouring particularities. Be-cause the UN's comparative advantage in human rights lies in its authority, global reach and capacity to speak as the sole universal intergovernmental body, the defence of universality became a central goal of the conference.

Indeed, every government that argued in favour of particularities at the Vienna Conference also paid lip service to the universality of human rights, noting that the rights are accepted by the international community. Iran, for example, stated that human rights are 'inherent in human beings ... [and] cannot be subject to cultural relativism'.[24] Indonesia, speaking as chair of the Non-Aligned Move-ment, cited 'our shared view on the universal validity of basic human rights'.[25] But those challenging universality also raised familiar arguments regarding national sovereignty and noninterference in the internal affairs of states, the pre-eminence of economic and social rights over civil and political rights, and the interests of the state over those of the individual. They challenged the validity of the UN's human rights machinery that criticises abusive actions by states.

The UN Secretary-General and government representatives defended univer-sality. They were spurred on by thousands of NGO representatives and by the active presence of the international media. Vocal, visible and decisive support for universality came from nongovernmental organisations from the same countries that defend particularities. Representatives of such groups insisted that human rights were universal and rooted in the cultural, historical, religious and legal traditions of their own societies. They expressed impatience with argu-ments about particularities advanced by the very governments committing atrocious abuses—the same governments that sought to keep them out of the conference proceedings. Ultimately, the NGOs succeeded in conveying the validity and importance of their message when the World Conference on Human Rights itself reaffirmed universality.[26]

A High Commissioner for Human Rights

The 1994 establishment of a UN High Commissioner for Human Rights has raised hopes that the world body's capacity to respond to and stop serious violations of human rights will improve dramatically. On the UN's drawing boards since San Francisco, the precise idea for a high commissioner was shaped in 1963 by Jacob Blaustein in his Dag Hammarskjöld Memorial Lecture at Columbia University. The United States backed it; NGOs, particularly the International League for Human Rights, lobbied for it, convincing Costa Rica to introduce the proposal formally. Thereafter, the idea bounced back and forth between the Commission on Human Rights and the subcommission until the early 1980s, when it was stripped of substance by the subcommission and otherwise abandoned by the Reagan administration and others.

The approach of the World Conference on Human Rights revived the idea, which was ardently supported by nongovernmental organisations. Official satellite meetings convened by NGOs worldwide endorsed it. Amnesty International called for establishment of a 'Special Commissioner for Human Rights', noting that the term 'high commissioner' carried with it the baggage of British colonial nomenclature. Each of the three Third World regional preparatory meetings of governments was paralleled by a nongovernmental regional meeting; and each NGO session endorsed the idea of a high commissioner. At the official Latin American regional meeting, Costa Rica succeeded in obtaining endorsement by the governmental conference of a study of the feasibility of establishing the post.[27]

By the time the fourth preparatory conference convened in Geneva in April 1993, US-based human rights NGOs, working in effective coalitions, had convinced the Clinton Administration to break with the Reagan–Bush policy of rejecting the need for a high commissioner on the grounds that enough high-level UN posts already existed. The Clinton Administration introduced this proposal at the fourth PrepCom—from which it emerged in 'brackets', signifying a lack of consensus. As the conference approached, few governments considered that the concept had any chance of survival, given the destructive mood of many rejectionist states. Predictably, the NGO Forum strongly endorsed the proposal for a high commissioner as 'a new, high-level independent authority within the United Nations system, with the capacity to act rapidly in emergency situations of human rights violations' and to ensure system-coordination and integration of human rights in all UN programmes.[28] About 60 top government officials, speaking to the plenary session of the Vienna Conference, referred to the concept. Some two-thirds favoured it, while most of the others—particularly those from Asia—called for 'further study' and cautioned about duplication of machinery and wasted resources. Hard and often creative negotiating was needed.

Lacking legislative power, the Vienna Conference did not create a high commissioner for human rights. Instead, it invigorated the idea by recommending that the UN General Assembly, which has such authority, consider the establishment of this post as a matter of priority.[29] After a 10-year hiatus, the high commissioner was back on the agenda.

At the General Assembly in September 1993, President Clinton placed the full authority of the United States, and of his office, behind the idea, urging the United Nations to create the post of high commissioner 'soon and with vigor and energy and conviction'. The foreign ministers of Belgium (for the EU), Germany, Canada, Hungary, Russia, the Gambia, Costa Rica and Sweden also spoke in favour. Cuba, setting the tone for the opposition, cautioned that it should be 'considered without undue haste, which we could in the future regret'.

Nongovernmental organisations pressed for early action and for a strong mandate, and formed a New York-based working coalition to bolster support. At the centre of this were the Jacob Blaustein Institute for the Advancement of Human Rights (recalling Blaustein's own early support), Amnesty International, Human Rights Watch, the International League for Human Rights, the International Federation for Human Rights, the International Human Rights Law Group, and the Lawyers Committee for Human Rights. Timely ideas, media commentaries, proposals and interaction with governments were strategic elements. There were comparatively few NGOs pursuing this issue in New York; and the frenzied pressure of Vienna, with Third World NGO presence, was absent. NGOs exerted pressure through strategic interventions, with the chair of the committee set up to consider the question, as well as through reports in the press and comments on various draft papers proposed by governments. Local sections and national affiliates of these groups were encouraged to intervene with their governments. The 'outside story' has been described by one participant, who emphasises the key NGO contributions during the drafting process and after the first High Commissioner was elected.[30]

The high commissioner's mandate is less specific and less activist than the proposals of NGOs or supportive governments. Still, it is flexible enough to give hope that a committed human rights leader could shape the post in the direction that nongovernmental organisations favour. The high commissioner's specific responsibilities involve making recommendations to UN bodies for the promotion and protection of all rights, including the right to development; playing 'an active role' in the elimination and prevention of violations of human rights around the world; providing overall coordination of human rights activities throughout the United Nations system; enhancing international cooperation in human rights, including the provision of technical assistance; coordinating education and public information programmes in human rights; and rationalising, adapting and strengthening UN human rights machinery. He is based in Geneva, but is supposed to have an office in New York.[31]

NGOs have emphasised that protection of human rights must assume the central role in the high commissioner's strategic planning and actions. This envisions the high commissioner responding effectively to human rights violations, wherever they occur, through effective fact-finding, public reporting, and securing relief and redress for victims of violations.

Human rights field operations

Until recently UN efforts to report and take action against abuses were conducted from afar, through Geneva-based complaint procedures or reporting based largely on NGO information, with occasional short missions by UN special rapporteurs. The situation changed as the United Nations launched human rights operations as part of multifaceted peacekeeping operations in El Salvador and Cambodia, and sent a monitoring mission to Haiti. Conceived and run in New York, these human rights missions have opened the door to other on-site UN human rights field operations in peacekeeping, humanitarian emergencies and development activities. Since 1993 new human rights monitoring offices opened in former Yugoslavia, Rwanda and Guatemala. Additionally, the Vienna Conference has encouraged an array of UN-run technical assistance human rights programmes.

The relationship of human rights to UN peacekeeping operations of the post-Cold War era have largely reflected their traditional role as outsider advocate–critics. Human Rights Watch and Amnesty International have analysed the Salvador and Cambodia operations, relying on observations of locally-based NGO groups and their own field missions, offering hortatory action-orientated recommendations about the performance of UN human rights monitoring or policing personnel. These critiques are premised on the shared assumption that human rights factors must be central to the design and execution of the peacekeeping mandates in each of the field operations. Each analysis is itself an advocacy document for the sponsoring NGOs call for stronger UN on-site presence.[32]

In spring 1995 two other New York-based human rights programmes issued book-length analyses of UN human rights field operations in El Salvador, Cambodia and Haiti.[33] With substantial detail on the planning, mandate, operation and implementation of each programme, these studies identify shortcomings and propose creating a special unit in the Department of Peacekeeping Operations (DPKO) at UN headquarters to ensure pre-mission planning, consistency and coordination across other departments, proper personnel training, appropriate relationships with local NGOs and due consideration for security. Like the earlier Amnesty International study, these reports emphasise the centrality of human rights in the design of peacekeeping mandates, particularly for those engaged in the post-conflict rebuilding of civic institutions.

Amnesty International has set forth human rights principles to be followed in designing all peacekeeping operations, calling for UN peacekeepers to be more than silent or indifferent witnesses, demanding that troops be impartial, properly trained and ready to uphold international law and to adhere to it in their own conduct as well. It does not yet offer detailed operational strategies with standard operating procedures suitable for use by soldiers or aid workers. None of the studies has yet explored such key issues as what procedures could advance on-site mission effectiveness without compromising security of mission personnel, or whether effectiveness depends more on being organisationally separate, or being integrated with the entire peacekeeping operation and its command. Neither has the United Nations itself.

The UN High Commissioner for Human Rights established a human rights monitoring mission in Rwanda as a response to the 1994 genocide. Instrumental to this was effective advocacy by Human Rights Watch, directed both at the Security Council in New York and at the high commissioner in Geneva. The Human Rights Watch Committee's expertise on Rwanda, staff contacts with locally based Rwandan human rights defenders, and high-profile media-oriented reporting—aimed at New York but also at Paris—were key factors in their effective advocacy for an expanded presence by the United Nations. Amnesty International, whose earlier campaigns on Burundi evoked only modest government attention, also played a significant role on the Geneva side. It was the first to demand an emergency session on Rwanda of the Commission on Human Rights, which in turn appointed a special rapporteur who—like his predecessor in former Yugoslavia—pressed for the more active presence of human rights field monitors.

The Centre for Human Rights has virtually no field staff experience or operational capacity, which means that there is much to do. Just as its other mechanisms have been dependent upon NGOs, field operations will probably show a similar dependency until the financing and operational experience grow dramatically.

Several of the most senior officials engaged to run the UN human rights operations have been drawn from human rights NGOs, including Ian Martin (former head of Amnesty International) for Haiti, and Diego Garcia Sayan (Andean Commission of Jurists) and Reed Brody (International Human Rights Law Group) for Salvador. Many staffers dispatched to work on-site come to the United Nations with NGO backgrounds, often in the field. Local nongovernmental organisations are not part of the UN monitoring teams, and there has been criticism that they have been inadequately consulted and often patronisingly ignored.[34] Human rights NGOs will probably continue to be the principal sources of personnel for future UN human rights monitoring missions.

The high commissioner has identified the establishment and maintenance of an 'international roster of specialized staff' available at short notice for human rights field missions as one of the long-term needs for rapid and effective responses to serious human rights violations.[35] Many if not most of the human rights officers able to depart for such emergency assignments will be drawn from experienced NGOs.

New challenges face human rights NGOs in their advocacy at and through the United Nations, even as the mandates set forth by the world organisation shift. Despite the growth in procedures and mechanisms, and the expansion of human rights into peacekeeping and other UN operations, the tasks before them become more complex and require greater skills. No situation has brought this home more clearly than the experiences in Rwanda, where political, humanitarian and human rights priorities of the UN and many nongovernmental organisations on the scene often seemed to be at odds. London-based Africa Rights, whose director formerly headed Human Rights Watch/Africa, has outlined the cognitive and operational contradictions facing humanitarian NGOs, UN agencies and peacekeepers. Tackling the argument that humanitarian field operations must be 'neutral', Africa Rights points out the distinction between 'operational neutrality' and human rights 'objectivity', and the latter's necessary focus on and solidarity with the victims of injustice and genocide.[36] In so doing, Africa Rights has challenged humanitarian NGOs to reassess their purpose and to develop new operational procedures that take account of the reality in which these groups operate and the principles of human rights that underlie UN humanitarian action.

Challenges ahead

There has been a continuing—some would argue, growing—backlash by several governments against legitimation of the engagement of human rights NGOs in UN programmes, whether they are humanitarian, peacekeeping, development or the programmes of the Centre for Human Rights. Sometimes, such backlash takes the form of opposing fact-finding mechanisms or field missions. Often, governments launch transparent attacks upon NGO information by declaring the organisations to be politically motivated, or smearing them as 'terrorists'. Ten years after its initial introduction, a UN draft declaration affirming the right of human rights NGOs to function continues to be delayed and diffused.

Since the Vienna Conference, priority has been placed on the development of technical assistance in human rights. Today, human rights NGOs seem on the verge of being offered the prospect of becoming 'insiders', working through and with the UN to achieve what has not been possible or desirable for them in the past—the delivery of legal services. Until now, programmes run by the Centre for Human Rights have purported to carry out such technical assistance, but have done so without working with or through local nongovernmental organisations. It is unclear whether international and national NGOs will join in this aspect of the UN's work and whether, if they do, it will influence their independence, impartiality, and outspokenness.

The arrival of so many new national NGOs onto the UN human rights scene has raised questions about participation in meetings. Time pressures at the 1995 Commission on Human Rights led its Malaysian chair to reduce by half the speaking time of all participants—governments and NGOs alike. Some governments argue that this should diminish NGO 'speechifying' in favour of on-the-record debate and discussion among member states. Some nongovernmental organisations have proposed that new national groups and single-issue representatives coming to the commission must show more self-discipline by grouping their statements. Others report that government speeches have grown in number and length, and that further curtailment of NGO speeches will diminish their ability to bring out real facts and build public pressure.

The impact of nongovernmental organisations is now greatest as a source of independent information that triggers special mechanisms and engenders action by UN special rapporteurs. Human rights NGOs can so profoundly influence attentiveness to human rights in UN peacekeeping, humanitarian or technical assistance programmes that an ongoing operational role in these areas ranks with the submission of detailed complaints as more significant than NGO speeches and representational activities at the Commission on Human Rights, even though such activities maintain public pressure on governments for action.

Human rights NGOs have grown in size and number, have become increasingly professional, and are located across the world. Their information now receives more acceptance and use within the UN system. As their impact grows, the political struggle waged against them—and against their access and legitimacy—intensifies. The strategic choices facing nongovernmental organisations include the issue of where to focus their resources: at home, on the core human rights reporting and action programmes in Geneva, or on the many operational programmes throughout the UN system, conceived and launched from New York. New coalitions are necessary for effectiveness throughout the UN system.

However, the political base is fragile, and the core activity for human rights NGOs in the UN remains effective interactions with the expert mechanisms of the Centre for Human Rights to build an early emergency response capacity. The great achievement of human rights NGOs has been to focus public attention on violations, mobilise outrage and maintain pressure for policy changes. Working with the high commissioner is one way to achieve this, but human rights NGOs will need to plan their strategies carefully to have an even greater system-wide impact on the United Nations.

Strategic, technical and organisational leadership in UN human rights programming has always come from the NGO sector. This must continue—to help prevent violations, to respond to those that occur and to make a reality of the hopes of those who fought so hard to ensure that human rights was one of the core purposes of the United Nations.

Notes

[1] Compare the draft language in Principle 25, UN Doc. A/CONF.157/PC/82, Fourth Preparatory Committee, World Conference on Human Rights, April 1993, and the final text in paragraph 38, Vienna Declaration and Programme of Action, World Conference on Human Rights, June 1993.

[2] Bangladesh insisted that 'tribute' to NGOs be dropped from the draft PC/82; Pakistan called for excision of positive references to NGO contributions; Indonesia proposed that the call for 'facilitating' work of NGOs be replaced by the more passive code words 'cooperation' and 'dialogue'. See Jan Bauer, 'Report on the UN World Conference on Human Rights, 31 October 1993', unpublished manuscript. The final text also added a reference to national laws notoriously restrictive to human rights NGOs.

[3] Joseph Proskauer, A Segment of My Times, New York: Farrar, Strauss, 1950, p 225.

[4] See Sidney Liskofsky, American Jewish Yearbook, 1945–46, New York: American Jewish Committee, 1946, pp 491–492; Clark M Eichelberger, Organizing for Peace, New York: Harper and Row, 1977, pp 268–273; V Riesel, New York Post, 4 May 1945; and P Edson, San Francisco News, 16 May 1945.

[5] Tom J Farer & Felice Gaer, 'The UN and human rights: at the end of the beginning', in: Adam Roberts & Benedict Kingsbury (eds), United Nations, Divided World, Oxford and New York: Oxford University Press, 1993, p 248.

[6] Roger S Clark, A United Nations High Commissioner for Human Rights, The Hague: Martinus Nijhoff, 1972.

[7] See Jerome Shestack, 'Sisyphus endures: the international human rights NGO', New York Law School Law Review, XXIV, (1), 1978, pp 89–123; and 'UN Review of the League and Other NGOs', Memorandum of the International League for Human Rights, February 1978.

[8] United Nations Action in the Field of Human Rights, New York: United Nations, 1988, pp 264–282. Also see Farer & Gaer 'The UN and human rights'.

[9] See Iain Guest, Behind the Disappearances: Argentina's Dirty War Against Human Rights and the United Nations, Philadelphia, PA: University of Pennsylvania Press, 1990, pp 79–86 and passim.

[10] See Shestack, 'Sisyphus' and 'Memorandum'.

[11] Nigel Rodley, The Treatment of Prisoners Under International Law, New York: Oxford University Press, 1987, p 196.

[12] David Kramer & David Weissbrodt, 'The 1980 Commission on Human Rights and the disappeared', Human Rights Quarterly, 1981.

[13] UN Doc. E/CN.4/1995/5, para. 26 (h).

[14] UN Doc. E/CN/4/1995/5/Add.1

[15] Helena Cook, 'Amnesty International at the UN', forthcoming in: Peter Willetts (ed), *We the Peoples*, Washington, DC: Brookings Institution, 1995.

[16] UN Doc. E/CN.4/1995/47, p 12, para 48.

[17] Ibid, 17, 52.

[18] However, Article 45 of the Convention on the Rights of the Child provides that, in reviewing implementation of the Convention, 'the Committee may invite ... other competent bodies as it may consider appropriate to provide expert advice on the implementation of the Convention ... ' This has been used to permit NGOs to interact actively with the treaty body.

[19] UN Doc. A/49/537, 19 October 1994, para 41.

[20] UN Doc. E/CN.4/1995/53, para 6.

[21] See Laurie S Wiseberg, 'Human rights non-governmental organizations', in R Claude & B Weston, *Human Rights in the World Community*, Philadelphia, PA: University of Pennsylvania Press, 1992, pp 372–382; and Shestack, 'Sisyphus'.

[22] Ludwig Boltzmann Institute of Human Rights, 'World Conference on Human Rights', *NGO-Newsletter*, 4.

[23] Ibid.

[24] See Bauer, 'Report on the UN', pp 131–132.

[25] UN Doc. A/48/214, 4.

[26] Vienna Declaration and Programme of Action (VDPA), UN Doc. A/CONF.157/23, Section I, para 5.

[27] UN Doc. A/CONF.157/58, 7.

[28] See UN Doc. A/CONF.157/7, 4.

[29] VDPA, II.B., para 18.

[30] Andrew Clapham, 'Creating the High Commissioner for Human Rights: the outside story', *European Journal of International Law*, 5, (4), 1994, pp 556–568.

[31] See General Assembly Resolution A/Res/48/141.

[32] See Americas Watch, *El Salvador-Peace and Human Rights: Successes and Shortcomings of the UN Observer Mission in El Salvador (ONUSAL)*, New York: Americas Watch, 2 September 1992; Human Rights Watch, *The Lost Agenda: Human Rights and UN Field Operations*, New York: Human Rights Watch, 1993; and Amnesty International, *Peacekeeping and Human Rights*, London, Amnesty International, January 1994.

[33] Lawyers' Committee for Human Rights, *Haiti: Learning the Hard Way. The UN/OAS Human Rights Monitoring Operation in Haiti, 1993–94*, New York: The Lawyers' Committee for Human Rights, 1995; and *Honoring Human Rights and Keeping the Peace: Lessons from El Salvador, Cambodia and Haiti*, New York: The Justice and Society Program, Aspen Institute, 1995.

[34] See Rakiya Omaar & Alex de Waal, *Humanitarianism Unbound*, Working Paper No 5, London: Africa Rights, November 1994, pp 18–33.

[35] UN Doc. E/CN.4/1995/98/ paras 32, 23.

[36] Omaar & de Waal, *Humanitarianism Unbound*.

NGOs and the UN System in Complex Humanitarian Emergencies: Conflict or Cooperation?

ANDREW S NATSIOS

This article explores the evolving relationship between the United Nations (UN) system and nongovernmental organisations (NGOs) in responding to complex humanitarian emergencies, and describes the two sets of actors, their organisational cultures, governance and mandates. It examines why the two sets of organisations have been drawn into a closer collaboration in dealing with civil conflicts and famines, how that interaction is working from both an operational and policy perspective and whether both are suited as currently constituted to respond to ongoing challenges. What are the unique institutional competencies and weaknesses each brings to relief responses? How is the friction between the UN and NGOs manifested in their diverse missions, operational styles and organisational cultures?

This essay focuses on operational and organisational cooperation between NGOs and the UN system, but not on the role of the military or the media in the humanitarian response system, subjects that have been well covered elsewhere.[1] Although operational NGOs in particular have been increasing their activity in policy and advocacy work in complex emergencies, this essay also does not address this work, which would require another essay in itself.

In Africa, the Balkans, the Middle East and the former Soviet Union, the growing number of failed states has produced a widening level of chaos to which NGOs and the UN have tried to respond. However, even the most charitable assessment must conclude that their responses have had mixed results. These complex humanitarian emergencies are defined by five common characteristics: the deterioration or complete collapse of central government authority; ethnic or religious conflict and widespread human rights abuses; episodic food insecurity, frequently deteriorating into mass starvation; macroeconomic collapse involving hyperinflation, massive unemployment and net decreases in GNP; and mass population movements of displaced people and refugees escaping conflict or searching for food. This instability does not respect national boundaries and frequently spills over into neighbouring countries, many of which are themselves unstable. The spreading chaos does not appear to be subsiding and presents the international community with a major challenge.

Some observers have argued that these emergencies have caused a shift of increasingly scarce resources away from sustainable development to life-saving humanitarian interventions. The amount of funding provided by the United States Agency for International Development (US AID) to UN organisations, the International Organization for Migrations (IOM), the International Committee of the Red Cross (ICRC) and NGOs for relief interventions in complex humanitarian emergencies has risen dramatically beginning in the late 1980s. In 1989 the Office of Foreign Disaster Assistance (OFDA) and Food for Peace (FFP), both US AID offices, provided $297 million in cash and food grants for humanitarian relief; by 1993 that had increased to $1.2 billion.[2]

Funding for relief work is derived from four US government accounts: the OFDA, Title II of P.L. 480, Section 416 food aid (from the Department of Agriculture), and the refugee programme budget (in the State Department). Much of the actual increase during this period has been in food aid, which would probably not have been used for development purposes, and which is now in precipitous decline. These funds would not have been used for sustainable development, which is not as politically popular as disaster relief in the US Congress or among the American people. This ambivalence over development assistance is reflected in Washington's relative contribution to relief efforts compared to other developed countries. The USA proportionally provides the tenth highest level of relief assistance among OECD countries, although it trails at 20th place in development assistance. It is not that relief funding is so high, it is that development assistance is so low.[3]

A complex response system has evolved to spend this money and respond to these emergencies, more by accident than design; it is composed of three sets of institutional actors: NGOs, UN organisations and the International Red Cross movement.

Nongovernmental organisations

NGOs are perhaps the most complex and diverse of these three sets of actors, particularly those involved in complex humanitarian emergencies. Although there are 1500 NGOs registered with the UN system as having observer status, only 400 are registered with US AID, a process necessary for them to receive US government grants.[4]

When Operation Restore Hope was deployed to Somalia in December 1992, there were 40 international NGOs working in the country. In November 1993, 76 NGOs had mail boxes at the UN High Commissioner for Refugees (UNHCR) offices at the Rwandan refugee camps in Goma, Zaire.[5] These NGOs were almost entirely based in the Western democracies. Although a mailbox in Goma is certainly an indication of some activity, these numbers are misleading. Many of these nongovernmental organisations provided services in Goma and Somalia on a modest scale for a few months and then left. Many others delivered gifts in kind—such as pharmaceuticals and clothing—to operational NGOs which then provided them to people in the refugee camps. Others are the national offices of the same international NGO: for example, Médicins Sans Frontières has national chapters in Spain, France, Belgium and the Netherlands, and members of these chapters worked together at Goma.

In short, most NGOs are not involved in relief. There are perhaps 20 in the USA and another 20 in Europe that work in complex emergencies. This work is sustained, technically sound and widespread enough to have an impact on the situation on the ground. Of these 40 NGOs, perhaps 10 US and another 10

European NGOs receive 75% of all the public funds spent by NGOs in complex emergencies. Ten US NGOs received 76% of all cash grants to NGOs for relief purposes from the US government in fiscal year (FY) 1993 and over 87% of all food aid for relief purposes in FY 1993.[6] The European Union gave 65% of all relief grants to 20 nongovernmental organisations in FY 1994.

These relief NGOs frequently specialise in one or more of the five activities that are commonly understood to compose the relief discipline: food distribution, shelter, water, sanitation and medical care. To this may be added the rehabilitation efforts to bring a society traumatised by a complex emergency to minimum self-sufficiency: animal husbandry, agriculture and primary health care. Perhaps half of these NGOs perform relief work exclusively, whereas the other half work in both relief and development. The larger development NGOs (CARE, Catholic Relief Services, World Vision, Save the Children, and Oxfam/ UK) have the added advantage in many complex emergencies of having had development programmes and staff to run them in the countries before the onset of the emergency. This advantage gives them a familiarity with the culture, ethnic groups and development programmes of the country as well as with indigenous staff.

Since the Ethiopian famine of 1985—a watershed event for most of the 10 major NGOs that work in relief—a quiet revolution has taken place in doctrine and practice between relief and development.[7] Traditional relief efforts were commodity-driven and logistically-based, with little programmatic, economic or developmental thought given to how the relief effort might be more than simply pushing down death rates and saving lives. Most NGOs, as a matter of policy, will now try to integrate into their relief work developmental components particularly focused in agriculture, microenterprise, primary health care, reforestation and road construction. This is done through food or cash for which recipients are assigned a specific project that community leaders have determined is of longer-term importance in the area. Much more effort now is spent on examining the economics of what is happening in famine, with the major food NGOs conducting household, food price and market surveys as a regular part of their relief interventions. A recent study of the USAID/OFDA effort in the Somalia emergency showed that 50% of its relief grants to NGOs contained developmental interventions.[8]

NGOs derive their financial support from both public and private sources. A few will accept no public sector money, while others get between 60%–70% of their income from donor governments.[9] Although UN funds and programmes have increasingly been making relief grants to NGOs, these grants do not yet approach the level of donor government grant assistance, a condition that may shortly change if present trends continue. NGO private funding resources come primarily from mass media appeals (most notably television), direct mail and major donor government contributions. US law requires an NGO to raise at least 20% of its aggregate resources privately to be eligible to apply for government funding. Most donor governments have created disaster relief offices—such as Agency for International Development's OFDA, Food for Peace and the European Community Humanitarian Office (ECHO) of the European Union—to provide grant assistance to NGOs, the ICRC and UN organisations.

How these NGOs are organised and governed affects their work. They have chosen four models to organise themselves internationally. First, all began and some remain with one headquarters based entirely in one country, even though they work internationally in others, for example, the International Rescue Committee and the International Medical Corps. Second, some have many autonomous national chapters with independent field organisations, each reporting back to the home offices. This means several offices may work independently of each other in the same country, for example Save the Children and Oxfam. Third, some have chosen to create many national fund-raising offices that pool their collective funds and spend them through a single worldwide field organisations, which is indigenously staffed and managed, such as World Vision International and the International Federation of Red Cross and Red Crescent Societies. A variation of this is a hybrid of the second and third models, in which each national headquarters has its own field organisation but is assigned specific emergencies in which to work by a central international organisation to avoid competition in the same country, e.g. CARE. Fourth, others only work through indigenous local NGOs that are not part of their organisational structure; they have no independent operational capacity in the field outside such indigenous partner agencies as the Church World Service, Oxfam/US, and Christian Children's Fund.

Each model has particular advantages and drawbacks. The first model tends to be the fastest in operations and decision making and the least bureaucratic; the second tends to be the most flexible, internally competitive and, at times, organisationally contentious; the third tends to have deeper community roots and capacity to aggregate large amounts of money rapidly for a particular relief programme; and the fourth has the deepest community roots but does not have a field staff that it may direct to a particular emergency and so lacks flexibility and quality control.

NGOs are governed by boards of directors that tend to reflect the particular culture, history and mandates of the organisations concerned. The board of directors of the International Medical Corps, a US NGO that specialises in emergency medical care in conflict, for instance, has been dominated by the medical professionals who founded it. Catholic bishops serving on the board of directors of Catholic Relief Services is another example. Since most NGOs raise money among a particular market segment of the American people, they must design their field programmes around the interests of their constituency or they may not survive. Under the NGO standards required by InterAction (the American nongovernmental organisation partnership association) of its 160 members, NGO bylaws must provide for term limits to ensure rotation of board members, require some racial and gender diversity, avoid appointing relatives of NGO executives, and limit the number of senior staff who serve on their boards. A similar set of standards exists for European and Third World NGOs which are members of the International Council of voluntary Agencies (ICVA), the European equivalent of InterAction. Most major relief NGOs belong to either of these two associations and most try to conform to these standards. Their boards of directors approve annual budgets; hire; review and fire the chief executive officer; and control major corporate policy decisions. Some are involved in operations, approving, for example, each new programme initiative and advocacy position on public policy taken by the organisation.

The rash of recent emergencies has created the impression that NGOs are in the business of ambulance chasing as they appear on the scene in large numbers to provide assistance. This impression is somewhat accurate. To attract private contributions to run their programmes, the NGOs must make use of news events and media coverage, which raise public awareness in a way that no paid advertisement could ever achieve. The more dramatic the event, the greater the media coverage, and the greater the ease of fundraising around it. Overhead rates for nongovernmental organisations are one of the few constant measures of success used to judge their worthiness as charities in the annual rankings of NGO efficiency in such publications as *Money Magazine* and the *Wall Street Journal*. These rankings affect NGO fundraising success in a self-reinforcing cycle that ultimately puts a high premium on early and visible involvement in relief operations. Fundraising around highly visible humanitarian crises raises more money at a lower cost than any other form of advertising or publicity. Certain NGOs have been attacked for what some critics call 'relief pornography'—raising money by showing scenes of starving children that wrench the donor's heart and portray a sense of helplessness. This distorts an organisation's judgment on where to work and when, but it is not an easily addressed problem since without funding they cannot work at all.

Nongovernmental organisations are accountable to their boards, but accountability to their contributors and beneficiaries is more tenuous. Unlike a profit-making business where customers can judge the quality of the service or product that they have purchased, the beneficiaries of the NGO contributions in a relief intervention have no regular way of registering individually their approval or dissatisfaction to donors of an organisation, or for that matter ICRC or UN performance. Likewise, private donors have no direct experience with the quality of the work that their contributions support. Good marketing does not necessarily ensure good programming. As a general proposition, NGOs make an effort in good faith—given the altruistic motivation of most of their workers and managers—to involve the people they serve in the field with how resources are spent. Community participation is an elemental axiom of NGO work. The wide variation in the quality of field programmes and the technical competence of staffs is a testament to the limitations of the existing system of accountability. Larger NGOs—the combined budgets of CARE, World Vision and Catholic Relief Services, the three largest NGOs, exceed $1 billion—have developed many of the management information, evaluation and control systems of private sector corporations to monitor quality in their projects.

Perhaps the most encouraging recent trend in the NGO community has been the growing presence of indigenous nongovernmental organisations working in their own countries to provide services during complex emergencies. In Liberia, during the worst period of chaos in the capital city, Monrovia, in the summer and autumn of 1990, all UN agencies, international NGOs, and even the ICRC had evacuated. The only Western presence at the time was a team of five operational staff from OFDA to run a relief effort to feed and provide medical care to 500 000 people in desperate conditions as four undisciplined militias fought for control of the city. The OFDA team enlisted the support of the local community to run the relief effort by forming an indigenous Liberian NGO that effectively distributed food, water and medical services. While the OFDA team withdrew six months later, the indigenous NGO did not and it continues its work today. The ICRC formed Somali women's committees to run hundreds of open air soup kitchens in Somalia in 1992, which fed hundreds of thousands of people during the worst of the chaos. These women's committees, independent of the ICRC, resurrected the moribund school system of Mogadishu and put 500 teachers and 20 000 students back in the classroom by using ICRC food aid to pay the teachers. The World Food Programme (WFP) worked with CARE and gave grants of local currency generated by the monetisation of food aid in Somalia in 1993 and 1994 to local Somali NGOs, which from all reports were quite effective on smaller scale projects. Bosnian Muslim NGOs have been the most effective in providing assistance during the conflict because they have been willing to take risks that international NGOs would never consider. Also they know the terrain and feel the suffering themselves. These indigenous NGOs are perhaps the fastest growing part of the relief response system and provide an intuitive understanding of local conditions that international NGOs could not hope to equal.

The UN system

Four UN organisations have become such visible players in most complex humanitarian emergencies that describing their functions and mandates will describe most if not all of the operational work of the entire UN system in relief operations. They are the World Food Programme, the Office of the United Nations High Commissioner for Refugees, the United Nations Children's Fund (UNICEF) and the United Nations Development Programme (UNDP). The first three are clearly the strongest and most indispensable. Although UNDP technically has the mandate to manage UN emergency operations in the field, it has been unwilling or perhaps unable to manage and technically fulfil its assigned role, and it has not distinguished itself by the work it has done either in quality or speed. The creation of the Department of Humanitarian Affairs (DHA) in the UN secretariat in December 1991 to coordinate UN work in complex emergencies is testimony to UNDP's failure—coordination had been the assigned task of the UNDP for two decades. A half dozen other UN agencies, seeing the movement of donor resources to complex emergencies, have flung themselves into the organisational chaos, but they arguably lack serious operational capacity or experience, and have only limited relief resources.

The WFP functions as the food aid agency of the UN system, providing a central coordinating role in developing crop production estimates, food aid requirements and logistics planning for major relief operations. At $1.8 billion its annual budget is the largest of the big four. It signed its first worldwide NGO cooperative agreement for relief operations in February 1995 with Catholic Relief Services and it is now engaged in negotiations over similar agreements with three other NGOs. WFP has had only a limited history of work with international NGOs, a historical reality that it is fast overcoming. Although WFP is organisationally subordinate to the United Nations and the Food and Agriculture Organization (FAO), it has become virtually independent since the 1991 reforms.

UNICEF's special mandate is to focus on the relief and development needs of women and children, which has made it the focal point among the big four UN agencies for emergency medical interventions, mass inoculation campaigns for children, water and sanitation programmes and therapeutic feeding programmes for severely malnourished children in emergencies. This work has placed it for some time in closer contact with NGOs at the village level than any other of the big four organisations. UNICEF is the only one of the UN entities with a substantial popular following in donor countries and a contributor base that provides significant private support for its work.

UNHCR has the longest history of the big four funds and programmes; its predecessor was created during the 1920s under the League of Nations. It also has the longest history of work with NGOs and spends the largest amount of money—at least $300 million annually—in grants to 130 NGOs, many of them indigenous. Although the bulk of its funding still goes to host governments to run refugee camps, the rush of events and the need for speed has made the NGO–UNHCR partnership more intimate and frequent in recent years, particularly in complex emergencies.[10]

UNDP, the development programme of the UN system, does only limited work with international or indigenous NGOs in emergencies. By tradition, as well as General Assembly guidelines, the UNDP resident representative in each country normally acts as the UN's resident coordinator with pre-eminent executive authority to coordinate other UN agencies. This authority also extends to disasters, although UNDP field representatives have been remarkably unprepared and unwilling to perform this function, with a few notable exceptions, for example Michael Priestley's strong leadership in Sudan during the civil war as UNDP resident representative was of consistently high quality. UNDP has occasionally funded certain public service projects in complex emergencies, such as managing airport facilities, city water and electrical systems, and other public services needed to support life, particularly in urban areas. The UNDP niche in the provision of public services in complex emergencies is the least developed and most needed of functions of the UN system.

The International Red Cross system

The International Red Cross movement arose out of the horrific conditions on the battlefield at Solferino in 1859, and its mandate has now been extended to alleviate suffering during conventional armed conflicts. The movement is the oldest, most disciplined and best organised of the three sets of actors of the international relief response system, with a worldwide budget of about $600 million. The ICRC also conveys family messages across conflict lines, reunites families separated by war and protects prisoners of war.[11] Its budget is primarily funded by annual block grants from donor governments, and to a lesser degree national Red Cross and Red Crescent societies, in much the same way as the UN funds and programmes obtain their funding. The ICRC operates under a set of inviolate principles that have been integrated into the nine governing principles of the national Red Cross and Red Crescent societies. These include absolute political neutrality in a conflict; indeed, the Red Cross symbol is the visual embodiment of the principle of neutrality in war. ICRC operating procedures require that they work on both sides of any armed conflict and that they respond to and practise complete transparency in all operations, notifying both sides each time a convoy departs, arrives or is delayed. These procedures sometimes put them at odds with NGOs and the UN agencies, and it encourages their insularity as an organisation, although their rules make it possible for them to work in armed conflicts where few other institutions dare go.

The age, doctrine, funding mechanism and mandates of the ICRC set it apart from both the UN system and the NGO community. Other than UNHCR, no other humanitarian relief organisation has a mandate assigned to it under international law, as are the cases of UNHCR under the UN Charter and the ICRC under the Geneva Conventions and Additional Protocols. The ICRC is an international organisation, not an NGO, and yet it is outside the UN system. As an international organisation, the ICRC more jealously guards its autonomy and prerogatives than any of the other institutional actors—UN or NGO—and resists coordination, but it shares information, sometimes reluctantly, and will attend organising meetings. For the most part, however, it must be discussed separately from either nongovernmental or intergovernmental organisations.

Collaboration of NGOs with the 'big four'

The collaboration of NGOs and the major four funds and programmes active in the humanitarian arena has increased dramatically over a short time. In most complex emergencies, host governments do not exist or exist in such anaemic form that they are ineffective as an interlocutor for the UN system, which deals with NGOs increasingly as the first responders. UN agencies have traditionally focused their attention on governments, their primary constituency, while NGOs focus on grassroots development at the village level and cooperate with developing country governments only at the regional or provincial level during emergency operations. Under this traditional paradigm, UN agencies viewed NGOs as subcontractors in a clearly subordinate position—paid for services performed—not as equal partners with unique capacities, particularly in humanitarian relief operations. This has caused the resentment by UN agencies of nongovernmental organisations when they do not act in the way expected, and by NGOs when they are treated as contractors rather than equal partners.

The UN system and the NGO community have made some progress at improved collaboration as the international humanitarian response system has matured. The Department of Humanitarian Affairs initiated monthly coordination meetings with NGOs in New York and Geneva to exchange information and discuss policy disputes in complex emergencies. UNHCR is well under way with its Partnership in Action (PARinAC) initiative to develop an operational and policy framework for working with NGOs. In complex emergencies, UN field offices have provided a natural coordination mechanism for nongovernmental organisations and UN organisations that has at least improved the exchange of information among the response agencies.

This recent UN and NGO marriage is more a relationship of convenience arranged by the press of events and overbearing donor governments than a passionate romance. The partners remain distrustful and moody when working together and are uncomfortable with the contrived arrangement. This discomfort is not based on an absence of familiarity with one another; they have good reason to be uncomfortable. The two sets of institutions compete for scarce donor government resources, speak to quite different constituencies that are frequently hostile to each other, recruit different kinds of people to work for them and move at distinctly different speeds. One institution measures success by whether host governments are pleased, the other by whether public and private donors are happy. One is more centralised, the other highly decentralised. NGO field directors generally have much more authority over the programme and management than their UN field counterparts, a situation about which many of the latter complain a great deal. One encourages risk-taking (some would argue cowboyism) and informality; the other advocates regular procedures and bureaucratic propriety. There are some overlapping functional claims between UN organisations and NGOs in complex emergencies, which means turf wars over competing roles and mandates. The UN system is more feudal than integrated, while the four agencies work essentially independently of one another.

While UN agencies and NGOs may wish for a discrete divorce or at least separation, in the chaos of complex emergencies they need each other more than they may want to admit. Each brings unique mandates and potential competencies to the relief response discipline, which are essential if collapsed societies are to be assisted in restoring some measure of self-sufficiency. The challenge now is to reach a consensus about who does what best to clarify institutional mandates and limitations, and better define roles.

As a general proposition, NGOs do their relief and development work at the grassroots level, which is labour intensive from a staff perspective, both expatriate and indigenous. Thus, they tend to have large field staffs that can carry out complex operations in remote areas. Philosophically, they are committed to empowering people at the lowest level of social organisation—the family and the village—to work collectively towards the sort of social and economic services that would typically be run by municipal government; however, NGOs are sometimes inconsistent in following their own ideology. Some services succeed more than others. These include community-based health care, primary and secondary education, agricultural extension work, water and sanitation projects, small-scale enterprise typically through cooperatives or small loans, road and bridge construction, and environmental programmes, particularly reforestation. These are the same operational and sectoral skills NGOs use in their relief response operations.

These strengths are at the same time weaknesses. The greatest single endemic weakness of NGOs is their reluctance to cede managerial or programme autonomy towards the goal of greater strategic coherence or managerial efficiency. Most lack either the will or the self-discipline to surrender autonomy and integrate their work with other actors. Their focus on the village and neighbourhood has been at the expense of dealing with national problems of governance, economic reform, planning and policy—which, when done badly, can cancel out overnight any grassroots successes their programmes may have enjoyed. NGOs have a problem of scale in their field programmes; they produce patches of green in barren landscapes, patches that are small, fragile and usually unconnected to each other.

UN funds and programmes are comparatively weak in field operations, with a modest presence usually in the country capital. They work under the UN Charter with the host government in each country. Most UN assistance then moves through host government ministries where UN organisations cultivate relationships with senior policy makers and managers. They are not heavily involved with grassroots organisations, with the possible exception of UNICEF because of the nature of its mandate. This means that the UN is much more familiar with central government bureaucracies and public services than most NGOs.

These two quite different sets of NGO and UN missions mean that when countries sink into civil war or ethnic conflict, their relief roles not unnaturally reflect their missions and unique competencies; they do what they know best. The UN tries to negotiate country-wide access in conflict areas, exemptions from customs duties for relief commodities and protection agreements for relief workers from the violence of the conflicts—essential tasks at which NGOs have little experience or success. UN agencies are reluctant to violate the sovereignty of any of the organisations constituencies and member states. This recalcitrance is not merely a function of the UN Charter, but also the prejudice of some UN staff, who are drawn from the educated elites of developing countries and retain a suspicion of Western colonial ambitions reasserting themselves under the guise of humanitarian interventionism. Only when the Security Council has voted for resolutions permitting a violation of state sovereignty will the system respond. NGOs have fewer inhibitions, except where they are working on both sides of a conflict and risk censure or danger from the national government. In fact, NGOs have violated state sovereignty over extended periods of time in at least four civil wars in Africa, Iraq and Bosnia. This same paradigm functions with respect to advocacy on human rights and diplomatic issues: UN staff are hesitant to criticise publicly a member state during a civil war, while NGOs do this more often in the context of their normal advocacy efforts.

There have been four reform efforts over the past three years to force UN agencies to work in a more cohesive and integrated way in complex emergencies. These reforms may have the combined effect of encouraging the UN system to design a single defined strategy in each complex emergency. NGOs look, however reluctantly, to the UN to provide some measure of operational coordination during complex emergencies, and these reforms strengthen the UN's capacity for doing so.

This coordination function was the major rationale for the creation of the DHA, led by an under-secretary general in New York, the first of these reforms. Although DHA has made some progress in fulfilling its mandate, there are intrinsic institutional limitations built into the UN system itself that make this task unenviable. Although the secretary-general (to which the under-secretary general who heads DHA reports) has legal authority over the big four UN programmes, they do what they want in practice. Their policy, budgets, personnel and procurement are self-contained, controlled internally by these independent UN organisations. Their governing boards reflect donor and recipient country politics more than those of the central bureaucracy at the secretariat or of the secretary-general himself, which are not necessarily the same thing. The field offices of UN organisations in emergencies are not necessarily responsive to the special representative of the secretary-general or of the representative of DHA who is theoretically in charge of the coordination of the UN's relief operations in an emergency. These field offices report back to their organisational headquarters and not to DHA directors in the field. Agency field directors are not deliberately uncooperative. However, the DHA representative does not have the institutional authority to resolve any disputes over policy, management and strategy among the big four in the field except by intellect or personality. This is not easily remedied in the absence of unlikely changes in the basic authority of the secretary-general.

The second of these reforms was proposed by the Nordic countries and approved by the General Assembly in 1993. The reform gives the Economic and Social Council (ECOSOC) oversight over the policy, budget and management of the big four funds and programmes. This administrative innovation may begin to put some pressure on these agencies to work more intimately together in emergency situations and force some measure of accountability when they do not. It remains to be seen whether this innovation will have salutary operational or strategic consequences.

The third reform is now being drafted within the UN secretariat. It would encourage a greater degree of information sharing, joint policy and strategy development, and overall management among the under-secretary-generals in charge of the political, military and humanitarian functions in the departments of Humanitarian Affairs, Peace-keeping Operations and Political Affairs during complex emergencies. There has been until now no formal mechanism for integrating these functions in headquarters, a situation that has not encouraged coordination among these three functions in the field. If this reform is successful, it may lead to the UN equivalent of Washington's National Security Council as a coordination and management mechanism for more coherent direction in field operations during complex humanitarian emergencies.

The fourth and perhaps most important innovation has been the creation of the Inter-Agency Standing Committee (IASC): a coordination mechanism chaired by the UN under-secretary-general for Humanitarian Affairs. Created in January 1992, it is composed of the 'big four' UN organisations: the World Health Organization; the Food and Agriculture Organization which should not have been included in the group because of its lack of expertise and operational capacity in disaster response; the ICRC (the Federation of Red Cross and Crescent Societies); and the International Organization for Migrations; and representatives of the European and US NGOs. The IASC meets quarterly, but only its principals are allowed to attend. Between meetings, working groups do much of the staff work on specific issues. This mechanism has improved the flow of information, but has been unable to design comprehensive strategies or enforce discipline in the response system. It has two major weaknesses. The donor aid agencies that fund much of this work are not members, and DHA has not had the bureaucratic power to force integration of UN organisations. It is, however, a step in the right direction.

Conclusion

Perhaps the single most serious challenge to the international community is developing and implementing strategies for dealing with failed states or preventing their collapse in the first instance. There is by no means a consensus among donor governments, NGOs, the ICRC and UN agencies on the need for a unified strategy in each complex emergency. Some argue that a thousand flowers should bloom and every agency should do its own thing. Information is shared reluctantly if donors insist, but nothing more. Given the gap between resources and needs, resources need to be leveraged to increase their influence. Conflicting strategies and objectives, or their abysmal absence, in complex emergencies with multiple actors frequently cancel each other out. Conversely, a single coherent strategy could allow the aggregation of sufficient resources to change the course of a conflict. Without clear objectives, the managers of the international response system will never know whether they have achieved their goals. Such achievements could convince wary parliamentarians, media and public opinion in donor countries that the heavy investment of public funds in relief response serves some successful purpose other than just keeping people alive so that they can die later. Given the declining donor resources for development and reconstruction after conflicts, as many developmental components as possible need to be built into relief responses. All these arguments suggest the need for a single unified strategy. Neither NGOs nor UN agencies are in a position to impose this sort of discipline. DHA, which might logically be charged with such a mission, has neither the political clout nor the resources to inject some discipline into this unruly, feudal response system.

While the UN system and particularly DHA will argue that their coordination work in complex emergencies amounts to a strategic plan, few of the actors—UN organisations or NGOs—wish to be coordinated, much less conform to a single strategy. Coordination has many meanings in management theory. In the present context of complex emergencies, it has become a mechanism for combining the wish lists of the UN and NGO relief agencies, even if the programmes have little chance of being funded, or even contradict each other. It can become a lowest common denominator rather than a higher standard of policy or performance. Coordination in this context is not particularly helpful. It certainly does not solve the strategy problem.

Even if all actors in the response system agreed that some unified strategy were essential, one serious impediment remains. The highly decentralised, feudal nature of the response system itself is made up of the UN system, with three central headquarters staff directorates in the secretariat (humanitarian affairs, peacekeeping operations and political affairs); the big four UN organisations (UNDP, UNICEF, WFP and UNHCR); 40 major relief NGOs; the ICRC (and the Red Cross Movement, which is an organisationally discrete entity); the military units making up international forces (all of which report back operationally to their military command structures in their home countries rather than to the UN force commander in the field); the US State Department and foreign ministries of other interested countries; and the foreign disaster response offices of donor countries (OFDA and ECHO). If one were present at the creation of this Byzantine system, one could not have created a more complex and convoluted structure.

Wildavsky and Pressman argue persuasively that the more organisational entities involved in a decision-making process, the greater the opportunity for delay, if not paralysis.[12] They point out that the mathematical probability of reaching a decision on a public policy issue is quite low when dozens of organisations have veto power or the power to delay a decision. Maximum feasible participation in decision making, given the lengthy list of actors, equates to operational chaos, deadly delay and inevitable failure in disaster response. It is noteworthy that the most successful humanitarian response effort in the post-Cold War era—Kurdistan in 1991—initially involved no UN organisations or UN peacekeeping forces but rather three military commands that had just fought in the Gulf War together, one donor country response office and no more than half a dozen NGOs. Limited organisational participation in this context translated into operational success.

Absent is a complete reorganisation of the relief response structure, which is politically and administratively infeasible and perhaps even undesirable from a policy perspective, but we must focus on incremental reform of the existing humanitarian order. The most feasible and salutary changes that might now be made would be to aggregate relief actors within each organisational sector. The United Nations would centralise authority for the formulation of a single UN strategy in one entity, which after all was the original concept behind DHA. NGOs would similarly organise themselves through InterAction and ICVA. Donor disaster response offices would do the same. Then a small group of representatives, one for each set of actors (UN, NGO, ICRC, military representatives if peacekeeping troops were involved and donor aid agencies), could meet and design a strategy. This ultimately would involve a workable entity of no more than half a dozen people. Any serious attempt at aggregation would require a commitment by the actors to would cede much organisational autonomy, something that is now jealously guarded. Such structural reform would require a high degree of organisational discipline and perhaps even some sanctions for organisations which refuse to participate in good faith. This reform stretches even the most expansive definition of coordination, perhaps the most abused and ill-defined word in the disaster response vocabulary. It is perhaps the best we can do under the circumstances.

The response system cannot continue to function as it does now; it is on the verge of breakdown. With the exception of military forces, all the organisations are seriously overcommitted in coping with the demands being placed on them. The rolling tide of complex emergencies is moving so rapidly that organisations have been drawn into each new major crisis before completing work on the last. The emotional toll that these emergencies are taking on relief staff cannot be calculated quantitatively, but it is significant. What is the psychological toll on staff watching the genocide in Rwanda or the atrocities in Bosnia? This has meant that NGOs and UN organisations are increasingly sending inexperienced staff to the field to run massive operations that even seasoned managers would find intimidating. This work is not a nine-to-five, Monday to Friday job. A rationalisation of the existing response system would progress some way towards relieving at least some of the organisational stress at a time when institutions are at a breaking point. More importantly, these reforms would increase, but not guarantee, the chances for designing successful strategies for managing and perhaps resolving these crises.

The marriage of convenience between NGOs and the UN system in relief responses over time may become comfortable enough that *ad hoc* arrangements will work, even if a passionate love affair never occurs. For most NGOs and most UN organisations, the marriage is a recent affair, beginning sometime over the last half decade. The organisational cultures are understanding each other better, perhaps at times even respecting each other. Given the horrific circumstances in the field in which this marriage of convenience has been consummated, problems are hardly surprising. Both sets of actors need each other, and that organisational need may be the key to the success of the relationship. The rationalisation of the design and execution of a unified strategy will increase the chances for success of the responses to complex emergencies. Nothing works better than success—however it is defined—to cement a partnership. There have been precious few successes, which has resulted in name-calling and finger-pointing among the actors. Success encourages collaboration and cooperation, failure discourages it. As the system matures, the marriage of convenience may ultimately work, but it will take time and patience.

Notes

[1] See Jonathan Benthall, *Disasters, Relief and the Media* (London: Tauris, 1993); and Andrew Natsios, 'International humanitarian response system', *Parameters*, Spring 1995; pp 68–81.

[2] See *Office of Foreign Disaster Assistance Annual Report, FY 1991*, Washington, DC: Government Printing Office, 1991 pp 8–9. However, little of this increased funding was initiated by the Bush Administration, with the exception of the Kurdish emergency, where a special appropriation was requested. Congress offered the increased funding in the face of escalating disasters frequently in special appropriations outside the budget cycle. Without this rising tide of emergencies, appropriations for development assistance would have been no higher. Development assistance has never been a particularly popular programme in the US Congress, but disaster relief (cash and food) continues to enjoy broad congressional and public support across party and ideological divides. In the case of food assistance for relief, much of the additional resources for complex emergencies has come from the Section 416 programme of the US Department of Agriculture, food aid which would probably not have been programmed for development purposes. With the depletion of Section 416, surplus stocks in FY 1993 and changes in the agricultural price supports that ensure that this depletion will not be restocked, increased food aid for emergencies will undoubtedly come at the expense of food for development under Title II of the Office of Food for Peace. The World Food Programme's (WFP) relief and development programmes have traditionally received equal shares of resources until the late 1980s when an appreciable shift began. At present, relief receives two-thirds of total resources, while the rest is programmed to development. This increased food aid for relief has not resulted in an actual decline in food aid for development; relief resources pledged by donor governments have increased markedly.

[3] See Department of Humanitarian Affairs rankings of ODC countries response to consolidated humanitarian appeals.

[4] See AID 1994 Annual Report, entitled *Voluntary Foreign Aid Programs, Bureau for Humanitarian Response*, Washington, DC: Government Printing Office, 1994, pp 70–97.

[5] I visited the UNHCR headquarters at Goma in November 1994 and counted the mailboxes.

[6] This figure is an estimate based on the grant-making experience of OFDA and the Office of Food for Peace. Four NGOs (CARE, Catholic Relief Services, World Vision and the Adventist Development and Relief Agency) received 87% of all NGO food aid grants for relief and development under Title II of P.L. 480. See Office of Foreign Disaster Assistance rankings of cash grants to NGOs for FY 1993.

[7] See Mary Anderson & Peter Woodrow, *Rising From the Ashes: Disaster Response to Development*, Boulder, CO: Westview Press), 1989.

[8] See Refugee Policy Group, *Humanitarian Aid in Somalia: The Role of the Office of US Foreign Disaster Assistance (OFDA) 1990–1994*, Washington, DC: Refugee Policy Group, November 1994, p 27.

[9] *Voluntary Foreign Aid Programs*, pp 70–97.

[10] UN High Commissioner for Refugees, *Refugees*, 97, 1994, p 8. This issue is devoted to NGOs and UNHCR, with particular emphasis on PARinAC.

[11] See International Committee of the Red Cross, *ICRC 1993 Annual Report*, Geneva; ICRC, 1993, pp 273, 277.

[12] Aaron Wildavsky & Jeffrey Pressman, *Implementation*, Berkeley, CA: University of California Press, 1979, pp 105–108, 147.

restraints

■ 4 ■

The Bureaucracy and the Free Spirits: Stagnation and Innovation in the Relationship Between the UN and NGOs

ANTONIO DONINI

The emergence of nongovernmental organisations (NGOs) in national and international society is a significant development of the last two decades. The theoretical and practical implications of how this sea change affects the functioning of the international system are analysed elsewhere in this issue. Suffice it to say here that the United Nations (UN), despite the fact that it is a polity of states, is one of the privileged venues for this escalating dialectical relationship between states and non-states. New issues and actors are knocking at the UN's door. It is no longer possible to keep them out; if the door is locked they will come in through the window or the cracks in the floor. There is no single area of UN activity that is not in some way shaped or touched by this relationship. Interactions between the world institution and the variegated torch-bearers and stakeholders of civil society express themselves in a multitude of ways. Not surprisingly, it is the informal interactions rather than the formal variety that are the most interesting; the outside world has been changing much faster than the official rule book can record. In fact, an increasing number of protagonists are ignoring the rule book altogether or have never even heard of its existence.

The aim of this essay is to throw some light on the changing institutional interactions between the rapidly evolving 'NGO galaxy' and the not-so-rapidly evolving 'UN solar system'. It examines what is new in the process—how a structured bureaucracy deals with the unstructured, and how ideas percolate from one to the other. It also looks at how formal and informal linkages are created, and how practical cases of cooperation have evolved. The emphasis is on innovation rather than inertia. The selection of illustrative material is by no means exhaustive, shaped more by personal experience than scholarly research. Some general considerations about the meaning of recent shifts in policy and practice are offered as conclusions. The vantage point is that of the bureaucrat who looks upon the free spirits with a mixture of admiration (often) and irritation (sometimes), but who recognises that the Temple of States would be a rather dull place without nongovernmental organisations.

Changes at the top

The basic rule book is Economic and Social Council (ECOSOC) Resolution 1296. Adopted in 1968, this resolution acts as gatekeeper and grants formal access, or consultative status, to NGOs. Procedures have changed little over the years, and it is not necessary to describe them here.[1] Changes may, however, be in the offing. The widespread recognition that these procedures, and those relating to NGO participation in international conferences, need a face lift has led to the establishment of an Open-Ended Working Group of ECOSOC. The working group met in June 1994 and in the spring of 1995. At the time this essay was written, a draft revision of Resolution 1296 had been tabled but not yet approved.[2] Whatever the final language, the new resolution is likely to take some stock of the changes in the relationship that have taken place in the past 27 years. The new text may give a clearer recognition of the two-way interaction between the UN and NGOs rather than continuing to consider, somewhat paternalistically as the present wording implies, the NGO community mainly as a cha l to disseminate UN policies and information.

The fact that the floodgates were opened at the Rio Conference on Environment and Development has been significant for this process. 'Competent and relevant' NGOs, whether in consultative status or not, were invited to become accredited (over 1 400 were accredited, the largest number at any UN conference). More importantly, NGOs played a significant role in shaping the agenda of the conference and in the international mobilisation around the concept of sustainable development. They also contributed to building the political consensus that made adoption of the Rio Declaration possible. Nongovernmental organisations were rewarded for this role in chapter 27 of Agenda 21, which gave full recognition to the role of 'major groups' in implementing and monitoring the agenda; it further emphasised the vital role played by NGOs in shaping and implementing participatory democracy. Another interesting development occurred after the conference. The General Assembly and ECOSOC adopted resolutions governing participation of NGOs in the work of the new Commission on Sustainable Development,[3] which allowed NGOs that had been accredited to the conference to be granted near automatic roster status. As a result, 550 NGOs were accredited (about half of the NGOs accredited to UNCED that were not in consultative status with ECOSOC). The consultative status machinery was by-passed, and this created an important precedent.

The Rio example is a clear demonstration of the crucial role that NGOs can play as policy shapers in an intergovernmental setting. So far, this is 'the closest approximation to direct popular participation'[4] that the UN has been able to accommodate. Other, less visible approximations are happening all the time. For example, both the preparatory work towards and the reporting on the implementation of the UN Convention on the Rights of the Child owe a lot to NGO action. The convention gives a unique monitoring role to 'other competent bodies' in recognition of the fact that despite its intergovernmental nature, many other actors are involved in realising the rights enshrined in the convention.[5]

The United Nations has no institutional or even informal framework for citizen representation and no political forum for the world's peoples. Other segments of the UN system have long been more advanced in this respect. The International Labour Organisation (ILO), thanks to its constitutional links with trade unions and its tripartite system, provides elements of citizen representation and participation in decision-making. National commissions of the United

Nations Educational, Scientific, and Cultural Organization (UNESCO) and national committees of the United Nations Children's Fund (UNICEF) have built strong bridges with professional groups, NGOs and even individual citizens. The same applies to the Food and Agriculture Organization's (FAO) Freedom from Hunger Campaign. Not so in the UN, where it has been observed that 'until quite recently the hauteur of secretariat and diplomatic officials about NGOs was matched by the disinterest and disdain of large portions of the NGO community for the UN as merely "another bureaucracy".'[6]

In any event, the current debate in ECOSOC will not proceed much further in the direction of a world parliament or a world consultative forum for civil society (although it must be noted that such avenues will continue to be pursued more aggressively on the UN's periphery[7]). It is even doubtful that ECOSOC will reach a consensus on the representation of civil society interests in the political *sancta sanctorum* of the General Assembly and the Security Council. However, this is already happening, or at least much more is happening than meets the eye of the custodians of the consultative process. Since the sessions of the General Assembly's main committees are public, current practice allows NGOs in consultative status with ECOSOC to attend, albeit without the right to circulate documents or make statements. But much goes on informally, to the point that many NGOs that have representatives in New York are now more active in the General Assembly than in the Economic and Social Council.[8] In addition, several subsidiary bodies of the General Assembly have devised informal arrangements allowing NGOs to take the floor or circulate documentation. Similarly, NGOs have participated actively in hearings of special committees (for example on apartheid) or in special sessions of the General Assembly (for example on disarmament or development). NGOs were invited, along with academics and entrepreneurs, to the hearings on the secretary-general's *An Agenda for Development*, convened by the president of the General Assembly in June 1994. Several NGO personalities have also been recently appointed by the secretary-general to serve on high-level advisory bodies (for example on sustainable development and on social and gender issues).

Interactions between NGOs and the Security Council are more low-key and indirect, but are nonetheless significant. The end of the Cold War and the de-compartmentalisation of hitherto separate regimes of UN activity—in particular of security and humanitarian issues—has greatly increased the humanitarian traffic that reaches this body, which in many ways has become a 'Humanitarian Security Council'.[9] Humanitarian and human rights NGOs have been following these deliberations with increasing attention. Although there has been no attempt yet to obtain formal representation with the council, much of the significant activity actually goes on outside the council's chambers, in the corridors of the UN in New York and in the capitals of key member states. Governments cannot ignore the nuisance potential of NGOs back home, with their capacity to alert the media and public opinion. For example, the shape of the belated international response to the Rwanda crisis was determined by the pressures of the humanitarian lobby, including Africa Watch in Washington, Médecins Sans Frontières (MSF) in Paris and Brussels, Oxfam and African Rights in London. Nongovernmental organisations are also an invaluable source of information on complex emergencies because of their direct contacts on the ground, where there is much informal exchange in and around embassies. NGOs are in frequent contact with ministries and the media in donor capitals. Some of this undoubtedly trickles up to the Security Council and influences its debates.

The importance of the NGO perspective in political forums is demonstrated by its increasing relevance in official delegations or in humanitarian cells in capitals. A couple of examples should illustrate this point. A former senior manager of MSF heads the 'humanitarian crisis reflection cell' of the French Ministry of Defence; a former Oxfam executive is the key official dealing with humanitarian issues in the UK's permanent mission to the UN; and NGO representatives are routinely included in official delegations to General Assembly sessions and special conferences. Revolving-door assignments also are widespread between NGO and UN positions, particularly in operational programmes such as those of the UN High Commissioner for Refugees (UNHCR), the UN Children's Fund (UNICEF) and the World Food Programme (WFP), where there is a tradition of picking talent from NGOs. No Amnesty International activist has yet been appointed to a senior position in the UN Centre for Human Rights, but this is the exception rather than the rule—and, to be fair, a former Amnesty International official was appointed to a very high position in the joint Organization of American States (OAS)–UN human rights monitoring mission to Haiti. In many ways these links between nongovernmental and governmental spheres of activity are a novel and welcome feature of the UN scene. This would have been unimaginable only five years ago.

Perhaps the most significant example of institutional interaction between an NGO—albeit a very special one—and the highest political level of the world organisation is the regular consultation between the president of the Security Council and the New York delegate of the International Committee of the Red Cross (ICRC). The ICRC was granted observer status by the General Assembly in 1990.[10] Since then it has been patiently developing its net of political contacts within the United Nations. This has culminated in discreet monthly meetings with the serving president of the Security Council, a practice that has been taking place for nearly two years. Basically, this *tête à tête* allows both sides to raise issues of special concern and to ask for, or volunteer, information on specific country situations in an informal and confidential atmosphere. Although neither side is likely to comment on what has been on the agenda, both sides give considerable importance to the meetings, which now occur with Swiss precision.

Secretariat units at all levels have also developed routine contacts and exchanges of information with NGOs, whether in consultative status or not. Working relationships in the field are discussed later. At headquarters, an interesting trend seems to be emerging whereby NGOs are brought closer and closer to internal decision-making. An example is the participation of the main coalitions of humanitarian NGOs— InterAction and the International Council of Voluntary Agencies (ICVA)—alongside the ICRC and the International Federation of Red Cross and Red Crescent Societies (IFRC) in the meetings of the Inter-Agency Standing Committee (IASC), which are chaired by the UN under-secretary-general for humanitarian affairs. Interviews with secretariat and NGO participants confirm that this is not simply a token participation by representatives of non-UN organisations. Policy and operational issues are discussed seriously and sometimes argued. Given the importance of humanitarian NGOs in the mobilisation of the international response to complex emergencies, having them on board when priorities and problems are thrashed out is no small advantage for all concerned. It also helps to introduce better transparency and accountability and to ease misunderstandings with other parts of the international response, such as the military. The Department for Humanitarian Affairs (DHA) also hosts regular meetings every four to six weeks with the main operational NGOs in the humanitarian arena, like CARE, the International Rescue Committee (IRC), Save the Children Federation (SCF), World Vision, MSF, Oxfam, etc. Similar meetings of European NGOs are hosted by UNHCR and DHA in Geneva on a regular basis.

The importance of NGOs as shapers of policy and not merely as providers of information or services is recognised by the secretary-general himself in his public presentations, but also, and more practically, in his schedule of appointments. A comparison of the present incumbent's schedule with that of his predecessor would no doubt show how much the heads of prominent NGOs and other non-state actors have become frequent visitors to the 38th floor of UN headquarters. The secretary-general must see the heads of ICRC or Oxfam or the IRC if they request appointments in the same way that he must see the presidents of the International Chamber of Commerce, of the Society for International Development, or of the Socialist International or Liberal International. This is also a reflection of how much NGOs have become active in areas that were previously considered the near-exclusive preserve of states: peacemaking and its junior cousins, preventative and humanitarian diplomacy.

A useful illustration of this relationship would be the role of an Italian NGO, the Comunità di Sant'Egidio, in ushering in the peace process in Mozmabique. Thanks to its contacts with the Mozambican Catholic church and the Italian government, Sant'Egidio was instrumental in arranging for low-key talks between the Front for the Liberation of Mozambique (FRELIMO) government and its Mozambique National Resistance (RENAMO) guerrilla opponents. The talks were held in Rome at the Sant'Egidio headquarters in a non-threatening atmosphere, starting in July 1990. Although the Italian authorities, the USA, the countries of the region, and the UN were kept informed, Sant'Egidio was in the driver's seat as mediator at least until sufficient confidence had been built up between the two sides for them to agree to bring in the international community.[11] Because Sant'Egidio was not a state, it provided a venue that avoided the issue of the parties' legal status. This was particularly important because RENAMO, being basically a rural insurgent movement, was unfamiliar with legal and diplomatic usages. Sant'Egidio was instrumental in allowing RENAMO to express 'its ideas in terms consistent with the overall goal of reconciliation'.[12]

Sant'Egidio has been active but less successful so far in other theatres. Its current initiatives on the Algerian crisis are now in the public domain. After two meetings convened in Rome, some progress seems to have been made at least in devising an acceptable framework for talks, despite the initial disbelief of the Algerian government and some of its main sponsors. Sant'Egidio is by no means the only example of behind-the-scenes peacemaking efforts conducted by religious NGOs in particular. In the early 1970s the All African Council of Churches was the primary mover in the first attempts to bring an end to the civil war in southern Sudan. More recently, the Mennonite Central Committee was involved in creative bridge-building in Somalia and was instrumental in bringing all the clans together for a meeting in Madagascar; Norwegian Church Aid has been doing similar work in Guatemala. The lesson here is that NGOs are often in a better position to reach out to non-state traditional or *de facto* (that is, warlords) authorities, than states or intergovernmental organisations (IGOs) are. As one observer put it, 'peace-making and peace-building are too important to be left to governments and the UN alone'.[13]

Another indicator of the growing involvement by nongovernmental organisations in peace initiatives can be seen in the current mushrooming of preventive diplomacy NGOs, such as the recently launched US-based International Crisis Group (ICG) or the initiative of a group of Euro-parliamentarians who have set up their own NGO, the European Forum for Preventive Diplomacy, which intends to act as a stimulant on preventative issues and to conduct missions to prevent tensions from escalating into conflict.[14]

Towards oligopoly?

Before looking at the new interactions between the UN and NGOs in the field, a discussion of financial flows and their implications is in order. During the past 20 years there has been an exponential growth of financial transfers by and through NGOs from the industrialised to the developing world. The total flow is estimated by the Organization of Economic Cooperation and Development (OECD) at $8.3 billion in 1992, or a staggering 13% of all development assistance.[15] This is much more than the amount being transferred through the UN system (not including the Bretton Woods institutions). In terms of net transfers, NGOs collectively represent the second-largest source of development and relief assistance, second only to bilateral governmental donors. This is largely the result of the increasing volume of official funding that is being channelled through NGOs to developing countries. Public grants represented 1.5% of NGO income in 1970, 35% in 1988, and, with the explosion of humanitarian relief programmes in recent years, probably over 40% today. Co-financing arrangements and direct transfers of bilateral or multilateral funds for operations in the Third World have therefore radically changed the funding picture of the NGO community. From the donor perspective the change has been equally noteworthy: member countries of the Development Assistance Committee (DAC) now transfer about 9% of their official overseas development assistance (ODA) through nongovernmental organisations, with much higher percentages in some countries. The figure for Switzerland is 19%. In 1993 the USA was channelling 17% of its ODA through private groups; this has increased to an estimated 30% in 1995 and is likely to increase immediately to 40% under the 'New Partnership Initiative' announced by the USA at the World Summit for Social Development.[16]

These figures signal a major quantitative and qualitative change in the way NGOs function in the Third World; the causes and implications of this change deserve to be more fully analysed. Regrettably, data on the destination of funds channelled through NGOs—types of activities and beneficiaries, breakdown between development and relief—are notoriously sketchy and unreliable. As for the origins of such funds—that is, the precise mix of voluntary contributions from the general public, direct overseas development assistance funding, and indirect funding through multilateral institutions—the situation is at best one of 'creative accounting'. The notion of co-financing is undergoing radical change. Ten years ago the European Community (EC, now EU) and most governments insisted on a 50–50 rule; but the portion of NGO resources that is now going into the co-financing equation is shrinking rapidly. The EU and the USA are now down to a 90–10 co-financing arrangement, especially in the case of emergency relief assistance. In some cases the remaining 10% is financed by another public source, for example by a UN agency.

Although the expansion of the role of NGOs in North–South relations may simply be part of the larger, worldwide growth of the non-profit sector, it does seem that an important restructuring in the functioning of significant sectors of society, particularly weaker Third World societies, is taking place. NGOs are now increasingly assuming state-type functions, such as the provision of public services, in areas like health and education to an extent that was unimaginable only a decade ago.

One explanation of this shift is that it represents a lasting legacy of Reaganism–Thatcherism in the sense that it is an application of laissez-faire and anti-state ideology to international relations. A similar view holds that it is a manifestation of the North's loss of patience with the perceived ineffectiveness of UN organisations as conduits for international assistance and of the corresponding faith in the operational superiority of 'hands-on' NGOs. In any event, the end of the Cold War seems to have accelerated a process that was already underway—the emergence of political conditionality. The Northern NGO community has benefited collectively from the fact that, with the end of superpower confrontation, the need for political state-to-state North–South support has all but disappeared.[17] This has made it easier for Northern donors to say 'human rights (and privatisation) first, development later', a complete reversal of the conventional wisdom that ruled in the halcyon days of 'development (and state support) first, human rights later'.

Furthermore, the dramatic appearance in the international panorama of failed states, and their corollaries, failed and arrested development, has also spurred the growth of NGOs. In such situations, the normal interlocutors of aid bureaucracies—the ministers and functionaries of the recipient government—disappear. The recourse to NGOs for assistance imposes itself when there is no government or when there are competing claims on the state. In internal conflicts, signing projects or aid agreements with government officials becomes impractical or politically contentious. Bilateral donors and UN agencies are conceptually and institutionally grounded when governmental implementing partners exist the development or relief scene. UN operational agencies—UNHCR, UNICEF, WFP—are slowly building up competencies in complex emergencies and procedures for working in failed states and civil war situations, but it takes time to build this expertise. It is only natural, therefore, that the United Nations should seek the talent and flexibility of operational NGOs, especially those with a documented history of working in war zones.

Finally, while the number of claimants for stagnating resources increases, short-term emergency needs take precedence over longer-term development. For example, the World Food Programme used to be primarily a development and food-for-work organisation. Now, close to 80% of its food resources are being devoted to emergency feeding programmes. This increases the demand for operational capacity in the field. UN agencies are stretched to the limit and, for budgetary and cultural reasons, are unable to redistribute staff resources quickly among programmes or to scale up existing staffing. NGOs have the flexibility to redeploy and grow faster. From Bosnia to Somalia to Rwanda a growing number of NGOs has been launched on the wave of breaking emergencies. While some are run by and employ hardened professionals, others are more of the Indiana Jones variety, making up solutions as they go along.

It remains to be seen whether the current spate of complex emergencies will be a permanent operational reality for the international community or if it is only a transitory phase in the post-Cold War movement of tectonic plates. It also remains to be seen whether the donor community will be able to continue mobilising the political will and the resources for stop-gap emergency assistance and for longer-term development in the Third World. Although serious prevention initiatives are nowhere to be seen, donor exhaustion looms ominously. Without public and media pressure for humanitarian aid, the rhetoric of political conditionality may be used as an excuse for doing less.[18] The international NGO community is not indifferent in this debate. On one hand, it has greatly benefited from the increasing donor tendency to direct overseas development assistance away from Third World governments; on the other, this trend has fundamentally modified the nature of many operational NGOs. Free spirits who were at one time relatively independent in terms of policy choices and access to funding are finding that they have become implementers of donor or UN policies and contracts. A new generation of NGO, the 'public service contractor', has appeared, particularly on the relief scene, and it relies exclusively on public funding for its existence.[19] Hence the legitimate question: is an organization that receives 100% of its funding from public sources still an NGO?

The new rules of the game in the solidarity and charity business, or in the 'humanitarian international', as it has been called,[20] have serious implications for NGOs. Their members are torn between the double dilemmas of independence and subservience, and between a keep-it-simple grassroots culture and the imperatives of running a business. No figures are available on the numbers of Northern expatriates and support staff employed by NGOs at home and abroad. Certainly their numbers are sizeable and their lobby is powerful (and to some extent humanitarian assistance functions as an unemployment subsidy for young people in the North). Two questions are worth asking: to what extent does the readiness of Northern NGOs to intervene in Southern theatres detract from local coping mechanisms (that is, might it be possible to use the same monies to generate many more jobs in the South)? Can Northern NGOs survive the quantum leap in interventionist capability without losing their soul, or at least without fundamental changes in their ethics and culture?

Some disturbing trends are starting to appear. While advocacy NGOs do not seem to run the risk of being expelled from the ever-expanding marketplace of ideas—civil society seems capable of absorbing unlimited competition of ideas and movements on all fronts—the market for operational NGOs is a very real one; the competition for finite and potentially contracting resources is increasingly tough. The explosion of humanitarian needs in the last five years seems to have resulted in a contradictory process of polarisation and concentration in the NGO community. At one end, many new and often 'truck-by-night' operations have made their entrance. At the other end, the more established actors appear to be engaged in a process of 'ganging up', primarily as a way of jockeying for position and resources and as a way of consolidating power and influence. One experienced observer has concluded that this is tantamount to an oligopoly, where eight major families or federations of international NGOs have come to control almost half an $8 billion market.[21] These eight market leaders control shares that are not far from $500 million a year each. They are: CARE (which has four main chapters in the USA, Canada, the UK and Australia and smaller ones in Germany, France, Italy, Denmark and Japan); World Vision International (a rapidly growing player with branches in the USA, Australia, Canada, the UK, New Zealand, Germany and elsewhere); the Oxfam federation (comprising nine chapters in the UK and Ireland, the USA, Canada, Quebec, Australia, New Zealand, Belgium, Hong Kong, and recently joined by Novib, a major Dutch NGO); the MSF group (chapters in France, Belgium, the Netherlands, Spain, the USA and MSF-International); the Save the Children Federation (chapters in the USA, UK and the Scandinavian countries); and the more traditional coalitions or consortia of operational NGOs, ie, CIDSE (Coopération internationale pour le développement et la solidarité, the coalition of Catholic development NGOs), APDOVE (Association of Protestant Development Organizations in Europe), and Eurostep (the main coalition of European secular NGOs).[22]

In most cases these groupings do not affect the individuality of their constituent members, who retain their operational and financial independence, except for World Vision, which is managed centrally. They do, however, engage in some coordination and organised division of labour within groupings, which greatly facilitates fundraising and helps in particular with access to European Union and UN funds. CARE, for example, has a lead agency approach whereby one of its branches is the principal partner in specific countries. The groupings are thus in a position to better coordinate policies on specific situations and to shape the market by their sheer presence in particular sectors or geographical areas.

The UN and the EU have facilitated, if not encouraged, this process of aggregation. It is easier to do business with semi-structured large consortia than with atomised individual NGOs. Indeed, both the EU and the UN have actively promoted the creation of networks and coalitions of issue-specific NGOs—in the development and humanitarian arenas in particular—at the international level. These include Eurostep for development NGOs in Brussels; International Council for Voluntary Agencies for refugee and humanitarian NGOs dealing with UNHCR in Geneva; and coalitions of humanitarian NGOs in the USA (InterAction) and in Europe (Actionaid) that act as a link to the UN Department of Humanitarian

Affairs and other UN bodies. UN organisations and some host governments have also fostered NGO coordination mechanisms and consortia in the field.

It is paradoxical that a process that owes so much to free-market ideology has resulted in an oligopoly, within which the smaller actors, not to mention indigenous ones in Third World countries, are at a distinct disadvantage. Perhaps deregulation has gone too far and some anti-trust control might be in order. It is also interesting to note that this process of concentration is paralleled by one of homogenisation in the practices, management style, and activities of NGOs.[23] To a large extent this results from donor pressure to conform to established norms and standards. NGOs have to fit into the mould that the system requires. It has been aptly noted that 'it is ironic that free trade theory, which emphasizes choice and freedom, brooks no opposition to itself'.[24]

The UN and NGOs in the field

Intervention by international non-state actors in the Third World is by no means a new phenomenon. Missionary activity has always accompanied colonisation. Although the ideological underpinnings may seem outdated—proselytising and the 'white man's burden' rather than sustainable human development—the activities carried out by the new 'missionaries' may not be altogether that different from those of colonial times. Often it has been the same individuals; in the 1960s and 1970s, especially in Africa, large numbers of former missionaries, colonial administrators and even military personnel transferred to NGOs, where they continued to do field work. This generation is now gone, though some old-timers still survive, but it can be argued that it was instrumental in shaping the ethos and culture of NGO work in developing countries and also in establishing the institutional framework for local groups to operate in. This is not meant to imply that all NGO expatriates are missionaries or pawns in the neocolonialist enterprise. It would be absurd to lump together NGOs that espouse Western values and those that deliberately challenge such values or actively promote social change, local and national self-reliance, or grassroots development. NGOs are, however, an inescapably Western concept, even though the system tends to export its antibodies as well as its values.

Nongovernmental organisations, often strong and healthy, obviously exist outside the first world—the figure of 5 000 NGOs in India is oft quoted. These can be either endogenous—with values, aspirations and operating modalities fundamentally alien to Western traditions—or entities with more familiar values and activities. The point is that the culture and standard operating procedures of the NGOs that are of interest here—that is, recognisable operational or advocacy organisations with a combination of voluntary support and external funding that implement discrete activities—are basically Western in origin.

The traditional operational relationships between the UN and NGOs in the field have undergone vast qualitative and quantitative changes in the last two decades. In the heyday of 'Third-Worldism', the development decades, and the quest for a New International Economic Order (NIEO), the UN and the donor community at large—with no significant differences between East and West—were promoting the mobilising myth of state planning. The official discourse was statist and did not really factor in non-state actors as independent variables in civil society. NGOs did not fit prominently into the picture and were treated at best with benign neglect. As far as the United Nations is concerned, the United Nations Development Programme (UNDP), the main interlocutor with governments on development issues, did not have a framework for dealing with NGOs at the field level until the late 1980s. International NGOs were often involved in social work and community development well before community development became a buzzword in UN circles. However, as the figures quoted in the preceding section indicate, the role of NGOs in shaping the development debate and as operational partners for the UN in the field was relatively marginal at least until the late 1970s. NGOs were active in certain sectors, particularly in relief work, and in many countries.[25] But there was little functional interaction between the UN system as such and international NGOs in the field. The only significant exception to this was UNHCR, which had traditionally devolved management and delivery of assistance to refugee camps to an array of specialised implementing partners (CARE, IRC, the many Caritas chapters, etc).

Moreover, the strictures of the Cold War did not allow for action by UN agencies or UN-sponsored programmes in civil wars. Cross-border humanitarian assistance was basically taboo for the UN since it was tantamount to a violation of sovereignty. Eritrea and Tigray are well documented cases of relatively large crossborder humanitarian assistance programmes implemented by consortia of nongovernmental organisations, with the humanitarian wings of the concerned liberation fronts but without any direct UN involvement.[26]

Meanwhile, UN assistance was being organised from the government side, and it reached mainly, if not exclusively, government-held territory. Similarly, crossborder assistance from Pakistan to mujahidin areas of Afghanistan became a growth industry for NGOs after the Soviet invasion. The role of UN agencies—UNHCR, WFP, UNICEF—was to provide assistance to refugees in Pakistan. The UN was not mandated, and was disinclined, to send anything to vulnerable groups across the border. The recognised government was in Kabul, and UN development activities there were largely unaffected by the war, except for the fact that they were limited to shrinking government-controlled areas. The situation changed only after the taboo was lifted by the Geneva Accords of April 1988. The government reluctantly agreed that the UN would work crossborder from Pakistan, Iran and the Soviet Union on the basis of a 'humanitarian consensus' of all warring parties. When, after the departure of the last Soviet troops, the UN stepped up its crossborder programmes using international NGOs as implementing partners, this was not without friction with mujahidin leaders and some NGOs that felt the UN was tainted because of its association with the Kabul government.

Coordination mechanisms among NGOs or between the NGO community and the UN have become more structured in recent years because of the mushrooming of complex emergencies and the parallel growth in the number of actors involved in them. Coordination mechanisms for development activities normally involve a prominent role for the host government, which is in a position to establish rules governing NGO presence and operations. In complex emergencies and in situations of internal conflict, there is often no meaningful government. A variety of coordination arrangements have been tested over the years. In some situations the chemistry and composition of the NGO community allow it to take the lead in coordinating its own activities and in providing a framework for interacting with the UN; in others, especially when there is a strong UN presence, the UN can provide a forum for UN–NGO coordination.

For instance, in the case of the cross-border programmes relating to Afghanistan, the 100 or so international and Afghan NGOs operating out of Pakistan developed a structured coordination framework with two regional bodies: Agency Coordination Body for Afghan Relief (ACBAR) for programmes originating from the North-West Frontier Province, and South-Western Afghanistan and Baluchistan Agency Coordination (SWABAC) for NGOs operating out of Baluchistan. ACBAR in particular was much more than a forum for exchange of information; it had a paid secretariat, geographical and sectoral committees (health, agriculture, education) that helped ensure a better division of labour, and some coherence in procedures and standards (for example, local salaries). Many NGOs 'did their own thing', however, and the Islamic NGOs tended to ignore ACBAR altogether. However, the UN found a reality that it could not ignore; it did not attempt to take over responsibility for coordination in an aggressive manner. In specific sectors it even allowed itself to be initially 'coordinated' by the key NGOs. For example, in the agricultural sector, one NGO, the Swedish Committee for Afghanistan, had far more competence and staff— including former senior government technicians and managers—than the UN agencies, which were considered the new kids on the block. Although much of the funding came from EC and UN sources, the Swedish Committee for Afghanistan successfully mounted and coordinated a multimillion-dollar pest control programme in eight or nine Afghan provinces, a task that the UN was initially unable to do or even to monitor.

The opposite happened in Rwanda. Over 100 NGOs were present in Kigali at the height of the emergency, but they were unable to agree on a coordination structure, despite an offer by ICVA to establish it. This was perhaps a recognition of the effectiveness of the leadership role in coordination exercised by the UN's Rwanda Emergency Office (UNREO), to which the NGOs flocked naturally. Paradoxically, it was the NGO community itself that provided assistance to UNREO, by seconding an NGO person to act as liaison officer with the community.

A number of new and significant operational interactions between the UN and NGOs in the field deserve to be highlighted. The fact that UNHCR, and to a lesser extent UNICEF and WFP, engage NGOs as privileged implementing partners in relief situations has been mentioned. Rather than relying exclusively on international NGOs for this purpose, UNHCR tries when possible to use trained local staff. When local NGOs are unavailable or when it is expedient to do so, UNHCR creates 'dedicated' NGOs to implement its programmes. These organisations receive all their funding from UNHCR and for all practical purposes are totally under its control, if not directly integrated into its local management structure. The financial and managerial advantages of the approach are obvious. The disadvantages are that the staff of these organisations are not UN staff and therefore have lesser protection in the face of high security risks. Often such dedicated NGOs employ expatriates as managers or in key positions. This allows UNHCR and the other UN agencies that have adopted this approach to circumvent the rigidities of creating new budgetary posts, normally a complicated and time-consuming procedure. While flexibility is an obvious asset, it does create a sort of subcategory of UN staff, locally recruited and less protected.

Perhaps the most interesting and large-scale example of the creation of dedicated NGOs by the UN is the de-mining programme in Afghanistan. Given the impossibility of setting up a national or government structure to address the mine problem in a fragmented if not war-torn country, the UN Office for the Coordination of Humanitarian Assistance to Afghanistan (UNOCA) set up facilities to train Afghan de-miners in Pakistan. This was done with the help of military experts provided by several donor countries and with the logistical support of the Pakistani army. Several thousand de-miners, mostly ex-mujahidin combatants, were thus trained. Rather than employing these de-miners itself, which as a coordination body it was not mandated to do, UNOCA drew up the terms of reference and created several Afghan NGOs to implement the programme. These organisations were fully funded by the United Nations and staffed by Afghans with a small number of expatriate consultants, mainly for planning, monitoring and quality control purposes. Overall coordination was provided by UNOCA's de-mining programme officers. Thus a Mine Clearance Planning Agency—which decided on the areas and the priority tasks to be performed and provided essential quality control—was created. Several regionally-based mine clearance agencies were created, each responsible for deploying mine clearance teams on the ground under the supervision of the planning agency. In 1991, while civil war was still raging in parts of the country, the United Nations was employing more than 1 000 Afghan de-miners through its dedicated NGOs. In mid-1995 this figure had risen to over 3 000.

A similar approach was followed for mine awareness campaigns. International NGOs were initially contracted to develop a strategy, publicity materials and training modules. The programme was subsequently 'Afghanised', with several regionally-based organisations providing training and deploying mine-awareness teams throughout the country (in government-held areas this was done through the Afghan Red Crescent Society, but using a common method). Without a viable and acceptable government structure, the overall coordination of the programme was provided by the UN, on the understanding that this would be transferred to the government when conditions permitted. This complex, ongoing, multimillion-dollar programme represented a unique effort to address a dramatically real problem and to encourage as much national self-reliance as local conditions permit. By and large it is considered a success story, the component of the UN Afghan programme that donors have consistently and generously funded.

A variant of the above is UN encouragement for the creation of indigenous NGOs that are not necessarily fully 'dedicated' and exclusively funded by UN sources, but that are semi-autonomous hybrids. Many such organisations have been deliberately established to act as implementing partners in humanitarian programmes. Others have been encouraged to come into existence to compete for UN resources, or they tend to germinate spontaneously. For instance, UNOCA in Pakistan and Afghanistan had a deliberate policy of 'Afghanization', which resulted in the rather liberal distribution of resources (cash, vehicles, office equipment) to nascent groups that were to act as implementing partners. This was done partly to encourage local self-reliance and a shift towards civilian reconstruction rather than military pursuits. It was done partly to undercut the hold that external NGOs had on certain areas, where they were sometimes simply providing a conduit for a rather peculiar type of 'humanitarian' aid to warring factions (for example, medical assistance to mujahidin groups). The idea was that the provision of such seed resources was the paying ticket to enter areas where humanitarian needs were not being met. This policy often ran into trouble because some of these nascent groups were not bona fide NGOs, but fronts for military/political entities. Institutional support to one group in one valley was naturally perceived as divisive and contentious by groups in neighbouring valleys. This approach is by no means unique to Afghanistan. In Somalia, the UN spawned colonies of clients. It has been noted that in Mogadishu in 1994 there were an estimated 1 000 'local NGOs set up by Somalis to channel foreign funds into worthy projects ... By the end of its mission, the UN was easily the biggest employer in Somalia ... supporting, according to some estimates, a hundred thousand people in Mogadishu.'[27]

Finally, a visible post-Cold War novelty in the field interactions between the UN and NGOs needs to be briefly mentioned—the increasing contact, friction, tension and synergies between NGOs and the UN military. From Angola to Bosnia, from Mozambique to Rwanda, the NGO community has been working in an environment where the presence of UN troops is the rule rather than the exception. New concepts and approaches are being tested and much fumbling has occurred in the encounter of hitherto antagonistic cultures. While there has been some initial enthusiasm for the role of the military in providing protection to NGO activities and security to staff, experience in Somalia and elsewhere has had a dampening effect. Most humanitarian actors would probably agree that direct military intervention in humanitarian programmes, whether UN or NGO, should be a last resort. This is not to deny the useful support role that the military can provide, particularly in the breaking phase of a complex emergency.

In Rwanda, and in the spillover areas of the Rwandan crisis, particularly in Goma, the military have been in many ways an important feature in the day-to-day life of the humanitarian community. The UN Assistance Mission in Rwanda (UNAMIR) and, for the period that they were there, the French, US, and other contingents were providing essential services to UN agencies, NGOs and even the media. These included security, logistics (transport of humanitarian commodities, free access to fuel, communications, medical support, air services, etc), information-sharing, and even the direct delivery of assistance. While these services were generally appreciated, there were mixed feelings in the humanitarian community, and in particular among NGOs, about the profile to be adopted, and the degree of proximity to be maintained in dealing with the UN military. Humanitarian NGOs were uneasy about being placed under a military umbrella, except when overwhelming security considerations dictated otherwise. It can also be argued that 'it is to the military's advantage to keep its profile and image distinct from those of the humanitarian agencies'.[28]

For reasons that are self-evident, the military is not best-suited to interact with civil society. In common with all military establishments, the UN military tends to cut itself off from society by setting up heavily fortified military compounds wherever it goes. Razor wire is enough to intimidate NGOs, not to mention the local population, even if the blue flag provides a reassuring presence. Less-intrusive forms of interaction with the military have been tried successfully in the context of the Rwanda crisis. This involved placing military assets under the direct control of the humanitarian agency. In one case, British troops in uniform from the corps of engineers were assigned to UNHCR to work at water and sanitation projects in refugee camps. In another, Irish military engineers clad in NGO T-shirts performed similar functions under the command and control of the Irish NGO, Goal. Such unobtrusive forms of collaboration between the military and NGOs are likely to be more effective and palatable to the humanitarian community than muscle-flexing.

The free spirits in a bind?

The preceding pages have attempted to outline some of the more significant innovations in the complex set of relationships between the NGO and UN communities. This general survey is somewhat biased by the writer's personal experience in the matter and is not exhaustive. There would be much to say from a UN perspective, for instance, on human rights NGOs, on development advocacy NGOs or on grassroots NGOs in the Third World. One must also be conscious of the dangers of sweeping statements and generalisations. The NGO community is not rational and uniform, but is an extremely diverse and sometimes fractious universe crisscrossed by contradictory forces. High levels of professionalism and contract-hungry or media-hungry amateurism coexist side by side, sometimes within the same organisation. Efforts by the NGO community to regulate its own behaviour—for example, through the elaboration of codes of conduct for relief organisations—often clash with the policy and practice of individual NGOs that are quick to jump on the relief bandwagon. In Goma, most NGOs seemed to have an inexhaustible supply of T-shirts with their coloured logo on display; some were more keen on jockeying for TV-friendly locations than on professionalism; and many appeared vulnerable to media and public opinion shifts at home. On the basis of research in various conflicts and emergencies, one observer concluded that 'we have yet to give the NGO community high marks for performance in even routine operational tasks' and that in the Gulf crisis 'the prevailing picture of NGOs was one of energy and determination, mixed with confusion and disarray. Distinguishing the charlatan from the humanitarian proved difficult in the panic of the crisis.'[29]

It has often been pointed out that the archetypal NGO is fundamentally a Western concept. It cannot be superimposed on indigenous self-help coping mechanisms, or on community-based structures for the protection of families or groups, or on the mechanisms to effect social change that may exist in rural or traditional societies. The notions of 'state' and 'civil society' are also basically Hegelian, Westphalian and Western.[30] While these terms have a relatively uniform meaning in the North, or at least in the West, they cover a wide range of different realities in the Third World. The relations between the individual, the community, civil society, the state and their representations in the collective unconscious are likely to be quite different in Bamiyan, Bandung, Bukavu and Boston.

Even with the best of intentions—solidarity, promotion of human rights, justice, grassroots sustainable development, life-saving emergency relief—helping hands extended by outside NGOs, UN agencies or bilaterals are fraught with risks for recipients. Deliberately or not, when they result in the imposition of Western values and approaches, the dangers are even greater. From this point of view, development assistance, whether through bilateral, UN or NGO channels, has often acted as a North–South conveyor belt for Western rationality. The key vehicle in this process is the ideology of the project as the privileged, discrete, time-limited, and budget-driven instrument to shape change. This approach, and the mimicry it encourages, may be fundamentally alien to the way that social change is perceived in non-Western cultures.[31] Or, as one observer put it, 'The development enterprise is oriented "North–South" by patterns of dominance between "uppers" and "lowers", and by funding, pressures to disburse and top-down accountability. These patterns increasingly affect NGOs, which may then become more like government organizations, in scale, staffing, hierarchical culture, procedures, and self-deception.'[32]

If development assistance breeds dependency, what should be said about relief? While humanitarian activities in Rwanda, Mozambique, Afghanistan or Somalia unquestionably provided succour and saved lives, the longer-term impact of the delivery of an overwhelming proportion of humanitarian assistance through external conduits—first and foremost NGOs—needs to be better understood. Hundreds of NGOs literally descended on Kigali and Goma at the onset of the crisis. More than 200 are currently active in humanitarian and development assistance in Mozambique. As crises come and go on the international community's selective radar screen, so does the humanitarian international. Apart from the chronic lack of consistency in the response, must not one ask what the consequences of this donor-driven invasion by humanitarians are likely to be for weakened or fledgling indigenous structures? In parts of the Third World, especially Africa, centralised authority has imploded. The weaker the government structures, the more difficult it is to resist the invasion.

In Mozambique, and to a lesser extent in other countries, the government has been obliged to surrender elements of sovereignty temporarily as a condition for the peace process to come to fruition. The donors and the relief community have been quick to fill the vacuum with operational plenum. Policies, privatisation and the like, are set by the donor consortium; implementation is in the hands of NGOs. Government entities have been weakened because they have been perceived as corrupt. They are being replaced by private companies, including many from industrialised countries. Relief agencies—and NGOs in particular, some of which have programmes larger than those of the largest bilateral donor[33]—have become the chief providers of public welfare and important sources of employment. They also further weaken government structures by siphoning off the remaining trained and competent local professionals, from deputy ministers to drivers, who are attracted by the higher and regular salaries paid by the outsiders.[34] The cost to the government of keeping track of thousands of projects represents an additional burden, if not a direct diversion of resources. A senior government official lamented that 'rivers of money were being spent on expatriate rather than on Mozambican talent'. Even some NGO representatives recognise that 'the government has lost all control', that the outsiders are 'arrogant', and that some are 'running amok in the most extraordinary way'.[35]

Western disengagement, the promotion of civil society and privatisation ideologies, and the quantum jump in NGO operations in the Third World are different elements in the same process. In many Third World countries, nongovernmental organisations are filling important short-term gaps because of the state's inability to provide essential services, particularly in the fields of health, education and welfare. Helping to fund the recovery of states as such, whether from conflict or from failed development, is not high on the international community's priority list.

The UN seems to have abandoned its traditional role of advocate of national self-reliance, a role it had played strongly in the 1970s and 1980s. The quest for a more equitable international economic order, Third World militancy and its attendant rhetoric—in such forums as UNCTAD, the Commission on Transnational Corporations, and the General Assembly—have all but disappeared. The mantra of national planning has been replaced by laissez-faire. It can even be argued that the liturgical invocation of the concept of 'sustainable human development', and of the role of civil society therein, further encourages people to bypass the shrinking powers of host governments. Even UNDP, once the steadfast proponent of statism and of the role of planning in development, is now turning to civil society organisations, like NGOs and the private sector, for project execution. Most Third World governments, whether they subscribe to the theory or not, are not in a position to resist. Nongovernmental organisations are part of this worldwide shift in the manner in which societies function. The growth of NGO funding and activities is unquestionable. Little is known, however, of the impact of this growth. From a UN perspective, one must ask, does it work? Can we document that privatisation, and the role of NGOs therein, promotes healthier and more democratic societies than previous models did?

Development as an aspiration for more *égalité* and *fraternité* not only within but between nations may soon be an idea whose time has gone.[36] The dialectics of globalisation and fragmentation is rapidly changing the shape of North–South relations and the terms of the debate. Development no longer seems to be the mobilising paradigm, but a replacement has yet to appear. It is no longer fashionable to shake the banner of social change, even as the urgency of relief makes operational choices simpler. Many NGOs with militant roots are being sucked into the business and are becoming service providers. Many others are simply born into the new world without the luxury of roots and values. The NGO community as a whole cannot afford to ignore the terms of this debate between values, consciousness-raising and advocacy on one side, and pressures to seek funds and to disburse them on the other.

Nongovernmental organisations, particularly those that act as implementing partners, find themselves at a difficult crossroads. It is to be hoped that the logic of self-criticism and accountability will prevail over subservience and the contract culture. Free spirits are sorely needed to protect and promote the interests of the victims of massive dislocations in the Third World. NGOs have been the traditional allies of the United Nations in the quest for more justice and solidarity. Often they have been the critical conscience of the UN, shaming it and pushing it forward. Overall this has been a positive relationship. And this is how it should be, provided that each side can be held accountable for what it does.

Notes

The author, a United Nations staff member, wrote this article while on a sabbatical leave with the Humanitarianism and War project, Watson Institute for International Studies, Brown University. He is solely responsible for the views expressed in this essay.

[1] For a discussion of the functioning of the consultative status mechanisms at the UN, see document E/AC.70/1994/5 of 26 May 1994, *General Review of Arrangements for Consultations with Non-Governmental Organizations*, Report of the Secretary-General, in particular paras 51 to 82 on the experience to date in the implementation of Resolution 1296.

[2] See UN document A/49/215-E/1994/99 of 5 July 1994, *Report of the open-ended working group on the review of arrangements for consultations with non-governmental organizations*, and E/AC.70/1995/CRP.1, which contains the draft revised text of the resolution.

[3] Resolutions 47/91, 1993/215 and 1993/220, respectively.

[4] Document E/AC.70/199/5, para 33.

[5] As Richard Jolly, deputy executive director of UNICEF put it, '... in issues of children's rights, NGOs can often do things or say things which UN bodies—as intergovernment bodies—no matter how forward thinking— find it difficult or impossible to do'. Statement to the ECOSOC open-ended working group to review arrangements for consultations with NGOs, 20 June, 1994.

[6] Erskine Childers & Brian Urquhart, *Renewing the United Nations System*, Uppsala: Dag Hammarskjöld Foundation, 1994, p 172.

[7] Structured proposals were put forth on the occasion of the 40th anniversary of the UN by Marc Nerfin, 'The future of the United Nations system: some questions on the occasion of an anniversary', *Development Dialogue* 1, Uppsala: Dag Hammarskjöld Foundation, 1985. Similar proposals have resurfaced 10 years later. See Childers & Urquhart, *Renewing*, p 171; Maurice Bertrand, *Une nouvelle charte pour l'organisation mondiale?*, paper presented to a seminar at IUHEI, Geneva, 27–28 February 1995; and Commission on Global Governance, *Our Global Neighbourhood*, Oxford: Oxford University Press, 1995.

[8] See document E/AC.70/1994/5, para 112, footnote.

[9] Maurice Bertrand, 'Une organisation perimée', *Le monde des débats*, July–August 1994.

[10] The Federation of Red Cross and Red Crescent Societies and the Order of Malta have also graduated from consultative to observer status, but they have not yet and are not likely to develop a similar relationship with the Security Council. Other coalitions of humanitarian NGOs, InterAction in particular, have requested observer status to be able to address the General Assembly and to have more document circulation rights, but this has been rejected by the General Assembly. In fact it is unlikely that the observer gates will be reopened soon. During the debate at the 49th session of the General Assembly, many delegations expressed the feeling that increasing the presence of non-state actors would run the risk of changing the nature of the organisation.

[11] The role of the Comunità di Sant'Egidio in the Mozambican peace process is described in detail in Cameron Hume, *Ending Mozambique's War. The Role of Mediation and Good Offices*, Washington DC: US Institute for Peace, 1994.

[12] Ibid p 73.

[13] Larry Minear, 'Humanitarian intervention in a New World Order: prospects for NGOs', in *NGOs and Refugees: Reflections at the turn of the Century*, Essays in honour of Arne Piel Christensen, Copenhagen: Danish Centre for Human Rights, 1993.

[14] European Parliament, *Liaison Info*, 3, 1994.

[15] The figures in this paragraph are drawn from UN document E/AC.70/1994/5, paras 16 and 28. Some authors place the NGO market share as high as $10 billion in 1993; on this see Ian Smillie, 'Changing partners: Northern NGOs, Northern governments', in *Non-Governmental Organizations and Governments, Stakeholders for Development*, Paris: OECD, 1993, p 14.

[16] Barbara Crossette, 'Gore says US will shift more foreign aid to private groups', *New York Times*, 13 March 1995.

[17] Mark Duffield, 'NGOs, disaster relief and asset transfer in the horn: political survival in a permanent emergency', *Development and Change*, 24, 1993, p 149.

[18] Ibid, p 151. See also Rakiya Omaar & Alex de Waal, *Humanitarianism Unbound, Current Dilemmas Facing Multi-Mandate Relief Operations in Political Emergencies*, Discussion Paper No 5, London: Africa Rights, 1994.

[19] Duffield, 'NGOS', p 141.

[20] See Omaar & de Waal, *Humanitarianism Unbound*.

[21] A senior UNDP official, interviewed on 28 February 1995.

[22] I am indebted to Ian Smillie for having provided me with empirical evidence to support the oligopoly thesis. According to information that he has assembled from various published sources, the annual income of World Vision International in 1992/1993 was on the order of $438 million (including $85 million of food aid and other in-kind contributions). It is reported to have increased significantly since then. CARE had a combined income of over $620 million in 1992, roughly half of which was for food and freight. Conservative estimates of the annual incomes of the SCF and Oxfam groups are on the order of $360 million and $250 million respectively. No figures were readily available for the other groupings, but they all are believed to be well above the $250 million mark.

[23] Smillie, 'Changing partners', p 23.

[24] Tim Lang & Colin Hines, *The New Protectionism*, London: Earthscan Publications, 1994, p 63.

[25] International NGOS started descending *en masse*, rather selectively, on several African countries in the late 1970s. In the early 1980s, when Sankara was in power, over 300 NGOS were active in Burkina Faso.

[26] Mark Duffield & John Prendergast, *Without Troops & Tanks: Humanitarian Intervention in Ethiopia and Eritrea*, Trenton, NJ: The Red Sea Press, 1994.

[27] William Finnegan, 'Letter from Mogadishu. A world of dust', *The New Yorker*, 20 March 1995.

[28] See Department of Humanitarian Affairs, *Report on the Coordination of Humanitarian Activities in Rwanda*, New York: United Nations, November 1994. A report on the use of military assets in Rwanda is being prepared under the auspices of the Humanitarianism and War Project of the Watson Institute. See Larry Minear & Philippe Guillot, *The Contribution of International Military Forces to Humanitarian Action in Rwanda*, Paris: OECD, 1996 forthcoming.

[29] See Larry Minear, 'Humanitarian intervention'.

[30] The argument here is that the Treaty of Westphalia and Hegel's *Philosophy of Right*, by defining the realms of sovereignty on the one hand, and of the state and civil society on the other, basically ordered our representations of how the archetypal Northern state functions. Hegelian and post-Hegelian (for example, Gramscian) theory are still relevant to capture the role of NGOS in civil society. This latter term is loosely understood here, as in Gramsci, to encompass everything that can be found between the economy and the state's political institutions—political parties, trade unions, professional associations, the media, NGOS, and so on. It has also been argued by Smillie (in 'Changing partners', p 18) that the theoretical basis of the NGO phenomenon is Tocquevillian. Be that as it may, it remains Western.

[31] For a detailed critique of 'project aid' see Bernard Lecomte, *L'aide par projet. Limites et alternatives*, Paris: OECD, p 1986.

[32] See Robert Chambers, 'NGOS and development: the primacy of the personal', draft paper for a workshop on 'NGOS and development: performance and accountability', Institute of Development Policy and Management, University of Manchester, 27–29 June 1994.

[33] It is reported that in 1993 and 1994 World Vision became the single largest donor in Mozambique, with total budgets of $90 million and $80 million, respectively.

[34] For a critical analysis of the role of the 'new missionaries' in Mozambique, see Joseph Hanlon, *Mozambique: Who Calls the Shots?* Bloomington, IN: Indiana University Press, 1991.

[35] Interviews in Maputo, December 1994.

[36] It has been pointed out that ' "Development" as an ever-growing populist project for the legitimation of Third World Governments, supported by the industrial powers, may go the way of decolonization. Analysts a generation hence may look on it as just another historically significant, but temporary, world political issue, a way of establishing manageable political cleavages among those with more and those with less power ... The new cleavages that will replace "development" at the center of the same politics are not yet clear.' Craig N Murphy & Enrico Augelli, 'International institutions, decolonization and development,' *International Political Science Review*, 14 (1), 1993, p 82.

■ 5 ■

Greening the UN:
Environmental Organisations
and the UN System

KEN CONCA

Environmental problems cry out for effective international governance. Pollution, habitat destruction and ecosystem degradation offer stark evidence of human power to transform the earth.[1] There are good reasons to doubt the effectiveness of centralised, hierarchical schemes of 'planetary management', and to worry about the political and social implications of such efforts.[2] But in a world where environmental damage and its social consequences ignore borders, substantial and effective international cooperation is essential.

It has been over two decades since the 1972 UN Conference on the Human Environment placed environmental problems on the global agenda. The period since the Stockholm meeting has witnessed a flurry of environmental diplomacy by governments. The list of multilateral environmental agreements has grown dramatically; states have crafted accords on problems as diverse as ocean pollution, acid rain, climate change, the ozone layer, the trade in endangered species, biological diversity, the hazardous waste trade and environmental protection in Antarctica.[3] The 1992 UN Conference on Environment and Development (UNCED), held on the 20th anniversary of the Stockholm conference, saw over 150 governments gather in Rio de Janeiro to endorse Agenda 21, an ambitious plan to promote ecologically sustainable development into the 21st century.

Nevertheless, it is difficult to avoid the conclusion that the problems are outpacing these displays of interstate cooperation. The effectiveness of most major international agreements remains to be demonstrated; most fail to grapple with the underlying political, economic and social practices that create environmental harm. Similarly, without clear political and financial commitments from most of the governments that endorsed it, Agenda 21 is being transformed from an ambitious plan of action into a tacit admission of failure. As Mostafa Tolba, former executive director of the UN Environment Programme (UNEP), suggested in 1992:

> I am obliged to report to governments and the public that progress has slowed. The commitment to set up ministries and to enter into international agreements has not always led to an equal commitment to action. Environment Ministries exist, but their role in national decision-making is frequently marginal. Agreements have been entered into freely, but the will to enforce them has often been lacking.
>
> There is a paradox here. On the one hand public concern has been growing steadily, as manifested by the growing power and influence of "green consumers" ... On the other hand, the pace of government action has faltered.[4]

There are several reasons for the ineffectiveness of state responses. Sovereignty fragments political authority, creating well-known barriers to international cooperation.[5] Environmental problems also challenge states to evolve new scientific and managerial capabilities, much as the socioeconomic crises of the industrial revolution forced the evolution of the welfare state in industrialised societies. These problems are exacerbated by economic globalisation and the growth of transnational economic power, which make it harder for states to control effectively or regulate environmentally harmful economic activities. Perhaps the biggest obstacle is that state power historically has been closely tied to environmental destruction, in both industrialised and post-colonial societies. The economic importance of natural resource extraction, the links between territorial control and sovereign recognition, the power that flows from the ability to assign property rights and define patterns of access to nature—for all these reasons, most states emerged historically from elite social bargains that have allowed for, or even demanded, dramatic forms of environmental transformation.

When states prove unwilling or unable to respond, nonstate actors represent hope for change. Paul Wapner describes two processes by which environmental organisations, and nongovernmental organisations (NGOs) more generally, may exert political influence in world politics.[6] First, and most obviously, they may be able to pressure, cajole, or otherwise influence states. But NGOs may also influence values, social behaviour and collective choice more generally among large groups of people-creating a form of 'world civic politics' in which state behaviour becomes less central to collective choice. This formulation is not unlike the two forms of influence attributed to international organisations, which may serve as institutions that shape the pattern of state-based bargaining, or as facilitators of broader processes of global dialogue, value convergence and social transformation.

In the more than two decades since the Stockholm conference, environmental organisations and the United Nations system have evolved a complex and multidimensional relationship, with many forms of engagement emerging on many levels. Both partners in the relationship contribute to this complexity. Environmental NGOs form a complex, multifaceted and often divided community. Similarly, even as the UN plays an important role in fostering international environmental dialogue and cooperation, its specialised agencies often behave in ways that constitute a significant part of the problem.

Environmental organisations and the UN system: an overview

Before the Stockholm conference, environmental organisations played only a limited role within the United Nations, just as the world organisation itself played only a limited role in environmental matters. The conservation of natural resources was made part of the constitutional mandate of the Food and Agriculture Organization (FAO), although its emphasis on natural resource production and extraction severely curtailed its environmental focus. The UN Educational, Social and Cultural Organization (UNESCO) played an important role in the 1948 formation of the International Union for the Conservation of Nature (IUCN), a body with governmental and NGO affiliates.[7] IUCN in turn spun off an important environmental NGO, the World Wildlife Fund (WWF), as an independent fund-raising body in 1961.[8] Other notable pre-Stockholm activities included the International Geophysical Year from 1957 to 1958, IUCN's First World Conference on National Parks in 1962 and UNESCO's Biosphere Conference of scientific experts in 1968.[9]

The Stockholm conference marked a watershed in UN deliberations on the environment and in the engagement of environmental NGOs with the United Nations system. Both the conference itself and the preparations for it raised international awareness.[10] Stockholm also led to the formation of the United Nations Environment Programme (UNEP), a small but at times effective body headquartered in Nairobi. In addition, Stockholm framed two of the core debates that dominate international environmental politics to this day: sharp disagreements over the relationship between environment and development, and governmental resistance to pressures that states compromise sovereign authority over natural resources and ecosystems within their territory.

Stockholm was also a milestone for international environmentalism. Environmental NGOs gathered in unprecedented numbers; 134 organisations engaged in the official proceedings, with many more involved in the protests, networking, consciousness-raising and other 'unofficial' activities linked to the conference.[11] Stockholm also marked the transition from a movement dominated by relatively depoliticised conservation groups to one heavily influenced by the 'new environmentalism' of the 1960s.[12] Finally, nongovernmental organisations at Stockholm reflected the pervasiveness of North–South divisions: southern NGOs accounted for only about 10% of those participating.[13]

Since then, as the United Nations has become a more important forum on environmental matters, environmental organisations have become more involved in several ways and on several levels. They lobby in the diverse bodies that make up the United Nations system, from the specialised agencies to broader forums such as the UN Conference on Trade and Development (UNCTAD) and the Economic and Social Council (ECOSOC). Environmental organisations also shape the positions of member states through domestic pressure and, increasingly, transnational efforts. NGOs also provide information, analysis and value-based interpretations that shape how problems, interests and solutions are defined. Finally, environmental organisations are playing a growing role in delivering services at the local, regional and even national level, receiving and administering UN funds in the process.

Within the United Nations system, these various forms of engagement take place on several levels: in specialised agencies and other functional bodies within the system; in relations with UNEP; in the various global conferences, international meetings and intergovernmental bargaining sessions that have occurred under UN auspices; and in the recently formed Commission on Sustainable Development, a high-level body within ECOSOC charged with monitoring the implementation of UNCED's Agenda 21.

It is difficult to estimate the number of environmental organisations engaged with the United Nations in these various ways. One reason is the fuzzy boundary between the environment and other issue areas. Many, but not all, of the larger and more influential NGOs define themselves as 'environmental' in relatively narrow terms. But it is often impossible to say where an environmental organisation ends and one dealing with a host of other issues—human rights, grassroots development, public health, the concerns of indigenous peoples, women in development—begins. These blurry boundaries and the alliances they make possible can be a source of great strength for environmental organisations and coalitions. Yet they make it difficult to describe a neatly delimited 'environmental' community.

 A second complication is that only a relative handful of environmental organisations are truly transnational. There is no question that within the environmental community, large and well-funded transnational organisations such as the Worldwide Fund for Nature or Greenpeace enjoy greater access to UN deliberations.[14] Limiting the definition of the relevant community of organisations to those with transnational operations would miss the important and growing role of local and regional NGOs, and would present a skewed subset of the full range of views, tactics, and strategies that environmental organisations bring to bear.[15] An important part of the international pressure on governments to live up to the rhetoric of UNCED has come from local organisations participating in national or transnational networks. Such networks can vary greatly in the formality of their organisation, the tightness of their coordination and the stability of their membership.[16] Emphasising only the most formally institutionalised organisations would also steer the focus toward traditional lobbying practices and away from the important consciousness-raising activities of environmentalists, many of which are relatively loosely coordinated and formalised.

Given these complexities, perhaps the best way to characterise the relevant set of environmental organisations is as a set of concentric circles. In the centre circle we find a handful of truly transnational organisations—those with well-institutionalised transnational operations, based on an organisational presence in many different countries.[17] This allows for a strong and consistent presence in international conferences, negotiations and deliberations by intergovernmental organisations. Examples include Greenpeace, with nearly six million members worldwide, affiliated offices in 30 countries and an annual budget of about $100 million; the Worldwide Fund for Nature, with three million members, 28 national affiliate groups and an annual budget of some $170 million; and Friends of the Earth International, with half a million members and national affiliate groups in 46 countries.[18]

Also included in the centre circle are a small number of important environmental think tanks, international NGO networks and informational clearinghouses—groups with the funding, reputation and transnational connections to have a consistent presence in the international arena. Some of the most influential think tanks are the Washington-based World Resources Institute (WRI) and Worldwatch Institute and the London-based International Institute for Environment and Development. Important networks include the Earth Council, a network of eminent persons formed by UNCED Secretary-General, Maurice Strong; the Centre for Our Common Future, a Geneva-based organisation emerging in the wake of the Brundtland Commission report, *Our Common Future*; and the Third World Network, a coalition of organisations and individuals engaged in research, information dissemination, organising and advocacy on issues related to development, the environment, the Third World and North–South relations.[19] International scientific groups also weigh in with substantial influence, derived in part from the technical complexity of environmental problems, but also from the relatively good access to governments that such groups often enjoy.

One step removed from this core group, the second circle captures a considerably larger set of organisations with some capacity to operate internationally or have a presence in international forums. The number of organisations falling into this circle is closer to a few hundred than to the few dozen found in the inner circle. Environmental organisations probably account for less than 10% of the roughly 1000 NGOs with ECOSOC accreditation. The recently formed UN Commission on Sustainable Development, which reports to ECOSOC, has accredited 550 NGOs within its first two years, and UNCED accredited more than 1400. Finger estimates that some 1600 groups participated in the NGO Global Forum held during the UNCED conference.[20]

The outermost circle in this simple model includes the large and apparently rapidly growing number of local, regional and national environmental organisations that enjoy only sporadic access to international debates. Although a comprehensive estimate of their number is impossible, most observers have put the figure in the tens of thousands or more. The Geneva-based Centre for Our Common Future distributes *The Independent Sectors' Network*, its monthly NGO newsletter, to over 30 000 organisations and individual subscribers. Fisher estimates that there are about 200 000 grassroots NGOs in the South and over 30 000 'grassroots support organisations' channelling funding, expertise and assistance to the grassroots.[21] Although these figures do not refer solely to 'environmental' NGOs, the distinction between environmental groups and those working on issues such as public health, basic human needs or family planning is often an arbitrary one at the local level.

The diversity of the groups in all three circles and the heterogeneity of their goals can be a source of great strength for environmentalism as a global social movement. For example, efforts to reform multilateral lending procedures for development assistance have been strengthened by South–North coalitions of NGOs able to pressure both donor and recipient governments simultaneously. But the concentric-circles model also reveals a highly unequal distribution of power and access, particularly in North–South terms. Roughly speaking, the further one moves out from the centre circle, the more difficult it becomes to have effective access to the United Nations system. And the further from the centre, the fuzzier the issue-area boundaries become between the environment and other concerns, reflecting the role of power and access in defining exactly what constitutes the 'environmental issue area' in international settings.

The experience of environmental groups within the UN system

Given the many forms of contemporary environmentalism, and the many levels on which nongovernmental organisations engage the United Nations, it is difficult to generalise about the experience of environmental organisations within the United Nations system. Efforts to work with or pressure the specialised agencies have varied greatly in effectiveness. UNEP has been an important resource or a useful entry point for some NGOs, but an irrelevancy or a missed opportunity for others. The picture is further complicated by the complex implications of the UNCED conference, and by the emergence of the Commission on Sustainable Development as a potential focal point in the post-UNCED era. What follows is not a comprehensive assessment of this complex and fluid situation, but rather a series of snapshots meant to show the range of NGO experience and the dilemmas of NGO engagement with the United Nations on environmental matters.

Engaging the specialized agencies

Before the 1990s most NGO attention focused on the specialised agencies for several reasons. To be sure, some—notably FAO, the World Health organization (WHO) and the World Bank group—have drawn attention because their functional mandates intersect with the environmental agenda in important ways. The focus on the specialised agencies also reflected their autonomy, and the absence of overarching UN institutions that dealt with questions of environmental governance, as well as the inability of UNEP to carry out its hopeless mandate as system-wide coordinator on environmental matters.

The specialised agencies date from a pre-environmental era. They have standard operating procedures that were formed, and deeply institutionalised, with little attention to environmental considerations. They are also classically bureaucratic entities that exhibit the full range of turf-grabbing, mission-defending and budget-enhancing behaviour common to large bureaucratic organisations. Most, when confronted with environmental demands in the post-Stockholm era, have exhibited a complex combination of turf-building and turf-defending behaviour. The environment has been a powerful argument for programmatic expansion, but also a threat to traditional operating procedures. Thus, it is no surprise that organisations such as FAO and the World Bank can embrace the concept of sustainable development, or that WHO has begun to redefine its view of health to include that of the planet.[22] At the same time, these organisations have often resisted change in the traditional practices that environmentalists find so disturbing, as in the resistance of FAO and WHO to stronger international standards on pesticides.[23]

This presents environmental NGOs with complex choices. On the innovative margin of an agency's activities, where core practices are not threatened, there may be opportunities for effective collaboration. But altering an agency's core practices generally requires a more confrontational stance, in which NGOs generate political pressure. Two campaigns of the 1980s—the effort for environmental reform of the World Bank's lending practices and the effort to institutionalise the Tropical Forestry Action Plan—illustrate the difficulties of sustaining this combined cooperative and conflictual stance.

The World Bank campaign.   Of all the agencies and intergovernmental organisations affiliated with the United Nations, the World Bank is perhaps the most consequential in environmental terms.[24] It maintains a lending portfolio on the order of $20 billion annually. Excluding the International Monetary Fund (IMF), which moves a similar amount on an annual basis, this figure is nearly an order of magnitude greater than the combined budgets of the approximately 20 other functional agencies affiliated with the UN system.[25]

The orientation of World Bank lending also has important environmental consequences. Its emphasis on infrastructural development such as roads, bridges, dams and power stations has produced several ecological disasters. The bank is also a central environmental actor because of its status as an intellectual and policy leader among development assistance institutions; its behaviour exerts a strong influence on a wide range of bilateral and multilateral organisations.

A loose coalition of environmental organisations began a public campaign in the mid-1980s to reform the World Bank's lending practices. Several high-profile examples of bank-funded disasters, including the Polonoroeste colonisation project in the Brazilian Amazon and the Sardar Sarovar dam in north-central India, were used to sharpen the critical focus and emerged as symbols of the Bank's failings. Nongovernmental organisations brought pressure on several levels at once by lobbying donor governments; pressuring and cajoling recipient governments; mounting public demonstrations and informational campaigns; advocating policy alternatives; and cultivating alliances with sympathetic staffers within the bank itself.[26]

NGOs realised significant gains through the World Bank campaign. Internal reorganisation has boosted staffing in environmental positions and created a somewhat greater incorporation of environmental considerations into project evaluation. The bank also began funding projects with an environmental focus (19 projects totalling $1.2 billion in fiscal 1992, according to the bank's figures).[27] In 1994 the bank also agreed, under strong NGO pressure, to create an inspection panel for public accountability. Affected parties in borrower countries may now file complaints that the World Bank has failed to follow its own policies, procedures and conditions in the context of a specific loan.[28] The panel is by no means a perfect vehicle for NGOs; the initial decision of whether to follow a complaint with an inspection remains shrouded in secrecy, and borrower countries must approve on-site inspections. Moreover, 'local representation' requirements prevent donor-country NGOs from filing claims. But the panel should be an important resource for NGOs to publicise the bank's failures and gain access to project records. Although the selection of panelists was shrouded in the usual bank secrecy, the procedures for filing claims are relatively open and simple.

The World Bank campaign has also been instructive for what has not changed. As Bruce Rich of the Environmental Defense Fund, a leader in the NGO campaign, said in 1990:

> Environmentalists were guardedly optimistic about [Bank President Barber] Conable's new-found commitment to reform at the time. Now, three years later, it is apparent that the emperor's new clothes bear only faint traces of green. Instead of becoming a leading environmental lender, the Bank has become an arena where the political, practical, and theoretical difficulties of reconciling economic development with ecological sustainability are most glaring. The Bank continues to stress

its commitment to the environment, but deep institutional and political contradictions prevent it from implementing reform in any meaningful way ... [29]

Rich identifies barriers on four levels: 'internal contradictions' in the bank's
hierarchical, segmented bureaucratic organisation; pressures from both donors
and borrower governments to keep the money moving; a lack of accountability
to either donors or borrowers; and contradictions between ecological sustainability and the bank's development model of growth, industrialisation and privatisation.

   The campaign's complex mix of successes and failures illustrates the challenge facing environmental organisations in trying to change the specialised
agencies. The campaign required consistent pressure, grounded in harsh criticism
and confrontation, to move the World Bank to action. At the same time,
however, forging cooperative relationships with potential allies in the bank and
among donor-government agencies was crucial to realise those gains.

The Tropical Forestry Action Plan. In 1983 FAO's Committee on Forest
Development in the Tropics charged FAO with developing an 'Action Programme' on the growing problem of tropical deforestation.[30] At that time, the
World Resources Institute, an influential Washington-based environmental policy institute, convened a series of meetings that produced an international task
force in conjunction with UNDP and the World Bank.[31] The FAO and WRI efforts
in the Tropical Forestry Action Plan (TFAP), converged a framework for guiding
development assistance in tropical forestry.

   TFAP encourages developing countries to submit national plans for sustainable
development in the forestry sector.[32] FAO coordinates review and implementation
of the plan for a range of bilateral and multilateral donors and UN agencies. TFAP
has produced both a substantial increase in forestry-sector aid and a consolidation of activities by the over 40 aid agencies active in tropical forestry. WRI
estimated that by 1990 funding commitments in forestry had 'at least doubled',
to more than $1 billion annually, and that this would rise to $2 billion if all
projects in the TFAP pipeline were indeed funded.[33] A 1994 FAO update reported
90 countries in Asia, Africa and Latin America involved in TFAP exercises,
ranging from initial planning to implementation of funded plans.[34]

   Together with bilateral and multilateral lenders, environmental organisations
were instrumental in creating TFAP. WRI in particular played a crucial role in
generating momentum for the initiative and influencing its policy framework. An
unofficial body, the 'Forestry Advisors' Group', emerged as a regular contact
point between TFAP funders and mainstream nongovernmental organisations.[35]

   As its full implications have become clearer, however, TFAP has received
increasingly scathing criticism from environmentalists, including some groups
involved in its formulation.[36] The most common criticisms have been the failure
to involve local participation in planning; lack of NGO access to both implementation and review processes; a narrow forest-sector vision of the problem; and
the emphasis on expanding timber yields. Even when funded national plans have
genuinely sought to promote a sustainable timber yield, the FAO approach
frequently overlooks associated environmental concerns related to forest regener-

ation, biological diversity and climate.[37] Many critics argue that TFAP is a net contributor to tropical deforestation:

> Far from attempting to tackle the root causes of deforestation, TFAP focuses almost exclusively on promoting commercial forestry ... The focus on the administrative failings of TFAP has enabled FAO to sidestep the more substantive criticisms of TFAP's underlying policies ... FAO has learned little from its TFAP critics: although the rhetoric has changed, the approach is still top-down, commercially-oriented, and, if adopted, likely to exacerbate the deforestation crisis.[38]

Perhaps consistent NGO pressure will eventually yield a thorough overhaul of TFAP. It would be grossly overstating their power to lay full or even principal blame on the environmental organisations involved in its formulation. There were notable differences from the start, for example, between WRI's vision and the FAO formulation that TFAP has reflected in practice. But the participation of mainstream environmental organisations lent environmental legitimacy to a badly flawed process—one that has probably, on balance, done more harm than good to the world's tropical forests. TFAP therefore stands as a cautionary tale of the difficulties of striking an effective balance between cooperation and conflict with the specialised agencies.

Global conferencing: the implications of UNCED

The 1992 UN Conference on Environment and Development marked a watershed in NGO activities within the United Nations system for several reasons. Compared to Stockholm, UNCED saw explosive growth in the scale and scope of NGO participation. The greater NGO presence at UNCED reflected the general growth in environmental NGOs during the 1980s, particularly in the South. The multistage, protracted nature of the 'UNCED process'—the Brundtland Commission activities, the UNCED Preparatory Committee meetings, national reporting efforts and planning for the parallel Global Forum of NGOs—also played a key role in mobilising NGOs. UNCED also used accreditation rules for nongovernmental organisations that were loose by UN standards, establishing what may be an important precedent. By the end of the fourth and final PrepCom, 1 420 NGOs had been accredited in addition to those already accredited to ECOSOC.[39]

Nongovernmental organisations enjoyed not only an unprecedented presence at UNCED but also greater influence. The most important vehicle for influence was the relative success of NGOs in getting on national delegations; Finger reports that at least 14 countries had environmental NGO representatives on their national delegations.[40] But accredited NGOs also gained access to PrepCom sessions and some albeit limited access to draft materials and working documents. This afforded the opportunity to at least comment and lobby during PrepCom sessions, where much of the actual politicking took place.[41] Five environmental NGOs—IUCN, Greenpeace, Environment and Development Action in the Third World, the Conservation Foundation and the Environmental Defense Fund—were able to place a representative among the 120 individuals making up the working parties of the PrepCom sessions.[44]

Despite these tangible gains, both UNCED and the parallel Global Forum revealed deep divisions within the environmental movement. Although accredited nongovernmental organisations had access to official working sessions during the PrepComs, they enjoyed no such access to the official session at UNCED, except as national delegation members. Despite the relatively looser accreditation standards and greater access to draft materials, the main source of NGO influence during official proceedings was to have a presence on national delegations. This meant that NGOs on the national delegations of the most influential states enjoyed the greatest influence among NGOs. Not surprisingly, this amplified the voice of relatively well-heeled, mainstream, northern environmental organisations and, in particular, several of the larger groups that were within the NGO community based in the USA.

The Global Forum, a concurrent meeting among nongovernmental organisations during UNCED, also revealed tensions among environmental NGOs. Several of the more progressive ones chafed at the way in which the forum was organised by the International Facilitating Committee, an offshoot of the Centre for Our Common Future in Geneva.[43] Led by the Nairobi-based Environmental Liaison Committee International, these groups organised an International NGO Forum, in which alternatives to the official UNCED agreements were negotiated among nongovernmental organisations. These alternative negotiations proved contentious; according to Grubb:

> These negotiations between the NGOs at UNCED were certainly not as difficult as the official negotiations, but they were hardly easy, and it requires little imagination to foresee the depth of disputes had they been negotiating real policy and trying to take account of the full range of viewpoints and affected parties (for example by including NGOs from industry or trade unions).[44]

Finger describes three increasingly distinct factions clearly visible at UNCED. 'Mainstream' NGOs, mostly US-based, enjoyed the most influence and exhibited the greatest willingness to compromise with actors wielding political and economic power. 'Political' NGOs, including the European Greens as well as many Third World NGOs, were frustrated with the relatively technocratic proceedings, the limits of NGO political influence and the tendency of UNCED to reproduce the debates of Stockholm 20 years earlier. 'Consciousness-raising' NGOs, more interested in promoting broad social transformation through consciousness-raising than in direct engagement in lobbying, exerting pressure and related forms of political action, represented yet another distinct group.[45]

UNEP: a missed opportunity?

Though small, chronically underfunded and marginal within the UN constellation, the United Nations Environment Programme has evolved into a relatively effective organisation. With a professional staff and budget akin to a small liberal arts college, UNEP officials quickly realised that the organisation's marginal status within the UN system would prevent it from accomplishing its coordinating mandate. Instead, UNEP came to define its role as a catalyst for international cooperation.[46]

UNEP's record is uneven. The South's power within UNEP's Governing Council provoked destabilising conflict with its principal funders during UNEP's early years. There have also been some notably failed initiatives, most glaringly the campaign on desertification.[47] Yet several UNEP initiatives to foster international cooperation have met with substantial success, including its regional seas programme and its role in the negotiations on stratospheric ozone depletion.

NGOs have been a key part of UNEP's approach. UNEP has fostered the growth of the Environmental Liaison Centre (ELC), a Nairobi-based network and informational clearing house for over 6 000 NGOs with an emphasis on environment–development concerns. UNEP also played a crucial role in providing NGOs access to the international negotiations on stratospheric ozone.[48] UNEP's relative openness to nongovernmental organisations can be explained in part by its small size and marginal status, which created a continual need to build alliances. However, UNEP's attempt to define itself as an 'honest broker' of knowledge and information has also been an important factor.[49]

UNEP's openness to and support for NGOs has not always been reciprocated. As momentum grew within the United Nations system during the 1980s for a major review of environment and development issues, UNEP lost its bid to play a central role. Several developments marginalised UNEP's role: the decision to form the independent World Commission on Environment and Development; the choice of Stockholm Conference organiser Maurice Strong as UNCED secretary-general rather than UNEP's Mostafa Tolba; and the decision that UNCED would report to the General Assembly rather than UNEP, breaking precedent with the first post-Stockholm review, held in Nairobi in 1982.[50] Strong NGO support may not have reversed any of these decisions, but would probably have enabled a stronger role for UNEP. In hindsight, a stronger UNEP role might well have facilitated more meaningful NGO access to some of UNCED's deliberations, particularly for southern nongovernmental organisations.

In the post-UNCED era, UNEP's role and status are uncertain. Member governments have supported substantial growth in its budget in recent years, to $100 million in 1993 compared with $20 million in 1973, its first year of operation.[51] Further growth may be a mixed blessing; as Imber points out, 'The role UNEP enjoys has been secured by virtue of resisting the inherently inflationary tendencies characteristic of UN agencies ... '[52] It is clear that even a dramatically expanded UNEP will not evolve into the sort of system-wide coordinating body that states envisioned at Stockholm, but never funded.

The Commission on Sustainable Development

Just as UNEP was the only official UN institutional reform after Stockholm, UNCED also produced a single formal institutional reform: the Commission on Sustainable Development (CSD). Just as UNEP received an unworkable mandate of system-wide coordination, so too has the CSD. Established in 1993, the commission's official purpose is to coordinate UN activities on the environment and to monitor national and international implementation of Agenda 21. Its 53 member states are chosen by a regional formula; Germany is the current chair, with Brazil, India, Namibia and Poland as vice chairs. The commission has met annually since 1993. The first two meetings were devoted principally to commission rules and procedures, as well as setting an agenda for those aspects of Agenda 21 upon which it will focus in upcoming meetings.

In principle, the CSD affords an important opportunity for NGO involvement. The General Assembly has stated that the commission should 'provide for non-governmental organisations, including those related to major groups as well as industry and the scientific and business communities, to participate effectively in its work ... '[53] As of this writing, 550 nongovernmental organisations have been accredited, using procedures less stringent than those of ECOSOC.[54] Accredited NGOs can work the halls, coordinate activities, make brief oral statements, and submit written statements, although they pay for reproduction and distribution themselves, unlike ECOSOC. NGOs with Category I consultative status may also propose agenda items.

It remains to be seen whether the commission can effectively coordinate system wide activities on the environment. Arguing that UNCED revealed the UN's institutional 'Catch 22', Bergesen voiced a common belief among sceptics: 'You cannot change the institutional structure without [first] changing the institutional structure'.[55] Even if the CSD fails in this regard, it may still afford opportunities for environmental NGOs. The UN Association of the United States, for example, argues several potential benefits. These include not only the commission's substantive work, the informational value of the proceedings and the chance to improve NGO–UN relations, but also such factors as the opportunity for long-range planning afforded by the annual meeting format and pre-set agenda, the value of an accurate historical record in the post-UNCED era and the chance to reinforce NGO efforts elsewhere within the United Nations system.[56]

Dilemmas of engaging the United Nations

Environmental organisations seeking to work within the UN system must make fundamentally political choices such as where best to target NGO efforts, how best to effectively broaden NGO access and how to translate the many strands of environmentalism into a source of strength in diversity as opposed to internal divisiveness and friction. These choices will help shape the future direction of environmentalism as a global social movement; they will also help determine whether the United Nations is to be a more effective mechanism of environmental governance, an irrelevant bureaucracy or an obstacle to the global transformations that are so urgently required.

The choice of entry points. Most environmental organisations are all too familiar with the need to establish priorities in the face of resource constraints. With regard to the United Nations, the most difficult choice may be between the traditional focus on the specialised agencies and the growing need to raise environmental concerns in broader, cross-cutting arenas. In the post-UNCED era, the discourse of environmentalism is clearly moving in the direction of cross-cutting themes. The traditional ecosystemic focus on air, land, water and species is giving way to a social-systems focus on international trade, global finance, sovereignty, development and other key processes and institutions. The old focus was consistent with the functional organisation of the United Nations into specialised agencies; the emerging focus demands a new forum.

The temptation is great to shift attention to institutions such as the Commission on Sustainable Development, which hold out the possibility of broader policy coordination that cuts across the traditional functional categories. The danger is that this shift will draw NGO and other resources away from the specialised agencies, just as engagement and pressure have begun to make inroads. There is a critical need for a forum in which to debate questions of sovereignty, ecology, political economy and North–South relations in a broader, more representative setting than the G-7 or the World Trade Organization (WTO) can provide. The question is whether the Commission on Sustainable Development, an adjunct of ECOSOC, can provide such a forum when ECOSOC itself has largely failed to do so.

The question of access. UNCED established an important precedent for NGO participation and the trend has continued with the relative openness of the Commission on Sustainable Development. Broadening participation typically yields a messier, less manageable process; consequently, there were tensions between older nongovernmental organisations with long-standing consultative status and the newer generation at UNCED.

Such tensions will deepen unless expanding access also transforms the nature of NGO participation. If the total amount of time and space for NGOs remain tightly controlled, and if most NGOs continue to be excluded from crucial informal and 'formal–informal' discussions, then expanding access may mean no more than forcing more nongovernmental organisations to crowd their literature onto the same display tables or compete for a fixed amount of speaking time. Under such conditions, organisations with their foot already in the door are unlikely to remain champions of greater NGO access for long. The tensions will be particularly acute—as they were at UNCED—between those organisations seeking to achieve specific policy-based outcomes and those seeking to use the United Nations system as a broader forum for global dialogue. The challenge facing nongovernmental organisations, and particularly those with relatively good access already, is to use the pressures to expand access as a way to transform the nature of NGO participation.

Coalition dynamics, power and the North–South divide. The emergence of the concept of 'sustainable development' is sometimes said to have transcended traditional North–South conflict on environment and development. UNCED revealed that deep North–South divisions remain, and that they are not limited to governments. According to Grubb, '... At UNCED, the gulf between the biggest environmental NGOs and many Southern NGOs in particular seemed almost as huge as that between their respective governments on some (though not all) issues'.[57]

Effective North–South alliances have been built when interests have converged, as in the World Bank campaign. Institutionalising such alliances will require moving beyond utilitarian cooperation and towards greater convergence in the message itself. Again, the burden falls principally on the large, mainstream organisations of the North. These groups have grown increasingly pragmatic— some would say too pragmatic—in their willingness to compromise their agenda in return for a dialogue with political and economic power. Although individual organisations vary greatly, the mainstream northern organisations as a group have been slow to show the same pragmatism in working with nongovernmental organisations and movement groups in the South. Failure to do so will only exacerbate the tensions that surround the potentially divisive questions of access and priorities already discussed in this essay.

How much to cooperate?   The growth of transnational economic power and the entrenchment of conservative, anti-environmental governments throughout the West in the 1980s forced environmentalists across the political spectrum to confront questions of political power and economic organisation. The result has polarised the movement: the debate over the North American Free Trade Association (NAFTA) in the USA, which split the normally united mainstream environmental organisations, is probably a harbinger of future divisions within the movement.

This raises the enduring question of whether and how nongovernmental organisations can collaborate with powerful institutions while retaining some portion of their oppositional character. Again, the question of access is central. If environmental NGOs gain influence within the UN system principally through national delegations, bringing consistent pressure to bear on the specialised agencies may require muting one's criticism at home. Similarly, using the United Nations to increase pressures on states may mean building bridges to the same specialised agencies many NGOs are wont to criticise. Both strategies are plausible, but few nongovernmental organisations are sufficiently large, multi-faceted and politically adroit to sustain both at once. Also, neither strategy works for the simultaneous transformation of both states and the UN system.

Conclusion

Without question, the emergence of a global network of environmental organisations has transformed the environmental debate. Individual governments can no longer easily ignore environmental problems, and governments are collectively being pushed, prodded and cajoled towards internationally coordinated action. At the same time, environmentalism has offered new paradigms and resurrected traditional ones that guide the behaviour and beliefs of millions of people worldwide, sometimes in ways that bypass governments entirely.

These gains notwithstanding, environmental organisations seeking to consolidate and strengthen what remains a relatively weak and loosely coordinated movement face many obstacles. Governments resist the encroachment onto their traditional domain of authority, even as they seek to use nongovernmental organisations to bolster their own legitimacy. NGO resources and access to political power pale in comparison to the forces driving environmental destruction. Cultural and ideological differences among environmentalists make coordinated global action difficult. The same North–South tensions that pervade relations among states can spill over into charges of paternalism or parochialism within and among nongovernmental organisations. These obstacles are formidable if NGOs seek to pressure governments, build effective mechanisms of international governance or transform social values.

Thanks to the efforts of environmentalists, the global environmental governance that states have manifestly failed to deliver may yet become a possibility. If the United Nations system can be a vehicle for strengthening the diverse voices of environmentalism without homogenising them, it will have made a major contribution towards that end.

Notes

I am grateful to Tina Blumel, Andy Knight, Rene Marlin-Bennett, Paul Wapner and Tom Weiss for comments on an earlier draft.

[1] On the many dimensions of the global environmental challenge, see Mostafa K Tolba et al., The World Environment 1972–1992: Two Decades of Challenge, London: Chapman & Hall, 1992.

[2] For a critique of the 'planetary management' approach, see Wolfgang Sachs (ed), Global Ecology: A New Arena of Political Conflict, London: Zed Books, 1993.

[3] Karen Litfin estimates that by the early 1990s there were more than 650 such agreements in operation. Most of these are bilateral or regional agreements with a relatively narrow focus on specific environmental problems or disputes. See Litfin, 'Eco-regimes: playing tug of war with the nation-state', in Ronnie D Lipschutz & Ken Conca (eds), The State and Social Power in Global Environmental Politics, New York: Columbia University Press, 1993, pp 94–117. Harold K Jacobson and Edith Brown-Weiss estimate the number at close to 900 in 'Strengthening compliance with international environmental accords: preliminary observations from a collaborative project', Global Governance, 1 (2), 1995, pp 119–148.

[4] Tolba, The World Environment 1972–1992.

[5] On barriers to international environmental cooperation, see Oran Young, International Cooperation: Building Regimes for Natural Resources and the Environment, Ithaca, NY: Cornell University Press, 1989.

[6] Paul Wapner, 'Politics beyond the state: environmental activism and world civic politics', World Politics, 47, 1995, pp 311–340.

[7] IUCN was originally named the International Union for the Protection of Nature, before changing its name in 1956. The organisation later changed its name to the International Union for the Conservation of Nature and Natural Resources before adopting the current name of The World Conservation Union. On the origins of IUCN see John McCormick, Reclaiming Paradise: The Global Environmental Movement, Bloomington, IN: Indiana University Press, 1989, pp 31–41.

[8] Ibid, pp 41–43.

[9] Ibid, chs 2 and 5.

[10] For a discussion of the Stockholm Conference and its significance see Ibid, ch 5. See also Lynton Caldwell, International Environmental Policy: Emergence and Dimensions, Durham, NC: Duke University Press, 1990.

[11] Peter M Haas, Marc A Levy & Edward A Parson, 'Appraising the Earth Summit: how should we judge UNCED's success?', Environment, 34 (8), 1992, pp 7–11, 26–32. As the authors point out, 'Such numbers must be taken with a grain of salt because not all NGOs reported their attendance to the secretariat'.

[12] See McCormick, Reclaiming Paradise, especially chapters 3 and 5.

[13] Haas, Levy & Parson, 'Appraising the Earth Summit'.

[14] The Worldwide Fund for Nature was previously known as the World Wildlife Fund and retains the acronym WWF. The US affiliate still employs the name World Wildlife Fund.

[15] See Thomas Princen & Matthias Finger, 'Introduction', in Finger & Princen, Environmental NGOs in World Politics: Linking the Local and the Global, New York: Routledge, 1994.

[16] See Julie Fisher, The Road from Rio: Sustainable Development and the Nongovernmental Movement in the Third World, Westport, CT: Praeger, 1993.

[17] One effort to identify transnational environmental organisations is found in Helge Ole Bergesen, Magnar Norderhaug & Georg Parmann (eds), Green Globe Yearbook 1992, New York: Oxford University Press, 1992. The editors list 25 organisations described as 'multinational and [having] a substantial part of their activities in environment and development' (p 14). The list excludes research institutions and ad hoc

networks. Of those listed, several are best described not as 'environmental', but rather as organisations with a broader mandate that may intersect with environmental matters; examples include the International Chamber of Commerce, the International Organisation of Consumer Unions, and the International Confederation of Free Trade Unions. Removing such organisations from the list leaves 10 multinational NGOs and one mixed-membership body, the World Conservation Union.

18 Data on national affiliate groups and budgets are from the appendix to Bergesen, *Green Globe Yearbook 1992*, and Paul Wapner, 'Environmental activism and global civil society', *Dissent*, Summer 1994, pp 389–393.

19 The international secretariat of the Third World Network is based in Penang, Malaysia, with offices in Accra, Delhi, Geneva, London and Montevideo.

20 Matthias Finger, 'Environmental NGOs in the UNCED process', in Finger & Princen, *Environmental NGOs in World Politics*, p 204.

21 Julie Fisher, 'Third World NGOs: a missing piece to the population puzzle', *Environment*, 36 (7), 1994, pp 6–11, 37–41.

22 For an example of the Bank's rhetorical embrace of sustainable development, see the 1992 edition of *World Development Report*, Washington, DC: World Bank, 1992. On WHO see World Health Organization, *Our Planet, Our Health: Report of the WHO Commission on Health and Environment*, Geneva: WHO, 1992.

23 Khalil Sesmou, 'FAO: an insider's view', *The Ecologist*, 21 (2), 1991, pp 47–56. The author, writing under a pseudonym, is identified as a 'senior FAO official'.

24 On the Bank and the environment, see Bruce Rich, *Mortgaging the Earth: The World Bank, Environmental Impoverishment, and the Crisis of Development*, Boston, MA: Beacon Press, 1994; and Philippe G Le Prestre, *The World Bank and the Environmental Challenge*, Selinsgrove, PA: Susquehanna University Press, 1989. See also the Bank's annual reports *The World Bank and the Environment*, a series begun in 1990.

25 Calculated from Peter R Baehr & Leon Gordenker, *The United Nations in the 1990s* New York: St Martin's Press, 1992, Table 2.1.

26 See Pat Aufderheide & Bruce Rich, 'Environmental reform and the multilateral banks', *World Policy Journal*, 5 (2) 1988, pp 301–321.

27 World Bank, *The World Bank and the Environment: Fiscal 1992*, Washington, DC: International Bank for Reconstruction and Development 1992.

28 The following summary draws upon David B Hunter & Lori Udall, The World Bank's new inspection panel' *Environment*, 36 (9), 1994, pp 2–3, 44–45. The authors are affiliated with the Center for International Environmental Law and the Environmental Defense Fund, respectively, two NGOs instrumental in pressuring the Bank on this issue.

29 Bruce Rich, 'The emperor's new clothes: the World Bank and environmental reform', *World Policy Journal*, 7 (2) 1990, pp 305–329. A more hopeful view is offered by Kenneth Piddington, 'The role of the World Bank', in Andrew Hurrell & Benedict Kingsbury (eds), *The International Politics of the Environment*, Oxford: Clarendon Press, 1992. Piddington was Director of the Bank's Environment Department, 1988–1991.

30 On the history of the Tropical Forestry Action Plan, see Robert Winterbottom, *Taking Stock: The Tropical Forestry Action Plan After Five Years*, Washington, DC: World Resources Institute, June 1990.

31 Task force recommendations were published in 1985; see World Resources Institute, *Tropical Forests: A Call for Action*, Washington, DC: WRI, October 1985.

32 Winterbottom concludes that TFAP's planning framework has focused in particular on land use, forest-based industrial development, fuelwood and energy issues, conservation of tropical forest ecosystems, and institution building at the local and national level. See Winterbottom, *Taking Stock*, p 4.

33 Ibid, p 13.

34 FAO, TFAP *Update 31*, Rome: FAO, June 1994. TFAP reporting is handled by the TFAP Coordinating Unit within FAO's Forestry Department.

35 Winterbottom lists WRI, The World Conservation Union (IUCN), the International Institute for Environment and Development (IIED), the International Union of Forestry Research Organizations (IUFRO), the Environmental Liaison Committee International (ELCI) and the Worldwide Fund for Nature (WWF) as regular participants. See Winterbottom, *Taking Stock*, p 8ff.

36 See for example Rich, 'The emperor's new clothes' or the special edition on FAO of *The Ecologist*, 21 (2) 1991. WRI itself produced a strongly critical assessment of the TFAP in 1991, emphasising the narrowness of TFAP's vision and a wide range of implementation failures. See Winterbottom, *Taking Stock*.

37 See Nels Johnson & Bruce Cabarle, *Surviving the Cut: Natural Forest Management in the Humid Tropics*, Washington, DC: World Resources Institute, February 1993.

38 George Marshall, 'FAO and tropical forestry', *The Ecologist* 21 (2), 1991, pp 66–72.

39 Finger, 'Environmental NGOs in the UNCED process', p 200.

40 Ibid, p 208. The countries were Norway, Sweden, the UK, Denmark, Finland, Canada, New Zealand, the USA, Australia, the Netherlands, the Commonwealth of Independent States, India, Switzerland and France.

[41] Michael Grubb, Matthias Koch, Abby Munson, Francis Sullivan & Koy Thomson, *The Earth Summit Agreements: A Guide and Assessment*, London: Earthscan Publications, 1993, p 44.

[42] Finger, 'Environmental NGOs in the UNCED process', p 196.

[43] Ibid, pp 203–206.

[44] Grubb, *The Earth Summit Agreements*, p 46.

[45] Finger, 'Environmental NGOs in the UNCED process', pp 209–211.

[46] On the origins and workings of UNEP see Mark Imber, 'Too many cooks? The post-Rio reform of the United Nations', *International Affairs*, 69 (1), pp 55–70; Peter M Haas, 'Institutions: United Nations Environment Programme', *Environment*, 36 (7), 1994, pp 43–45; Caldwell, *International Environmental Policy*.

[47] McCormick, *Reclaiming Paradise*.

[48] Princen & Finger, 'Introduction', p 6.

[49] See Peter M Haas, *Saving the Mediterranean: The Politics of International Environmental Cooperation*, New York: Columbia University Press, 1990.

[50] Finger, 'Environmental NGOs in the UNCED process', p 195.

[51] Haas, 'Institutions'.

[52] Imber, 'Too many cooks?', p 69.

[53] Grubb, *The Earth Summit Agreements*, p 21.

[54] NGOs applying for consultative status with ECOSOC must be approved unanimously by the 19-member Committee on NGOs. If accredited, they submit written testimony and ask to be heard at Council meetings.

[55] Helge Ole Bergesen, 'Empty symbols or a process that can't be reversed?', *International Challenges*, 12 (3), cited in Grubb, *The Earth Summit Agreements*, p 43.

[56] See United Nations Association of the United States of America, 'NGO Guide to the UN Commission on Sustainable Development', UNA–USA Background Paper, June 1994.

[57] Grubb, *The Earth Summit Agreements*, p 46.

■ 6 ■

IGO-NGO Relations and HIV/AIDS: Innovation or Stalemate?

CHRISTER JÖNSSON AND PETER SÖDERHOLM

In 1981 the symptoms later labelled acquired immunodeficiency syndrome (AIDS) were encountered for the first time among five homosexual men in Los Angeles, California. Few people, if any, at that time could possibly have foreseen the consequences of the diagnosis. By the end of 1994 over one million AIDS cases had been reported to the World Health Organization (WHO). Taking under-reporting into account, WHO estimates that about 4.5 million men, women and children are now suffering from AIDS (see Fig. 1).

Projections into the future indicate that we have witnessed only the beginning of the pandemic. Over 14 million persons are carriers of HIV, the virus that causes AIDS. The average incubation time of 10 years, with asymptomatic carriers continuously spreading the virus, leads to estimates ranging from 40 million to 100 million HIV-infected individuals by the year 2000.[1]

In little more than a decade, AIDS has provoked responses on an unprecedented scale in the history of health. A gradual realisation that AIDS was not confined to certain high-risk groups, but was affecting every corner of the world, provoked calls for international action. The United Nations (UN) system, with its reputation and expertise in health as well as social and economic develop-

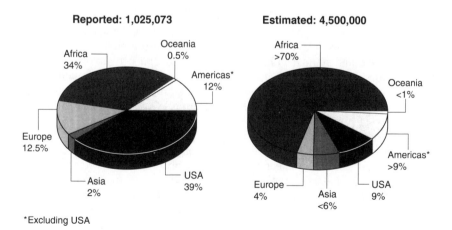

Source: WHO Global Programme on AIDS   GPA/SERSG95009 12 January 1995

FIG. 1. Total number of AIDS cases in adults and children from the late 1970s until late 1994. *Source*: WHO Global Programme on AIDS GPA/SERSG 95009 12 January 1995.

ment, was soon compelled to mount a response to the disease. The UN, it was thought, could substantially help mobilise governments and international organisations to develop policies to prevent and control HIV/AIDS, and to mitigate the economic and social consequences resulting from the virus.

A global offensive was launched in 1987, 'the year of global AIDS mobilization'.[2] In May of that year WHO initiated its Special Programme on AIDS, later known as the Global Programme on AIDS (GPA). In October AIDS was discussed by the UN General Assembly, the first time a specific disease was considered by that forum. Another watershed was the January 1988 world summit of health ministers, attended by delegates from 148 countries, which issued the so-called London Declaration on AIDS Prevention. Endorsing the WHO GPA, the document called for 'the involvement of all relevant governmental sectors and nongovernmental organizations in creating the supportive social environment needed to ensure the effective implementation of AIDS prevention programmes and humane care of affected individuals'.[3]

The stage was thus set for global collaboration by a broad range of organisational actors. This paper draws on a collaborative study, more fully reported elsewhere, which uses an interorganisational approach to trace the emergence of transnational cooperative structures in response to AIDS.[4] Of chief concern here are the efforts at creating and maintaining links among and between intergovernmental organizations (IGOs) in the UN system and the many heterogeneous organisations usually lumped together under the NGO label. After a discussion of the nature of the AIDS issue, we focus on two aspects of IGO–NGO relations: various ways of framing the AIDS issue, which tend to empower and disempower different sets of organisational actors; and the conscious efforts by GPA to coordinate IGO and NGO activities. In conclusion, we identify some lessons and insights of broader applicability emanating from the AIDS case.

The nature of AIDS

Several characteristics of the AIDS issue are germane to understanding organisational responses. First, AIDS provides a graphic illustration of the degree of interdependence and mutual vulnerability among peoples. It involves so many different actors that it cannot be dealt with effectively by a single organisation—whether a national government, international organisation, multinational business corporation or nongovernmental organisation.[5] 'AIDS cannot be stopped in any single country unless it is stopped in all countries.'[6]

Second, AIDS typifies an issue that spans global and community levels, in which penetrating societies is of utmost importance. It is an issue for which community and global connections are arguably more important than the national ones.[7] Global cooperation and community-based treatment, care, and education are the indispensable components of an effective AIDS strategy.

Third, efforts to prevent or halt the spread of AIDS encroach upon the private and personal spheres that are normally beyond the purview of states. AIDS is a fatal infection that spreads through behaviour considered private or even taboo, such as premarital sexual relationships, extramarital sex, commercial sex, sex between men and needle sharing when injecting drugs. Though present, these practices are seldom openly acknowledged in any society. Some governments even choose to deny them altogether.

Fourth, the long incubation period of HIV/AIDS, combined with the fact that young adults, the most productive and reproductive members of the population, are primary targets, makes this the first epidemic in medical history for which the infected have formed articulate and well-informed consumer lobbies. Impatient with bureaucratic responses, various coalitions of People with AIDS (PWAS) have demanded respect for those who are ill, and access to treatment for them. This has been said to represent a revolution in public health, a dramatic rupture with the past, with repercussions beyond the AIDS issue.[8]

These traits combine to challenge the orthodox state-centric view of international relations. States, either alone or collaborating in IGOs, cannot halt the spread of AIDS. Only through the interaction of states, IGOs and NGOs can care and education reach into societies. Only through interaction can a global policy that is responsive to the demands of those affected by the epidemic be formulated. In the next section, we analyse to what extent NGOs and IGOs have assumed prominent roles in the transnational processes triggered by the HIV/AIDS pandemic.

Framing the issue

Problem definition, or framing, is a crucial aspect of agenda-setting. Problems do not exist 'out there', but are the result of subjective interpretations of certain perceived conditions and events. Most of what we generally recognise as international problems can be framed in a variety of ways. The importance of framing a problem has been recognised in different research traditions. Prospect theory, for example, asserts that the way people frame a problem determines in part how they see the consequences of choice.[9] And cognitive scientists have shown that categorisation is not independent of who is doing the categorising. Categories do not exist in the world but have to do with the world as we interact with it.[10] Framing, in short, is a highly political process. Goals of organisations and systems of organisations are subordinated to the goals of those who control the categorisation process.[11] Moreover, different ways of framing an issue mobilise and empower different types of actors at the expense of others.

AIDS as a medical problem

The most obvious and orthodox way of framing AIDS is in terms of medical science. Within the biomedical paradigm, the causes of ill health are located within the body, and AIDS is conceptualised in an elaborate scientific vocabulary.[12] This framing of HIV/AIDS mobilised and empowered actors traditionally engaged in health-related activities such as epidemiological surveillance, biomedical research and health care.

Associated with a medical understanding are a set of practices established as a social institution. The social institution public health entails standard operating procedures understandable to those well versed in its discourse. Thus, a search for the causative agent of AIDS constituted the reflexive response by medical research institutes. As the Center for Disease Control (CDC) in Atlanta received the first reports from doctors in California and New York about homosexual men developing a rare form of skin cancer and pneumonia, the research apparatus at CDC's disposal was immediately set in motion, reports were disseminated, articles submitted for publication and public hearings arranged. Also, CDC reported the new strange medical condition to the WHO epidemiological surveillance unit, which started to compile information and to disseminate it around the world. Long-established international cooperative structures in the field of health were activated.

As discovery was followed by a search for the cause, the number of actors grew. Quasi-governmental organisations were given resources to start research. For example, the National Institutes of Health (NIH) in Maryland as well as the Pasteur Institute in Paris became engaged. As results accumulated, yet other nongovernmental actors were involved in the form of publishers of medical journals and professional organisations for public health specialists. Furthermore, as possibilities for vaccines and drugs were explored, pharmaceutical companies saw potential profits and began to think about new products and markets.

Medical experts were also the first to bring AIDS to the international agenda in earnest. In August 1983 the Panamerican Health Organization (PAHO), in cooperation with the US NIH and CDC, convened a regional meeting of scientists and public health workers in Washington, DC to exchange information on the occurrence of AIDS. Two months later a similar meeting in Aarhus, Denmark focused on AIDS in Europe. It was co-organised by the Danish Cancer Society, WHO and the European Organization for Cooperation in Cancer Prevention Studies.

The First International Conference on AIDS was convened in Atlanta in April 1985 and may be considered the beginning of worldwide mobilisation of the scientific community. The Atlanta conference, organised by CDC and co-sponsored by the US Department of Health and WHO, was attended by scientists and health authorities from 50 countries. International AIDS conferences have since become annual—since 1994, biennial—events, furnishing opportunities for exchange of viewpoints between specialists and for raising public awareness. Although their topics and participants have gradually expanded, medical framing remains the predominant approach. The International AIDS Society, a voluntary association of scientific interest groups and a co-sponsor of the annual AIDS conferences, is a principal NGO within this frame.

However, a medical understanding of the pandemic is far from simple. Traditional medical solutions to epidemics—a drug that would cure the disease, a vaccine that would prevent infection—have remained beyond reach. In this respect, AIDS is a medical problem thus far without a medical solution. Moreover, any approach to preventing or controlling AIDS needs to be informed by the particularities of the epidemiological patterns and the routes of infection. In short, medical framing tends to hide other aspects of the pandemic.

Jonathan Mann, former executive director of GPA, coined the notion of three epidemics to highlight its multifaceted nature. The first epidemic is the silent and unnoticed infection by HIV that began spreading from continent to continent in the 1970s. The global manifestations of the infection, the spread of AIDS cases, represents the second wave. The third epidemic concerns the social, economic, political and cultural reactions to, and consequences of, the first two epidemics. This includes social disruption as individuals, families, groups and societies are affected; the economic consequences of expensive health care and loss of income, families' losses of breadwinners and societies' losses of entire generations of workers; and the stigmatisation of and discrimination against those infected by the virus. The third epidemic, says Mann, is 'as central to the global AIDS challenge as the disease itself' and can be 'as destructive as the preceding ones'. It 'threatens increasingly to overshadow and overwhelm the epidemics of HIV and AIDS'.[13]

AIDS as a problem of human rights

The notion of a third epidemic implies several possible framings in addition to the medical one. Blame and stigmatisation represent one alternative conceptualisation, not only in the general public but also among policy-makers. AIDS is understood not in biomedical and scientific terms but in moral and sometimes even theological terms. The disease is viewed not primarily as the result of infection by a micro-organism but as a social, moral or spiritual affliction.[14] This includes calls for quarantine and other exclusionary policies as a response to the actual mode of transmission and also to the felt need to establish a boundary between 'us' and 'them'. In the mid-1980s several countries, including the USA, passed legislation restricting the entry of HIV-infected individuals. Aided by the discovery of the AIDS virus in 1983 to 1984 and the subsequent development of diagnostic tests, policy-makers were often prodded into such action by religious and conservative organisations.

An antithetical framing is in terms of human rights. Discrimination and violations of the human rights and dignity of HIV-infected people then become key aspects, and refinement of legal instruments and international conventions become the preferred solution. The human rights conceptualisation to a certain extent stands in stark contrast to the medical framing. Surveillance of the epidemic invokes practices that may raise questions of human rights. These practices include involuntary testing of high-risk groups, such as prostitutes, prisoners, intravenous drug users and homosexuals; users of health services, such as pregnant women and patients with sexually transmitted diseases; migrants or travellers; and certain occupation groups, such as military and health personnel. Notifying health authorities of cases of AIDS, ostensibly only a technical public health measure, also raises the human rights issues of confidentiality and anonymity.

Homosexual men in the USA and Europe were the first known AIDS victims and also the first to organise a response. People with AIDS reacted to what they perceived as grave injustices, such as loss of employment and housing, occupational restrictions, for example in health care and food handling, or social ostracism. Organisation was facilitated because homosexual communities, especially in the USA, were already well organised as a result of the struggle for respect and non-discrimination dating back to the civil rights era of the late

1960s. AIDS mobilised these gay organisations and provided them with a target for their frustration. They were relatively well equipped with organisational resources, such as office space, committed and educated staff and, not least, established contacts with policy-makers within city, state and national authorities. On the one hand, this mobilisation spawned numerous AIDS service organisations (ASOs) engaged in providing basic health care and counselling for the sick. Around the world, ASOs mushroomed and became institutional vehicles of volunteer, community-based AIDS prevention and care efforts. On the other hand, public advocacy and activist organisations, such as Gay Men's Health Crisis in the USA, quickly rose to prominence. ACT-UP (the AIDS Coalition to Unleash Power) is a prominent activist organisation that stages direct action, including civil disobedience, to target institutions that impede AIDS research or discriminate against HIV-infected people. Starting as a local activist group in New York's Greenwich Village, ACT-UP now has chapters in several countries around the world.

It is noteworthy that the first intergovernmental body to address the epidemic was a human rights organisation. In 1983 the Council of Europe pointed to the human rights aspects of the epidemic in a couple of remarkable resolutions.[15] The involvement of the Council of Europe at an early moment, when denial and dim recognition of the AIDS problem prevailed, may seem surprising. Human rights issues are traditionally given high priority on the organisation's agenda, but the various Council of Europe institutions have a conservative record. The council's action on a very sensitive issue can be attributed to the pre-existence of a specialised committee concerned with safe blood products and the precedent of a 1981 resolution on discrimination against homosexuals which, in turn, reflected a history of lobbying by homosexual activists.

Several international organisations, IGOs as well as NGOs, have established an elaborate set of practices and a discourse for dealing with human rights. However, the worlds of public health and human rights seldom meet. Yet human rights became a crucial element of GPA's global AIDS strategy. This reflected Jonathan Mann's growing consciousness of the human rights aspects of AIDS, developed in conversations with a handful of intellectuals. Not only did Mann accept that human rights of PWA/HIV should be respected because it was right, he also found a public health rationale for respecting them. If AIDS was a reason for discrimination, he argued, effective prevention campaigns would not reach the targets; the problem would be driven underground and allowed to fester undisturbed by public intervention.

GPA officials hosted consultations with human rights and AIDS-related NGOs in Geneva and New York in May 1988 and requested the British-based human rights NGO, Rights and Humanity, to prepare an internal briefing document on how to involve UN agencies in human rights aspects of AIDS. Attention to these aspects gradually gained momentum, as NGOs pressed for incorporation of human rights aspects of the AIDS pandemic in the annual international AIDS conferences, co-sponsored by WHO. An International Consultation on AIDS and Human Rights was convened in Geneva in July 1989 in collaboration with the UN Centre on Human Rights. Four dozen participants from a wide variety of professional fields and representing an array of international, regional and national civic-based and public organisations exchanged ideas and concerns. Although instrumental in clarifying issues, this meeting also unveiled organisational constraints. Specifically, GPA and the UN Centre on Human rights represented divergent organisational cultures and working habits. Their relations remained strained, and little result was achieved in the further development of policies at the intersection of AIDS and human rights.

AIDS as a socioeconomic problem

Yet another framing defines the epidemic as a socioeconomic problem. AIDS was initially perceived to be a 'disease of affluence' confined to the Western industrialised countries, but it has become ever more evident that AIDS is a 'disease of poverty'. In a global perspective, AIDS becomes a North–South problem, epitomising the gap between developed and developing countries. Foreign aid then constitutes the time-honoured response.

WHO's active involvement with AIDS coincided with the realisation that the epidemic was spreading rapidly in the Third World. Support to developing countries in providing health for all has been a mainstay of WHO's work since the late 1970s. It is therefore natural that WHO's growing involvement brought the North–South aspects of the AIDS problem into focus. By the same token, development NGOs also became potential actors.

WHO GPA assumed a coordinating role in providing AIDS-related foreign aid to the Third World. For many donor countries, channelling financial resources through WHO offered a convenient way out of a political quandary. WHO Director-General Halfdan Mahler put it succinctly during an informal meeting on AIDS in connection with the 40th World Health Assembly in May 1987: 'A number of major bilateral donors have stated clearly that their bilateral efforts to combat AIDS have been constrained by political sensitivities, and inadequate knowledge, expertise, experience, and financial and human resources ... That is why [they] have decided to complement WHO's programme and centrally-funded activities.'[16]

One limitation in WHO's ability to fulfil its coordinating role in foreign assistance results from having governmental agencies as its national counterparts. In the Third World, health ministries are notoriously weak and inefficient. GPA therefore first turned to UNDP to improve its access in developing countries, forming the 'WHO–UNDP Alliance to Combat AIDS' in March 1988. The purpose was to take advantage of UNDP's socioeconomic expertise and presence in most Third World countries. UNDP resident representatives were authorised to coordinate all external assistance to national AIDS programmes at the country level. The idea of combining the strengths of WHO and UNDP, while sound in theory, worked less well in practice. The envisaged collaboration was encumbered by duplication and turf battles.

In short, socioeconomic framing became predominant with WHO's involvement. At the same time, the very definition of AIDS as a North–South issue contributed to a gradual erosion of WHO's role as lead agency because donor countries and development IGOs and NGOs came to question WHO's competence. In the absence of medical solutions, development had to focus on education and behaviour change. The burden of design then passes from medical to social science. WHO's traditional partners in member states and among NGOs have primarily medical expertise. Although the number of NGOs in official relations with WHO is impressive, very few deal with development and hardly any deal with health service and education in rural settings.

As this brief account shows, there exists a confounding variety of framings of, and proposed solutions to, the AIDS problem—all with their concomitant sets of interested organisational actors. In the following section, we trace the efforts by WHO GPA to forge links with NGOs from various sectors in hammering out a global AIDS policy.

Forging IGO–NGO links

After the initiation of GPA, WHO's role as lead agency in AIDS-related international cooperation was endorsed by states and by a host of intergovernmental organisations. WHO's interest in NGOs increased as the implications of its ambitious Global Strategy for Health for All by the Year 2000 took hold.[17] That strategy represented a redirection of WHO towards a broader focus on health care and its role in development; and it required a partnership among governments, WHO and NGOs. Thus, when WHO developed its responses to HIV/AIDS, it acquired the potential to become a focal point for transnational NGO activity.

From the beginning of his tenure as head of GPA, Jonathan Mann demonstrated an enthusiastic, if initially lonely, conviction that cooperation with NGOs would prove to be essential. He and newly-recruited colleagues built up contacts and insights into the NGO world, while an increasing number of NGO representatives sought information and cooperation from GPA.

By the end of 1987, GPA had recruited Robert Grose, an experienced hand with NGO relations who came from the Overseas Development Administration of the United Kingdom. Grose's task included not merely direct contact with NGOs but the creation of an organised structure for that line of contacts. By that time, it had become obvious that a few NGOs were taking an interest in and occasionally carrying out loud and dramatic demonstrations at the international AIDS conferences that GPA was co-sponsoring. Other NGOs were becoming involved in the growing number of National AIDS Programs (NAPs) that GPA promoted.

However, most GPA staff had little experience in working with NGOs outside the public health and medical sectors; no consensus existed within GPA concerning the degree of influence that NGOs should be given in GPA policy and programme discussions. One group wanted NGOs to help GPA with the execution of programmes and with information gathering. NGOs, it was argued, 'do not possess an overall appreciation of the AIDS pandemic and all its manifestations and, moreover, usually represent a specific interest group and hence possess only a specific or limited orientation toward the dilemma as a whole'.[18] Another group, including Mann and Grose, wanted to include ASOs and AIDS-related NGOs in all aspects of the policy process. They proposed and started to build 'a small informal working group composed of those persons and organizations with whom we feel comfortable, to strategize and map out a framework'.[19]

The informal GPA-centred network included individuals who were nodes in regional networks and who multiplied discussions. Among them were key Red Cross officials in Geneva, a creative and bold homosexual man responsible for the AIDS activities of the Norwegian Red Cross and a Canadian physician and human rights activist plugged into the North American ASOs. On the whole, the picture began to emerge of a fairly small group of people in regular contact with each other.

Many ASOs pressed for official acknowledgement of their legitimacy and competence and for representation on AIDS-related bodies. In addition, they sought material support. Both as a matter of policy and of legal capacity, IGOs have been cautious in directly supporting NGOs. GPA sought an indirect route via national governments and the GPA-sponsored National AIDS Programs. In 1991 GPA officially recommended that NAPs commit at least 15% of the funds channelled through WHO to support NGO AIDS activities. In reality, however, collaboration between national programmes and NGOs remained limited, and resource flows to NGOs through the NAPs were small.[20] GPA also initiated a Partnership Program to distribute 'seed' grants directly to NGOs for specific projects. To qualify, projects had to be carried out jointly by transnational and local NGOs and required the approval of both national governments and national programmes.

An international NGO forum

Several leading AIDS activists lobbied GPA, requesting assistance in setting up an umbrella organisation to group the new ASOs and other NGOs. Ken Morrison of the Canadian AIDS Society recalls the early history:

> Early in 1988, the Canadian AIDS Society (CAS) wrote to WHO to request assistance in setting up an international forum. This was followed by more and more concrete proposals from CAS. Richard Rector, wandering American, was working hard in and out of WHO lobbying for such a forum. In Brazil, Walter Almeida, behind his computer, his telephone and fax machine, churned out proposals. The Canadian Council for International Co-operation, an umbrella organization of international development agencies, also put together a proposal for an international AIDS project.[21]

Grose and Mann encouraged these plans. Such a structure would explicitly recognise the role of NGOs, while at the same time responding to demands from within the WHO structure and elsewhere for more bureaucratic tidiness. After several informal consultations between GPA officials and a small group of NGO representatives, the first international meeting of ASOs was held in Vienna in late February 1989. Another ASO conference took place in Montreal in June the same year, just before the Fifth International AIDS Conference. Representatives of more than 100 AIDS-related NGOs participated. A task force of representatives from nine regions was established to develop the organisational structure and a programme of action for a proposed International Council of ASOs (ICASO).

Ratification was to take place at the Second International AIDS NGO Conference, set to coincide with the Sixth International AIDS Conference in San Francisco in 1990. As a result of a widespread boycott of the San Francisco conference because of US legislation restricting entry of HIV-infected travellers, the NGO conference was moved to Paris and convened in early November 1990. Ratification of ICASO proved to be controversial, since proponents of the new umbrella organisation had failed to involve counterparts at the local and regional level.

Africans took the lead in opposing ICASO. During the first African caucus session, three-fourths of the participants argued that they had never heard of ICASO. The sole African member of the ICASO planning committee claimed she had never been asked to contribute during the drafting process. Attitudes among the participants from other regions were mixed. Many felt that the structure of ICASO was being forced on them without prior consultation. The conference ended with the ICASO ratification left in suspense. In the end, the conferees agreed that the organisational development process was to go forward but opted for a more decentralised and regionalised structure, which was confirmed in 1991.

Formal representation of NGOs became an issue in connection with the GPA Global Management Committee (GMC), the highest policy-making body of GPA. Because almost all GPA funding derives from voluntary contributions by governments, their representatives sought an appropriate supervisory device. GMC consists of representatives of all governments making unearmarked contributions to the GPA budget. Other members represent WHO regions and the six IGOs that have cooperated most intensely with GPA. NGOs were at first limited to observer status at GMC meetings but, as early as January 1988, some NGOs requested representation in GMC. GMC anticipated success in the plans to create an umbrella organisation, and accepted one NGO representative as a full member. With the controversial nature of ICASO, it has become difficult to represent the varied perspectives and interests of NGOs, and the presence of a full NGO member has been postponed while a growing number of NGOs participate as observers.

Informal networking

Annual international AIDS conferences have been forums for informal networking. The earliest NGO meetings, as we have seen, were held in conjunction with these larger conferences. Since then, they have provided ample opportunities for contact among various NGOs and the establishment of *ad hoc* coalitions and networks.

For several years, non-medical issues played a subordinate role in official conference programmes. The 1992 conference in Amsterdam, by contrast, reflected a commitment by the organisers to bring social issues into a new balance with biomedical science and public health. The planners also made a special effort to involve People with AIDS and local organisations from the Third World. The conference programme reflected an integrated approach, and NGOs played an unprecedented role in the planning as well as the proceedings. A series of workshops were specifically aimed at empowering small organisations to grow and connect to other similar organisations. Skills such as producing newsletters, communicating with authorities and organising workshops were taught; and HIV-net, a computerised bulletin board connecting several organisations, was set up. Subsequent conferences have not matched the precedent set by Amsterdam concerning NGO involvement.

The Amsterdam conference included the prominent presence of a new organisation, Global AIDS Policy Coalition (GAPC), which was started by Mann from his new post at Harvard University, where he went after leaving WHO. It has assembled outstanding researchers, policy analysts, practitioners and community workers from around the world. A special area of interest is the nexus of AIDS, health and human rights issues. From his Harvard position and as head of GAPC, Mann has been able to stay at the forefront of the global policy process, despite his abrupt exit from WHO after a dispute with the director-general.

NGOs and AIDS-related foreign assistance

One particular area where NGOs have played an operational role, alone, or in collaboration with IGOs, is AIDS-related foreign assistance. From the outset, most multilateral aid was channelled through GPA. From 1987 to 1990, donors increased their funding annually, so that GPA's financial resources increased from $29.8 million in 1987 to $79.3 million in 1990.[22]

NGOs had a comparative advantage in the multilateral aid effort. Efficient AIDS programmes demanded sustained community commitment. In order to play a role in such programmes, GPA needed to establish credibility and trust among organisations with documented results in health service delivery and sex education. Without such contacts, little rationalisation could exist for using GPA for channelling resources from major donors. Naturally, GPA staff were aware of how donors like the US Agency for International Development (US AID) and the Swedish International Development Agency (SIDA) were enthusiastic about NGOs in general.

In November 1989 the bilateral donors and UN agencies represented on the GPA Global Management Committee decided to commission an external review of GPA. Although it conformed to WHO's usual practice, there were other signs of dissatisfaction with the way GPA performed its coordinating role. By 1990 there was a shift towards bilateral funding. Moreover, in 1991 for the first time contributions to GPA declined at the same time as total contributions (bilateral and multilateral) for AIDS prevention and care in the Third World decreased.[23]

The review criticised the deficient coordination among UN agencies, citing 'duplication of effort and territorial rivalries'.[24] In addition, the review pointed to problems in GPA's relations with NGOs. While praising the farsightedness of recognising the importance of NGOs in early policy documents, the review also stated that 'a number of NGOs felt that GPA was attempting to mediate and control their initiatives'.[25] Problems of NGO coordination were noted at the national level as well:

> During visits to countries, the ERC [External Review Committee] noted that NGOs (where they exist) receive few funds through NAPs [National AIDS Programs], and that collaboration appears to be a low priority. Donors have attempted to channel

funds directly to NGOs through their own institutional mechanisms. In addition, some have begun to explore new ways of channeling technical and financial assistance to NGOs: needs are being assessed and a range of possible measures will be explored.[26]

The review recommended that a new structure for coordination be formed at the global level, and called for stronger interagency coordination at country level, with special emphasis on NGO participation.[27] Succeeding designs for new coordination bodies were drafted by various *ad hoc* committees, only to be rejected. At the GMC meeting in November 1992, an informal working group managed to produce a proposal that was adopted unanimously. The proposal called for a GMC Task Force consisting of three representatives each from recipient governments, donor governments, the UN family and NGOs.

The task force idea originated from Nils-Arne Kastberg, a member of the Swedish mission in Geneva who had not previously dealt with cooperation on AIDS. Primarily a development expert, he had prior experience in UN coordination issues, had participated in the Nordic UN Project to reevaluate development efforts, and had taken an active part in the reorganisation of UN disaster relief. Kastberg was appointed chairperson of the task force and came to play a prominent role in informal interagency consultations that eventually resulted in a joint and co-sponsored UN programme on HIV/AIDS, endorsed by ECOSOC in July 1994.

While this new programme primarily concerns coordination within the UN family, it envisages NGO participation in a programme coordinating board and in the secretariat. Whereas the original plan for a joint and co-sponsored program called for collaboration with 'nongovernmental organizations, community-based organizations and groups of people living with HIV and AIDS',[28] this to date has received scant attention in the interagency bargaining process. Confronted with a *fait accompli*, NGOs have generally been wary of the new coordination scheme.

In sum, AIDS has raised several questions concerning IGO–NGO relations but provided few answers. For all the efforts at collaboration, a persistent element of mutual mistrust can be discerned. NGOs have feared that GPA wants control rather than coordination, and have balked at a too close identification with IGOs. At the same time, GPA has had to struggle with the confounding variety of NGOs, not all of which are seen as responsible partners. NGOs and GPA have remained 'reluctant partners'.[29]

Lessons and conclusions

Several lessons of broader applicability can be derived from the experience of IGO–NGO links in this specialised yet diffuse and elusive issue. In keeping with our interorganisational approach, we shall concentrate on five interrelated aspects: the problems of NGO representation and representativeness; the advantages and disadvantages of formal versus informal coordination; the costs of network building; the varying degrees of organisation among interested actors; and the kind of expertise needed in network building.

Representation

Problems of representation are inescapable facts of international coordination. IGOs face perennial discussions of representation. The dividing line typically separates the principle of one state, one vote and representation qualified by some special attribute of the state considered essential for the implementation of the organisation's task. In the case of the task force, for instance, donor countries agreed that their three members would represent the countries of the European Community (now Union); the countries of Scandinavia and the European Free Trade Association (EFTA); and North America, Japan and Australia. This division was obviously based on contributions to AIDS-related assistance.

NGO representation presents special difficulties. According to the GMC decision, the selection of three NGO representatives for the task force was to be made by 'appropriate NGO coordinating bodies'.[30] In the absence of an official, commonly accepted NGO forum, this deliberately vague formulation left open the selection procedure. The actual choice of the Amsterdam-based AIDS Coordination Group, the Senegal-based ENDA-Tiers Monde and the Global Network of People Living with HIV/AIDS was made through an informal consultation process involving established NGO networks. As network theory would predict, these selections depended on trusted persons rather than organisations as such. From the Amsterdam group, Maria de Bruyn had a central role in European development-orientated networks. From ENDA-Tiers Monde, El Hadj As Sy was the pivotal person linking African ASOs, although his organisation, founded in 1972 with support from the UN Environment Program (UNEP), had little claim to be a key actor in the AIDS field.

It is still unclear how a few organisations might represent the heterogeneous NGO community—in the task force or in any other contemplated coordination body. Whereas the task force symbolises official recognition of NGO access to decision-making and coordination, difficult questions concerning constituency and representation remain.[31] Representation problems, in short, arise in any formalisation of IGO–NGO links, and informal solutions are as valid as more formalistic procedures to elect participants.

Formal versus informal coordination

The case of AIDS illustrates the common tendency to search for formal mechanisms whenever a need for international coordination is perceived. Yet there are indications that informal network-like arrangements have certain advantages when it comes to complex coordination tasks. For example, Ernst Haas recommends that international organisations 'resist an overt reordering and centralization of authority', 'minimize hierarchies and regulations' and 'minimize the importance of the boundary between the organization and its environment'.[32] Proceeding from a study of the coordination of regional transport in the San Francisco Bay area, Donald Chisholm arrives at similar conclusions: 'While I do not quarrel with the contention that interdependence requires coordination, I strongly dispute the reflexive assumption that coordination is inexorably tied to centralized arrangements such as comprehensive plans and consolidated agencies'.[33]

Formalisation raises a host of problems, one of which is representation, as discussed above. Formal coordination structures inevitably limit the number of organisations represented, whereas informal coordination among many independent, partly overlapping organisations provides more points of access to the decision-making process.[34] Another problem is that formalisation normally introduces an element of hierarchy. And even hints of centralisation tend to invite controversy. To wit, everyone wants coordination but no one wants to be coordinated.

In the case of AIDS, the designation of WHO as the lead agency injected elements of hierarchy and centralisation from the outset. The degree of conflict and the variety of agencies concerned with AIDS were probably underestimated, but they became obvious in the process. The joint and cosponsored UN programme differs in that it aims to create a new structure between rather than above existing agencies. Explicitly seeking to avoid verticalisation, the UN programme promotes a multisectoral approach. Furthermore, one of the lessons learned from developing a joint and co-sponsored UN programme pertained to the participating organisations' need to preserve their identities, which are often endangered by hierarchical coordination designs.

Informal coordination structures also tend to be more flexible and adaptable than formal ones. Roles and definitions of tasks are determined not by a single authority but by the participating agencies themselves. Roles can be continuously redefined and specific tasks renegotiated. Moreover, information tends to flow more freely through informal structures than through formal channels, which are often ineffective when information is sensitive or politically charged. In effect, the informal yet crucial role played by the *ad hoc* task force, with representatives of IGOs and NGOs as well as donor governments, is an example of the advantages of informal coordination. The task force served as a clearinghouse for exchange of information and views among key actors in the institutional bargaining process. It would hardly have been able to transmit information to and from constituencies and forward comments and views to the involved agencies so freely had it been part of a formal, hierarchical coordination structure.

In international cooperation generally, and concerning AIDS in particular, the lack of trust among governments and between IGOs and NGOs is an irritant. One important advantage of informal over formal organisation is that it provides an opportunity for mutual mistrust gradually to be broken down and replaced by confidence.

Of course, informal organisation should not be idealised. There are disadvantages associated with informal channels based on personal relationships. They are extremely vulnerable to high rates of turnover among personnel, especially when they result in departures from the interorganisational system instead of movements within the system.[35] This is especially relevant in connection with AIDS, where high staff turnover and burnout occur at the managerial level of national AIDS programmes, and where people with HIV/AIDS—who are more susceptible than others to exhaustion, sickness and death—are often key links in national and international networks.[36] Thus, informal organisation is not a substitute for, but rather an important complement to, formal organisation.

Costs of network building

There is a variety of costs associated with network building. First, transaction costs, to borrow a term from economists, can be formidable for small and especially for poor NGOs. Face-to-face contacts constitute the foundation of transnational networks, which usually require generous travel funds. In the field of AIDS, this represents a significant obstacle to universal representation at international gatherings, since the participation of Third World NGO representatives has overwhelmingly depended on funding from industrialised countries. Financial dependencies stay in the way of closer IGO–NGO links in other issue areas as well.

In addition to these tangible costs, there are other, less material but equally significant ones. For many NGOs, opposing and criticising government policies have been traditional. To collaborate with governments and IGO in networks and to formulate and implement joint programmes may imply a profound change in identity with concomitant costs: 'Their *autonomy* is challenged: by engaging in coordinated programmes, NGOs surrender a certain degree of autonomy over their own actions and the external factors that might affect them. Finally, their *cohesion* is weakened, as new tensions emerge within the NGO.'[37]

It is obvious that anticipation of these kinds of costs contributed to the reluctance among NGOs for full-fledged cooperation with WHO's AIDS strategy.

Finally, individual leadership—a crucial ingredient in effective transnational networks—entails notable costs. The example of Jonathan Mann is illustrative. During his years as director of GPA, Mann provided vital leadership. He was an active network builder; his background in public health made him well equipped to integrate medical professionals and other AIDS activists; he made important contributions to the formulation of the goals of global AIDS cooperation; and in his travels around the world, he was in constant interaction with the work. In the process, he apparently failed in the internal functions pertaining to his constituent organisation, WHO; in 1990 he was replaced by a long-standing WHO official. As this and other examples indicate, successful leadership in a transnational network may endanger the leader's position within his or her home organisation, whether governmental, intergovernmental or nongovernmental. Leadership implies a readiness to depart from narrow organisational roles and to base initiatives on a conception of collective goals, however controversial.

Degree of organisation

One factor working against the creation of a tightly knit AIDS network is the varying degree of organisation among relevant actors. Among affected groups, homosexual men are incomparably the best organised. In several Western countries, they constitute influential pressure groups; they have been able to mobilise and articulate political demands; and they have developed well-functioning international networks. As the AIDS epidemic developed across the globe, it became apparent that this was not a disease restricted to the gay community. In fact, three-quarters of all adults with HIV in the world today have been infected through heterosexual transmission. Yet homosexual men remain key actors in transnational networks. Other affected groups—such as prostitutes, intravenous drug users, haemophiliacs, women or children—have few or no organisations to look after their interests; they thus play a peripheral role in transnational cooperation.

There are great geographical variations as well. The degree of organisation in the Third World and Eastern Europe is low compared with North America and Western Europe. The networking that goes on tends to link English-speaking representatives of industrialised countries. Even when it comes to addressing AIDS problems in the Third World, some of the most influential organisations are based in the industrialised world, such as the UK NGO AIDS Consortium for the Third World in London and the National Council for International Health in Washington. Lack of funding is a major obstacle to better organisation in the Third World. In Eastern Europe, in addition, there is a lack of experience of working in grassroots organisations and a heritage of distrust. After several decades of compulsory membership in voluntary organisations, volunteerism has a negative connotation.

Expertise

The popular notion that epistemic communities—knowledge-based networks of experts—play a key role in international policy coordination finds little support in our study of AIDS. Close informal relationships among individuals representing organisations appeared at crucial junctures in every instance of cooperation we found. However, they did not usually fit neatly with the notion of epistemic communities. Rather, the networks were looser in both intention and composition.

Our study suggests that international cooperation in a specialised issue area requires not only know-how but also 'know-who'. Expert knowledge of an issue such as AIDS needs to be combined with knowledge of the relevant organisational and individual actors who might contribute to a solution to the problem: who are they? Under what restraints do they work? How can they be accessed? This is precisely the kind of knowledge that is necessary for successfully building networks.

Among AIDS activists there has often been insufficient understanding of the workings and vagaries of international organisations, especially of the UN system. Conversely, the most successful network builders have developed expertise about organisational actors. It is also noteworthy that a person with absolutely no AIDS expertise but with solid knowledge of the UN system and other actors on the North–South arena assumed a central position in recent efforts at coordinating assistance to the Third World.

In sum, an interorganisational perspective on IGO–NGO links in the global response to AIDS reveals possibilities as well as limitations. NGOs are necessary partners, since they represent the victims of the epidemic, can span the local and global levels, and are better equipped than government authorities to deal with the sensitive, private issues involved in AIDS prevention. NGO representatives also have assumed central positions in informal transnational networks. Yet mutual mistrust, turf battles and the tendency to search for formal coordination mechanisms have stood in the way of closer links and greater efficiency in combating AIDS.

Notes

[1] Jonathan Mann, Daniel J M Tarantola & Thomas W Netter, *AIDS in the World: A Global Report*, Cambridge, MA: Harvard University Press, 1992, p 3.

[2] Jonathan Mann as quoted in Panos Institute, *AIDS in the Third World*, London: Panos Institute, 1988, p 94.

[3] The text of the document can be found, eg in WHO/GPA, *Global Programme on AIDS: Progress Report Number 4*, WHO/GPA/GEN/88.3, Geneva, October 1988, pp 87–88.

[4] Leon Gordenker, Roger A Coate, Christer Jönsson & Peter Söderholm, *International Cooperation in Response to AIDS*, London: Pinter Publishers, 1995.

[5] Such issues have been variously labelled 'global indivisibilities', 'interdependence issues', or 'international physical externalities'. See respectively, James A Caporaso, 'International Relations theory and multilateralism: the search for foundations', *International Organization*, 46, 1992, p 599. James N Rosenau, *Turbulence in World Politics*, London: Harvester Wheatsheaf, 1990, p 106; Mark W Zacher, 'The decaying pillars of the Westphalian temple: implications for international order and governance', in James N Rosenau & Ernst-Otto Czempiel (eds), *Governance without Government: Order and Change in World Politics*, Cambridge: Cambridge University Press, 1992, pp 76–80.

[6] WHO/GPA, *Special Programme on AIDS: Progress Report Number 1*, WHO/SPA/GEN/87.2, Geneva, April 1987, p 5.

[7] Jonathan Mann, 'Pandemic disease, NGOs and the future of public health', address to the Second International Conference of AIDS-related NGOs, Paris, 3 November 1990.

[8] Interview with Jonathan Mann, 'SIDA: Une révolution dans la santé', *L'Autre Journal*, 5, October 1990, pp 89–101.

[9] Daniel Kahneman & Amos Tversky, 'The psychology of preferences', *Scientific American*, 246, 1982, pp 160–173.

[10] George Lakoff, *Women, Fire, and Dangerous Things: What Categories Reveal about the Mind*, Chicago, IL: University of Chicago Press, 1987.

[11] Robert W Cox, 'Problems of global management', in Toby T Gati (ed), *The US, the UN, and the Management of Global Change*, New York: New York University Press, 1983, p 64.

[12] Ken Plummer, 'Organizing AIDS', in Peter Aggleton & Hilary Homans (eds), *Social Aspects of AIDS*, London, The Falmer Press, 1988, p 23.

[13] Panos Institute, *AIDS and the Third World*, p 69.

[14] Plummer, 'Organizing AIDS', p 28.

[15] Council of Europe, *R(83)8 and Resolution 812:1983*, Strasbourg, 1983.

[16] Halfdan Mahler quoted in WHO, *Report of the External Review of the World Health Organization Global Programme on AIDS*, GPA/GMC(8)/92.4, Geneva, 1992, p 4.

[17] The strategy was set out in World Health Assembly resolution WHA 34.36, 1981. See also Leon Gordenker, 'The World Health Organization: sectoral leader or occasional benefactor?', in Roger A Coate (ed), *US Policy and the Future of the United Nations*, New York: The Twentieth Century Fund Press, 1994, pp 171–172.

[18] WHO/GPA, Memorandum from Terry Mooney to Jonathan Mann, 7 March 1988.

[19] Ibid.

[20] WHO, *External Review*, p 19.

[21] *Opportunities for Solidarity*, final report of the Montreal Meeting of NGOs involved in community AIDS service, Montreal 2–4 June 1989, p 6.

[22] WHO, *1991 Progress Report: Global Program on AIDS*, Geneva: WHO, 1992, Annex 8.

[23] Mann et al, *AIDS in the World*, pp 511–12, 519.

[24] WHO, *External Review*, p 39.

[25] Ibid, p 35.

[26] Ibid.

[27] Ibid, pp 42–43, 47.

[28] WHO, *Executive Board document*, EB93/INF.DOC/5, Geneva, 1993, p 2.

[29] Compare John Farrington & Anthony Bebbington, *Reluctant Partners: Non-Governmental Organizations, the State and Sustainable Agricultural Development*, London: Routledge, 1993, p 26.

[30] WHO/GPA, *Extraordinary Meeting of the Management Committee 23–25 November 1992: Conclusions and Recommendations*, GPA/GMC(E)92.7, Geneva, 1992, Annex 2.

[31] The reference to 'nongovernmental organizations, community-based organizations and groups of people living with HIV and AIDS' in the *Study of a joint and cosponsored United Nations programme on HIV/AIDS*, WHO, EB93/INF.DOC./5, represents one attempt to distinguish different groups or constituencies.

[32] Ernst B Haas, *When Knowledge is Power: Three Models of Change in International Organizations*, Berkeley, CA: University of California Press, 1990, pp 201, 206, 207.

[33] Donald Chisholm, *Coordination Without Hierarchy: Informal Structures in Multiorganizational Systems*, Berkeley, CA: University of California Press, 1989, p 13.

[34] Ibid, pp 173–182.

[35] Ibid, pp 29, 142.

[36] Mann et al, *AIDS in the World*, pp 301–305.

[37] Farrington & Bebbington, *Reluctant Partners*, p 49.

■ 7 ■

Engendering World Conferences: The International Women's Movement and the UN

MARTHA ALTER CHEN

The Fourth World Conference on Women will have been held in Beijing in September 1995. Twenty years earlier, the First World Conference on Women, which launched the UN Decade for Women, was held in Mexico City. Two other world conferences for women marked the midpoint and end of the decade: Copenhagen in 1980 and Nairobi in 1985.[1] These UN world conferences for women have served to galvanise the international women's movement,[2] to increase the visibility of women and to show that women matter to world development.[3]

As the international women's movement has grown and matured, other world conferences have attracted its attention and energy. This is so because women recognise the importance of voicing women's perspectives, not only in special conferences for women but also at all conferences, and because these conferences deal with issues that are of interest and concern to women. The ability of the movement to influence these world conferences has increased steadily over time.

UN world conferences also have attracted the attention of such other NGO-led movements as the human rights and environmental groups. When people now speak about a world conference, they usually mean two separate but related conferences—the official UN conference and the NGO forum—held simultaneously or sequentially in the same city. The official conference is the place where government delegations meet to negotiate official policies and documents. The NGO forum is the place where NGOs meet, exchange experiences and develop new strategies.[4]

This essay presents a brief history of how the NGO-led international women's movement has shaped the UN Decade for Women, the World Conferences for Women, and other UN conferences. In so doing, it examines how the types of NGOs interact with the UN, how the relationships between the UN and NGOs have changed over time, and what strategies have proved effective in putting women's concerns on a variety of international agendas.

This is partly the story of women's efforts to influence world conferences and partly an analysis of the methods and strategies women developed in the process. The essay starts with a brief background and history of the UN Decade for Women. It then describes how women were able to shape the policy debates at three recent UN conferences—the Rio conference on environment, the Vienna conference on human rights and the Cairo conference on population. It ends on an uncertain note since many of the gains made by the movement in Rio, Vienna and Cairo have been challenged during the preparatory process leading towards the Fourth World Conference on Women held in Beijing.[5]

Making women visible: the UN decade for women

Over the first 30 years of its existence,[6] the United Nations made steady progress on women's rights within a framework laid out in its Charter of equality between men and women and nondiscrimination on the basis of gender.[7] In those early years, according to the UN accreditation rules at that time, the only women's NGOs that had consultative status with the UN were those that were both international and representative: for example, the Associated Country Women of the World, the International Alliance of Women, World Association of Girl Guides and Girl Scouts, World Young Women's Christian Association and Zonta International. Only a few were headquartered outside Europe or North America.[8]

Since 1975 the UN perspective on women has changed dramatically. The movement itself has also changed dramatically over the past 20 years. The number and variety of NGOs and NGO networks have increased exponentially, and the leadership of the movement has shifted perceptibly from women in the North to women in the South. Moreover, the women's movement has accumulated significant experience and expertise and coalesced in a remarkable way to influence the global policy agenda.

According to the oral history of the UN family, the idea of and initial demand for an International Women's Year came from an international women's organisation in consultative status with the UN: in the Women's International Democratic Federation. The idea was taken up by two official women representatives to the UN Commission on the Status of Women.[9] In 1972 the commission recommended to the General Assembly that 1975 be declared International Women's Year; it became the first of the UN theme years for which extensive preparations were undertaken at all levels.

Thus the International Women's Year is a prime example of an NGO initiative taken up by the UN system, one that exceeded all expectations. It developed into a UN Decade for Women which, in turn, generated 'a process with dimensions and repercussions such as the initiators had hardly dared to dream of'.[10] The International Women's Year also marked the beginning of a new 'women's era' in the UN and the emergence of a global women's movement.

The major event of the year was the First World Conference on Women in Mexico City. Over 6000 women participated in the NGO forum in Mexico City, more nonofficial participants than at any previous UN world conference. Delegations from 133 member states took part in the official conference. They adopted a World Plan of Action, which 'was the first such document the world had seen to concentrate specifically on problems and concerns of women, covering all possible aspects of their lives from food, health and education to family planning and political participation'.[11] However, its comprehensiveness and its lack of an underlying causal explanation of women's status led some feminist critics to refer to the plan as a 'shopping list' of issues relating to women.[12] In December that year, the General Assembly approved the recommendations of the Mexico City conference and declared 1976–1985 to be the UN Decade for Women.

In 1980 a second World Conference on Women was organised in Copenhagen to mark the midpoint of the decade and to assess how much the targets set in the World Plan of Action had been attained. At the official conference in Copenhagen, more so than at Mexico City, many wider political issues such as Zionism, apartheid and the new economic order were used to deflect attention from the World Plan of Action and the whole issue of women's equality. However, the official conference adopted a platform of action for the second half of the decade that emphasised employment, health, and education for women. Meanwhile, the 7000 people, mainly women, who had gathered at the NGO forum were able to communicate and find common ground, despite differences in political, ideological and cultural backgrounds. In the end, the Copenhagen conference covered a wider range of development issues and perspectives than were covered in Mexico City, including critiques of past approaches to women in development and of the new economic order's impact on women.

The Third World Conference on Women was held in Nairobi in 1985 to mark the end of the decade. The numbers for both the official conference and the NGO forum reached a record high. The number of delegates to the official conference was about one-third more than in Mexico City and Copenhagen—over 2000 delegates from 157 countries, and several hundred representatives of NGOs in consultative status to the United Nations.[13] More significant still, over 14 000 women from some 150 countries attended the NGO forum. The final document of the Nairobi Conference, called 'Forward Looking Strategies for the Advancement of Women', provided an analytical framework as well as prescriptive measures to address the obstacles to the advancement of women. After long and strenuous negotiations during the conference, the 'Forward Looking Strategies' were adopted unanimously.[14]

By far the most conspicuous change over the decade was the exponential increase in the number and types of women's NGOs in every country of the world, and the complex of alliances, networks and coalitions set up to unite them. While thousands of women had participated in the three conferences, 'tens of thousands were mobilised by the process in countries around the world'.[15] These new groups represented every hue in the ideological rainbow: secular, religious, radical, conservative, grassroots and elite. They were engaged in delivering welfare or development services to women, organising women for change, researching women's lives and work, advocating change for women and more.[16] They were local, national, regional and international.

These groups represent a new breed of NGOs quite distinct from the established international women's NGOs that have long had consultative status with the UN. This new breed brought energy, vitality and creativity to the international women's movement as well as important links with local organisations and networks. Their goals were to bring women together to share information, resources and strategies, and to create alternative spaces for them at the local, national and global levels.[17] By opting to remain within the framework of the UN, the older established women's organisations were soon outnumbered and overwhelmed by this new breed. However, the older established organisations not only spearheaded the campaigns for the International Women's Year but also coordinated the organisation of the NGO forum at the three women's conferences during the decade.

At the international level, the new breed of NGOs manifested itself primarily as networks. A notable example is Development Alternatives with Women for a New Era (DAWN): a network of scholars and activists in the South, which was established shortly before the Nairobi conference and has consistently articulated alternative development strategies. With the emergence of DAWN and other significant networks of women from the South, the leadership of the international women's movement shifted perceptibly—although not entirely—from North to South.

To maintain the emerging international networks of newer NGOs, a few more formal organisations have been formed. One of the first was the International Women's Tribune Center, which grew out of the NGO forum in Mexico City. Its location next to UN headquarters facilitates networking among grassroots women's organisations and between these organisations and the United Nations. The visions and aims of DAWN and other Third World NGOs have given impetus to the women's movement to set its own goals and aspirations.[18] The skills and contacts of the International Women's Tribune Center (and other networking NGOs) also have given practical skills and knowledge to the women's movement.

Another result of the decade's national and international meetings—and of the thousands of smaller local meetings, seminars, studies and projects that sprang up around the world—was that women around the world not only knew each other better but were also better understood and more widely listened to.[19] Women and development issues could no longer be overlooked by the United Nations or its member nations.

However, much of the Decade for Women was spent in addressing differences in approaches to feminism at the theoretical or ideological levels and differences between women from different social, cultural, historical and geographic locations at the practical level. By the end of the decade, the international women's movement had only begun to address these differences; the hierarchies of class, race and dependency that condition women's lives continued to divide them. Over the past decade, in contrast, the international women's movement has been able to forge remarkable consensus and coalitions around specific issues that affect women, namely environment, human rights and population.

Putting women on the agenda in Rio, Vienna and Cairo

The issues of concern to women, as well as their contributions and problems, came to the forefront in several conferences other than those specifically for women.[20] However, several other world conferences in the late 1970s 'failed totally to realize that there might be an important women's dimension to these topics, and that its recognition might enhance possibilities of solving some of the problems'.[21]

From their experience at these various world conferences, the international women's movement had learned several important lessons. The first was that women's voices have little chance of being heard at UN world conferences without deliberate and concerted efforts. When there have been a few active women on the delegations, in the UN secretariat responsible for the conference, or in NGOs concerned with the substantive issue, they have generally taken the initiative. When sufficiently well-versed in UN procedures, the women have been able to get draft resolutions and text in support of women through all the preparatory stages and the conferences themselves.[22]

The second lesson was that the best time to influence a world conference is during the preparatory process. Many groups and individuals went to the parallel NGO forum at the various women's conferences with the hope of being able to influence the resolutions of the intergovernmental conference. On the spot, however, this was very difficult. NGOs have to master lobbying techniques, understand UN conference procedures clearly and lobby effectively during the preparatory process to make an impact on the official debates. This was a bitter lesson.

The third lesson was that the international women's movement needed to build consensus and coalitions to bridge the ideological and material differences between women. To do so internationally, they first had to do so at the local, national and regional levels.

Coming out of the decade, the international women's movement was determined to build on these lessons and to put women on the agenda of all world conferences, not just of special conferences for women. The experiences shared, the networks and coalitions strengthened and the lessons learned during the 1970s and 1980s all had important consequences for the decade that followed. The international women's movement entered the 1990s with more political vision, know-how and strategies and with a wider political base than ever before.

Rio: women, environment and sustainable development

The UN Conference on Environment and Development (UNCED) held in Rio in 1992 is seen as a turning point for NGOs and as an example of strengthening partnerships between governments, the United Nations and NGOs. The number of NGO representatives who attended the official conference as well as the number of people who attended the NGO forum were the largest ever.[23] Because the UNCED planners adopted an inclusive accreditation process, over 1400 NGOs attended the official conference.[24] Thousands more were informally linked to the UNCED process through the preparatory meetings and the many regional meetings leading up to Rio: a record 30 000 people from 171 countries attended the Global Forum.[25] Increased access to NGOs proved to be a two-way street, giving NGOs information and access to policy-makers, and giving policy-makers expert advice from the diverse NGO community.[26]

For the international women's movement whose member NGOs had already turned out in record numbers in Nairobi, Rio marked a different type of turning point. They effectively put women's issues and concerns on the official global agenda; they established 'that women's issues are part of global agendas and must be incorporated there, rather than addressed separately',[27] and they first worked closely with another social movement, in this case, the environmental movement.[28]

Women's Congress. To build a consensus of women's perspectives and to prepare women to participate equally at Rio, the Women's Environment and Development Organization (WEDO), a US-based group guided by an International Policy Action Committee, organised a World Women's Congress for a Healthy Planet in late 1991. The congress was attended by 1500 women from 83 countries, and included women from UN agencies, governments, and organisations concerned with environment and development, religious organisations, grassroots groups, universities, foundations and the news media. It was the largest ever unofficial conference convened to prepare for and influence a UN world conference.[29]

Former US Congresswoman Bella Abzug and other WEDO members had attended the Mexico, Copenhagen and Nairobi conferences and the PrepComs leading up to Rio. They had learned what it would take 'to bring women's perspectives into the proceedings and to claim equal representation of women in the whole UNCED process, as well as in national delegations attending the Rio Conference'.[30] And they were determined to make both happen.

To organise the Women's World Congress on a Healthy Planet, WEDO formed a steering committee of 10 women representing the various regions of the world. Members of the steering committee agreed to organise campaigns in their own regions not only for the inclusion of equal numbers of women as men in the official delegations to Rio but also to make women's concerns an integral part of Agenda 21, the official document for Rio.

A notable feature of the Congress was a tribunal during which five judges heard 15 women from different countries testify on women's perspectives on various issues relating to the environment, including an environmental code of ethics; environment and development; and science, technology and population. The most notable outcome of the congress was a document reflecting the essence of the discussions at the congress, the Women's Action Agenda 21.[31]

During the months between the Congress in November 1991 and the official UNCED Conference in Rio in June 1992, WEDO set up task forces to analyse the draft of the official Agenda 21, to compare it with Women's Agenda 21, and to prepare amendments to strengthen the recommendations and make them reflect women's views. At the beginning of this process in the preliminary draft of Agenda 21, women's issues and concerns were mentioned only in the 'poverty' section or in the context of 'vulnerable groups'. By the end of this process, in the final draft of the official Agenda 21, women's issues and concerns were mentioned in hundreds of places, most notably in paragraphs that recognised women as actors and participants in the move towards more sustainable development.[32]

Women's Caucus. Much of this success was the result of concerted efforts by alliances of NGOs during the preparatory phase leading up to the conference. This concerted effort was facilitated by an innovative mechanism introduced by WEDO, a public forum called the 'Women's Caucus'. It provided a bridge between the official deliberations and the parallel NGO deliberations. Governmental delegates are invited to join NGO participants in a daily dialogue on key issues being addressed each day at the official deliberations.

The Women's Caucus was held each morning in the NGO forum to review the results of the previous day's official meetings, to share information and to plan daily strategies. Representatives of women's groups then used the daily statements to lobby their respective government delegations. By combining efforts and skills in caucus sessions, NGOs talked with delegates knowledgeably, gave helpful suggestions on possible changes and adaptations, and added specific issues and concerns where they had been left out.[33]

First organised during the UNCED preparatory process, the Women's Caucus has been organised at every preparatory meeting and conference since. In addition to providing a forum for all women to air their views, issues and concerns, a major function of the Women's Caucus is to monitor all amendments and rewrites of draft documents. To focus on specific subjects within drafts, the caucus breaks into task forces. Each task force organises around one or more priority areas within the draft documents. They study drafts within the context of their particular subject areas and make revisions or suggest changes. The task forces report back to the caucus daily. From their reports, statements are produced that relate to the part of the draft UN document being discussed by delegates that day.

The Women's Caucus is credited with contributing to a landmark decision that 'key elements relating to women's critical economic, social and environmental contributions to sustainable development be addressed ... in all the substantive documentation, particularly Agenda 21, the Earth Charter and the Convention'. It further requested that recommendations from relevant meetings held by governments, intergovernmental and nongovernmental organisations be made available to the Preparatory Committee. This enabled the recommendations from key NGO initiatives to be integrated into the UNCED documents.

Vienna: women's rights are human rights

By the late 1980s, various international, regional and local women's groups had begun meeting to strategise on how to make women's human rights perspectives more visible. Galvanised by the successes and lessons from the Rio process, the international women's movement reached the Vienna conference better prepared than ever before.

Global campaign. In 1991 the Center for Women's Global Leadership (Global Center) organised a strategic planning meeting of grassroots activists from 20 countries. At this meeting, the participants decided to target their activities on preparing for the upcoming UN World Conference on Human Rights and to focus on 'gender-based violence against women as the issue which demonstrates most clearly and urgently what it means to expand human rights to incorporate women'.[34] They called for a global campaign that would take up various strategies for linking women's rights to human rights, including an annual period of global action; an international consensus-building effort; a petition drive; local action by women's groups; documentation of violence against women; and drafting a consensus document on integrating women's rights into human rights.[35]

As part of the global campaign, local women's groups attended national preparatory meetings, and regional networks of women's groups attended the regional preparatory meetings. All worked to transform the limited interpretations of human rights.[36] National, regional and global documents were written, exchanged and revised by women in this process, and several international gatherings were held to develop some common points of emphasis to present in Vienna.

In 1993 the Global Center organised a second strategic planning meeting to focus on how women could most effectively influence events at the Vienna Conference. The meeting brought together a small group of women from around the world who had been effective at the national and regional meetings. The specific tasks of the meeting were to work on lobbying strategies; to develop a set of recommendations on women's human rights; and, in particular, to plan a global tribunal on women's human rights.

Women's caucuses.   The Global Campaign proved highly successful. In the final PrepCom before Vienna, the Women's Caucus—including women from both the North and South who worked in government, NGOs and in UN agencies—succeeded in exerting pressure to add text on women to the draft document and in forming the basis for many women to continue working together in Vienna.

Throughout the Vienna Conference, the NGO Women's Caucus met daily to assess the conference proceedings and their implications for women. A lobbying group from the caucus kept track of the drafting process in the official conference to ensure that the gains made in the preparatory process were not lost. In response to threats of new clauses inimical to women's human rights, they drafted new texts for delegates. The NGO Women's Caucus gained time slots for six short presentations from its members at the official conference.

Also, throughout the Vienna Conference, a daily Governmental Women's Caucus was organised by the United Nations Development Fund for Women (UNIFEM). This caucus brought together women from governmental delegations or UN agencies with representatives from the NGO Women's Caucus to explore possible means of collaborating to advance women's humans rights at the conference. Vienna was the first conference to have two parallel women's caucuses, which was necessary because most NGOs were denied access to the official conference.

Global tribunal.   Undoubtedly, the most dramatic event in this process was the Global Tribunal on Violations of Women's Human Rights, organised by the Global Center together with the International Women's Tribune Center and others at the NGO forum. The tribunal featured women from 25 countries who had survived a vast range of human rights abuses—from domestic violence to political persecution to violations of economic rights. Their collective testimonials provided graphic demonstration of how being female can be life threatening, subjecting some women to torture, terrorism and slavery every day.[37]

The idea of convening a Global Tribunal on Violations of Women's Human Rights emerged from discussions over several months among those active in the Global Campaign for Women's Human Rights in different regions.[38] In response, the Global Center and the International Women's Tribune Center sent out a call for local grassroots hearings on violations of women's rights. During the last six months leading up to Vienna, women around the world held hearings to document individual complaints and group cases of violations of women's human rights. The resulting testimonials were recorded and the documentation sent to the UN Center for Human Rights.

The Global Tribunal was presided over by four international judges. The testimonies gave vivid expression to the life and death consequences of women's human rights violations.[39] The judges, working in consultation with an advisory committee of women lawyers from different regions, sought to assess accountability for the human rights abuses presented by those testifying at the tribunal, to delineate the human rights principles and agreements that had been violated, and to make concrete suggestions on how to redress violations. The judges and their advisors drafted a final collective statement that was delivered at the tribunal's closing session.[40]

The organisers then secured time on the official agenda for a report on the tribunal and its recommendations. Presentations from the tribunal were followed by three speakers from the NGO Women's Caucus. One of the speakers called for a moment of silence and asked delegates to remember all the women around the world who had died or been badly injured by domestic violence during that minute. Leaders of the global campaign later reported, 'Women had arrived on the Conference agenda!!'[41]

Cairo: women's reproductive health and rights

In Cairo in September 1994, the United Nations hosted the Third World Conference on Population and Development. In many aspects, Cairo marked the culmination of a long struggle by the international women's movement to transform the public agenda. As one observer noted, the International Conference on Population and Development (ICPD) represented 'a giant leap for womankind'.

Global campaign. Having listened to the polarised and heated debates on population issues at Rio, a group of women decided to initiate an international campaign to build a consistent framework on population issues among women's groups and to bring women's voices to the upcoming conference on population and development. They approached the International Women's Health Coalition, which had been working with women's health activists around the world since 1980, to convene an expert group.

In September 1992, women's health advocates from Asia, Africa, Latin America, the Caribbean, the USA and Western Europe met to discuss how women's voices might best be heard during preparations for Cairo and in the conference itself. The group suggested that a strong positive statement from women around the world would make a unique contribution to reshaping the population agenda to better ensure reproductive health and rights. The group, which called itself the 'Women's Voices '94 Alliance', drafted a 'Women's Declaration on Population Policies', which was reviewed, modified and finalised by over 100 women's organisations across the globe.

Between September 1992 and September 1994, when the Cairo conference was held, at least 15 national, regional and international women's meetings reviewed the declaration. And the original London group convened a major women's conference—what it called a 'feminist PrepCom'—in Rio de Janeiro in January 1994. One of the aims of the Rio conference was to 'search for and identify common ground and universalities in women's perspectives on reproductive health and justice'. In five short days, 215 women from 79 countries who gathered in Rio generated a collective statement as well as a series of strategies and activities to ensure that women's perspectives and experiences were considered and acted upon at the Cairo conference.[42]

As a critical part of the follow-up strategy, the International Women's Health Coalition and a core group of colleagues worldwide focused their attention on the official draft document: entering what they refer to as the 'battle of the brackets'.[43] They decided that there were three ways to influence the official document—by influencing the composition of official delegations, by lobbying at all preparatory meetings and at the conference itself and by working with the media. Several of the Rio conference participants were appointed to their government delegations. Others mobilised a tightly planned strategy and process for the focused lobbying required in the final PrepCom and at the Cairo conference.

By the time they reached Cairo, the Women's Voices '94 Alliance and the Coalition were well prepared. They had reached remarkable consensus on key values (gender equality, reproductive rights and male responsibility) across the divides of ideology, culture and relative wealth and power.

Women's caucus. Throughout the two-year preparatory period, at all of the official and NGO meetings, WEDO facilitated a daily NGO Women's Caucus. Members negotiated with official delegations to ensure that the draft document incorporated women's concerns throughout and to secure inclusion of a chapter specifically on women.[44] These negotiations before and during the conference 'required delicate balancing of diverse values, stark political and economic power imbalances, and other significant social and cultural differences' among governments as well as women's groups.[45]

At the NGO forum in Cairo, as in Rio and Vienna, every morning started with a meeting of the Women's Caucus to review negotiations. After the advocacy priorities for the day were discussed, the more than 1000 members of the caucus went into action. Every afternoon the Women's Caucus shifted venue to the official conference site to facilitate a coordinating meeting among NGO representatives in the official conference, representatives of the Women's Caucus and members of the press. At the final caucus meeting, a 'post-Cairo Task Force' formed by the Women's Caucus presented its recommendations for an innovative new watchdog network called 'Women Watching ICPD'.

In addition, in Cairo as in Vienna, small groups of core lobbyists systematically intervened with government delegations on a timely basis not allowed by the large-group processes of the caucus. Although the negotiations bogged down over the 'brackets', in particular over one paragraph on abortion, the outcome was a clear victory for women's NGOs and for women. There is no doubt that the language used in the 'Programme of Action' document 'leads the way for new approaches to population and development, that places women's health, their empowerment, and rights at their center'.[46] By the end of the conference, governments had 'reached an unprecedented consensus' on the 20-year Programme of Action.[47]

A noteworthy feature of the Cairo Conference that undoubtedly contributed to the unprecedented consensus was the number of NGO representatives on official delegations and the remarkable dialogue between NGOs and the official delegations. In particular, the US delegation made every attempt to understand the concerns of women from the developing world. Over half its delegates were from NGOs, including the vice-president of the International Women's Health Coalition and the US co-chair of WEDO. The US delegation was led by Undersecretary of State Tim Wirth, who held a daily press briefing at the NGO forum, not at the official conference hall, as an expression of his openness to NGO concerns.

Even the Secretary-General of the Conference and Director of the United Nations Population Fund (UNFPA), Dr Nafis Sadik, visited the Women's Caucus at one of its daily morning meetings in the NGO forum.[48] She acknowledged that the efforts of the members of the Women's Caucus—in drafting, educating participants and the public about the complexity of the issues and lobbying official delegates—had been critical to the success of the conference.

In their analysis of the remarkable consensus that was reached in Cairo, the International Women's Health Coalition writes:

> The underlying basis for consensus was created by the constituency most concerned—women. For the first time, a wide range of representatives of women's organizations from every region of the world were central to the negotiation of an international population document. Working together with a common purpose, women engaged at every stage of conference preparations and at every level to gain access to negotiations. Gradually, through the conference preparations, governments and international agencies recognized women as legitimate players. Women served as members of many government delegations, and led NGO efforts to lobby governments both during preparatory sessions and at the conference in Cairo. This involvement, along with governments' consultation with women's groups in many countries and at the UN through the ICPD process, gives the Cairo Programme of Action a legitimacy and a political base of support that previous government policies and programs have never had.

> At numerous points throughout the process of drafting and finalizing the document, when language accepted by the majority of governments and NGOs was threatened by a handful of delegations, women were the ones who mobilized to protect the

emerging consensus. Because women have been most affected by population policies and programs, they emerged as an unassailable moral force.[49]

Shaping the policy agenda: critical changes and necessary strategies

Critical changes

The UN Decade for Women, and the decade that followed, radically reshaped the international women's movement and its relationship to the UN system and to the international community more broadly. There have been at least four dimensions: there are new players on the global stage; they have new skills and competencies; they have forged critical alliances and coalitions; and they have taken their place at the policy-making table.

New players. Within the international women's movement, as elsewhere, the older established NGOs have been supplemented by a new breed of NGOs. By far the most conspicuous change over the decade was the exponential increase in the number and types of women's groups and women's NGOs in every country of the world, and the complex of alliances, networks and coalitions set up to unite them. Most visibly, there has been a dramatic increase in women's groups and women's NGOs in developing countries.

New skills. The international women's movement has matured as well as grown and diversified. Women's NGOs have developed or strengthened their skills: substantive and technical; advocacy and political; research and policy analysis; and documentation and communication. They have learned how to operate on the global stage and how to make themselves seen and heard. Moreover, they have provided effective leadership to the development, environment, human rights and population fields.

New alliances. The number of NGO alliances, networks and coalitions have increased as well as the number of individual NGOs. Interestingly, many of these are alliances of international NGOs working with grassroots groups. Most critically, NGO networks and coalitions have been developed that cut across regional and North–South divides to build broad-based consensus on key issues.

New 'places'. Increasing numbers of women from NGOs have been offered or taken a place at policy-making tables, either national or international. They have demanded to be included, and they are increasingly recognised as important players with special competence on substantive issues.

Necessary strategies

The experience of the international women's movement offers important lessons about optimal strategies such as 'be prepared' and 'take part in the preparatory process'. To participate effectively in policy deliberations at all levels, the women's movement did its homework and came prepared. Without collecting, knowing and analysing their facts and without building broad-based coalitions, it would have been difficult for women to influence the policy agenda. They also recognised the importance of getting involved in the preparatory process that precedes world conferences because most of the negotiating work is completed before the formal deliberations begin, with only a few key issues left unresolved.

To participate effectively in the preparatory process as well as the formal policy-making sessions, the women's movement developed several key strategies, including the following:

1. *Mounting global campaigns.* To mount pressure on official policymakers and to build coalitions and consensus, women's NGOs mounted global campaigns calling for dialogue and action at the local level; for lobbying at the national, regional and international levels; for petition drives; for gathering evidence on and documenting violations against women's rights; for attending all local, national, regional and international meetings; and more.
2. *Building coalitions and consensus.* To build coalitions and consensus, women's NGOs held multiple strategic planning meetings with a representative cross-section of women and women's NGOs from around the world: at the local, national, regional and international levels.
3. *Preparing policy documents.* To influence policy makers and official policy documents, women's NGOs drafted their own resolutions, treaties, protocols, conventions and platform documents.
4. *Influencing official delegations.* To influence the position of national governments and the composition of official delegations, women's NGOs published reports, held briefings, lobbied and nominated women and NGO representatives to be members of official delegations.
5. *Bridging NGO and official deliberations.* To bridge NGO and official deliberations at international meetings, women's NGOs developed a mechanism called the women's caucus: a daily time and space at all policy making meetings for NGOs to strategise and to hold dialogues with official delegates and policy makers.

In pursuing these strategies, the international women's movement learned to focus on key issues and on official documents, to work with all players and to become serious lobbyists. To provide coherence to their global campaigns, women's NGOs focused on one or two key issues—for example violence against women in the campaign leading up to Vienna, and women's reproductive health and rights for Cairo. To influence the outcomes of world conferences, women's NGOs focused on the official platform document for each conference. They drafted alternative or additional texts to reflect women's interests, concerns and perspectives. To influence the outcomes of world conferences, women's NGOs worked deliberately and strategically with government delegates, UN agencies, media, influential persons and other NGOs. Finally, to become serious lobbyists, women's NGOs found they needed to 'have passion, solidarity, discipline, stamina, and money'.[50]

Beijing and beyond

Towards Beijing

The two decades from 1975 to 1995 have been the most dynamic in the history of the international women's movement, which was invigorated by Mexico City; grew and strengthened during the UN Decade for Women; and was empowered by the process leading up to and the victories gained in Rio, Vienna and Cairo. The international women's movement developed tremendous political and strategic skills in linking up to the UN system before and during the recent world conferences. Indeed, the movement helped change the way UN conferences are planned and conducted.

The immediate challenge before the international women's movement has been to maintain its momentum towards Beijing. To meet this challenge, it has had to keep the UN and national governments aware that the movement is watching to see how governments will deliver in Beijing on promises made in Rio, Vienna and Cairo.[51]

However, on the eve of the Fourth World Conference on Women to be held in Beijing in September 1995, there were signs of a well-organised and well-financed backlash to these promises. The final Beijing PrepCom, held in New York in March 1995, was marred by restrictions on NGO access and accreditation as well as cumbersome, inefficient and divisive drafting processes. After four weeks of mostly closed-door negotiations, the Draft Platform of Action was still far from a consensus document. About 35% of the draft was still bracketed, which meant that one or more governments were unwilling to accept the text's content or wording; this bracketed text would be subject to further negotiations and additional amendments in the official conference in Beijing. Most critically, all statements reaffirming the principles set forth in Vienna and Cairo remained bracketed.[52]

What accounts for the lack of consensus over the Draft Platform of Action? To begin with, the final draft of the document was introduced very late in the preparatory process, leaving little time for delegations to prepare positions. Second, the preparatory process itself is sufficiently participatory that minority voices can slow down, derail or obstruct the process. As noted above, even a single government can call for text that it is unwilling to accept to be bracketed. At the final Beijing PrepCom in March 1995, fewer than a dozen countries (out of 184) objected to most of the bracketed text coming out of the PrepCom. And there is evidence to suggest that most of these countries are members of a sophisticated, well-funded and well orchestrated backlash to the victories achieved in Vienna and Cairo.

Beyond Beijing

Whatever the outcome of the Beijing Conference, the next challenge for the international women's movement will be to implement the promises made to women in Rio, Vienna and Cairo. It must influence and monitor national policies and programmes to ensure that they reflect the goals and mandates from the recent world conferences; translate these goals and mandates into concrete projects; forge working relationships with the specialised agencies of the UN; train more women on how to use existing treaties, conventions and laws;[53] encourage women to continue to pursue many of the strategies used in the global campaigns; nurture the international networks and alliances forged during the global campaigns; and maintain links with the wider development community.

The international women's movement is well positioned, as it enters the 21st century, to consolidate and build on previous gains. The competence, solidarity, maturity, discipline, strength and will of the movement should not be underestimated. While one part of the movement has secured strategic gains for women at the global policy level, another part pursued practical gains at the local level by implementing concrete programmes, working with the specialised agencies of the UN and organising the grass roots. However, in the current global climate of social conservatism and fiscal austerity, the international women's movement will need allies and resources both from within and outside the UN system.

Notes

[1] The names of the cities that host world conferences are commonly used as a 'nickname' for the conferences held there. However, Mexico City hosted both the First World Conference on Women in 1975 and the Second International Conference on Population and Development in 1984. In this paper, Mexico City is used to refer to the first conference.

[2] Whether to use the singular 'women's movement' or the plural 'women's movements' is a thorny question. 'To speak of a single women's movement may attribute too great a unity to what can be perceived only as a plurality of activities and approaches, diversified by class, culture, region and the like. Yet to speak of women's movements in the plural raises concerns about what, if any, commonality there is among these groups and whether it is possible to speak of them in a global context.' Deborah Stienstra, *Women's Movements and International Organizations*, New York: St Martin's Press, 1994, p 160. I use the singular women's movement since it reflects the common goals and concerns around which women have organised at the global level and the remarkable consensus women have built in preparation for recent global conferences.

[3] The international women's movement is primarily composed of and led by nongovernmental organisations: local, national, regional and international. In addition to NGOs and individual women members, the international women's movement is composed of and has benefited from the leadership of a wide variety of institutions, including governmental agencies, donor agencies, academic groups, business groups, religious groups and more.

[4] The term 'NGO forum' is used here as a common term for the parallel NGO conference held at world conferences. Some variation on that term has been used at most but not all world conferences. For instance, the following terms were used for the parallel NGO conferences at the world conferences for women: International Women's Year Tribune in Mexico City; the NGO Forum in Copenhagen; and Forum '85 in Nairobi. The first major UN event at which a parallel NGO forum was held was the 1972 Conference on the Human Environment held in Stockholm.

[5] This paper draws on several published sources which spell out in far greater detail the key players and the substantive gains. At this writing in mid-1995, parts of the story have yet to be told, at least in written form—particularly those relating to the Social Summit held in March 1995, where women's NGOs were key players and the Beijing Conference itself, to be held in September 1995. So the paper also draws on discussions with several of the key players: Peggy Antrobus of DAWN; Charlotte Bunch of the Center for Women's Global Leadership; Marilyn Carr of UNIFEM; Susan Davis of the Women's Environment and Development Organization; Joan Dunlop of the International Women's Health Coalition; Adrienne Germain of the International Women's Health Coalition; Noeleen Heyser of UNIFEM; Vicki Semmler of the International Women's Tribune Center; Peg Snyder (formerly) of UNIFEM; and Anne Walker from the International Women's Tribune Center.

[6] It is important to note that the history of NGOs lobbying the international community on issues of concern to women predates the United Nations. Before World War II, for example, a number of nongovernmental organisations made a proposal to the League of Nations to prohibit sexual slavery, which was not adopted before the outbreak of the war. Soon after the formation of the United Nations in 1946, the issue resurfaced.

And by 1949, the Convention for the Suppression of Traffic in Persons and the Exploitation of the Prostitution of Others had been adopted.

[7] Several landmark years for the advancement of women within the UN system include: 1946, when the Commission on the Status of Women and the Branch for the Advancement of Women (within the Department of International Economic and Social Affairs) were established; 1948, when the Universal Declaration of Human Rights was adopted; and 1967, when the Declaration on the Elimination of All Forms of Discrimination Against Women was adopted. This declaration was the precursor to the Convention, which was adopted by the General Assembly in 1979 and ratified by the mandatory 20 countries in 1981.

[8] A study of 47 international women's organisations at that time found that nine were religious in orientation, 10 were in the international relations arena, 18 were for professional and working women, seven were educational and cultural, and three were for sportswomen. Elise Boulding, *Women in the Twentieth Century World*, New York: Sage, 1977, p 187. Only five were headquartered outside Europe or North America. The first international women's organisations were established in 1880.

[9] The two women representatives were the Romanian representative (Florica Andrei) and the Finnish representative (Helvi Sipila). Helvi Sipila was later to be appointed the first female Assistant Secretary-General.

[10] Hilkka Pietila & Jeanne Vickers, *Making Women Matter: The Role of the United Nations* London: Zed Books, 1994, p 76.

[11] Ibid pp 78–79.

[12] Rounaq Jahan, 'The International Women's Year Conference and Tribune', *International Development Review*, 3, 1975, p 38.

[13] Pietila & Vickers, *Making Women Matter*, p 7.

[14] Ibid, p 48. The conferences in Mexico City and Copenhagen were not able to reach consensus in their deliberations to adopt the final documents unanimously.

[15] Irene Tinker & Jane Jaquette, 'UN Decade for Women: its impact and legacy', *World Development*, 15 (3), 1987, p 419.

[16] Ibid, p. 426.

[17] Stienstra, *Women's Movements*, p 91.

[18] Pietila & Vickers, *Making Women Matter*, p 73.

[19] Tinker & Jaquette, 'UN Decade', p 426.

[20] Most notably at the 1974 International Conference on Population and Development; the 1974 World Food Conference; the 1979 World Conference on Agrarian Reform and Rural Development Conference; and the 1979 UN Conference on Science and Technology for Development. NGOs together with women staff in the UN system brought women's contributions and problems to the attention of all these conferences. The first female Assistant Secretary-General, together with US NGOs, organised a lobbying conference on the role of women as part of the preparatory process for the Population Conference. Women staff in the nutrition section of the Food and Agriculture Organization (FAO) lobbied for recognition of women's role in agriculture at the World Food Conference and an NGO group organised a parallel meeting which succeeded in influencing the conference. An NGO group distributed information to and carried out effective lobbying with delegates to the Agrarian Reform and Rural Development Conference (both before and during the conference). And a group of NGOs, together with female delegates to the Preparatory Committee meetings, lobbied to have women's perspective appropriately incorporated in the texts of the draft document during the preparatory process and, when the draft text met active opposition during the conference, regrouped to draft a resolution on women, science and technology, which was unanimously adopted.

[21] Pietila & Vickers, *Making Women Matter*, p 87. These were the conferences on Economic Cooperation, Water, Desertification, Technical Cooperation and Primary Health Care.

[22] Ibid, p 89.

[23] These 30 000 participants represented over 9000 organisations, groups and movements from 171 countries. Ibid, p 139.

[24] Only NGOs with consultative status at the UN's Economic and Social Council (ECOSOC) are automatically accredited to attend UN world conferences and the preparatory committee meetings (commonly referred to as PrepComs). In order to become accredited to attend a world conference and its PrepComs, NGOs that are not in consultative states with ECOSOC must submit specific information about their organisation and its work. For Rio, UNCED adopted an inclusive accreditation process that allowed 1420 NGOs to attend the official conference.

[25] Yolanda N Kakabadse & Sarah Burns, *Movers and Shapers: NGOs in International Affairs*, Washington, DC: World Resources Institute, 1994.

[26] Maurice Strong and the UNCED Secretariat can be credited with using an accreditation process that allowed 1420 NGOs to attend UNCED. When the Commission on Sustainable Development was formed to oversee implementation of the UNCED plan of action, they granted roster status to any NGO accredited at UNCED. This has opened the door for greater NGO access to the UN system.

[27] Charlotte Bunch, 'Organizing for women's human rights globally', in: Joanna Kerr (ed), *Ours By Right: Women's Rights as Human Rights*, London: Zed Books, 1993, p 148.

[28] Each of these brief descriptions focuses on a few key players, strategies and events. Admittedly, many other key players, strategies and events are not mentioned. For instance, in 1991 as part of the preparatory process for UNCED, the United Nations Environment Programme (UNEP) held a meeting called Global Assembly–Partners in Life. At that meeting, 218 success stories of women's roles in environmental management were showcased. United Nations Development Fund for Women and United Nations Non-Governmental Liaison Service, *Putting Gender on the Agenda*, New York: UNIFEM and UN/NGLS, 1995, p 4.

[29] Pietila & Vickers, *Making Women Matter*, p 135.

[30] Ibid, p 135.

[31] The Women's Congress was not the only body preparing alternative documents for Rio. One month after the Women's Congress, several hundred NGOs attended a People's Summit in Paris. They decided to undertake an Alternative Treaty Process, preparing drafts for numerous treaties to be discussed and developed in Rio among the NGO representatives. Altogether they produced 46 alternative treaties on diverse subjects related to the environment and sustainable development. Of these 46, two focused exclusively or predominantly on women while many of them integrated women's concerns into other functional themes.

[32] Pietila & Vickers, *Making Women Matter*, p 137.

[33] International Women's Tribune Center, 'Claiming our rights!', *The Tribune: A Woman and Development Quarterly*, Newsletter 51, New York: IWTC, March 1994.

[34] Bunch, 'Organizing for women's rights', p 146.

[35] The Global Campaign included the following: an annual period of global action called '16 Days of Activism Against Gender Violence'—during the 16 days that link International Day Against Violence Against Women on November 25 and Human Rights Day on December 10; an international consensus-building effort to bring women's human rights on to the agenda of the Vienna conference; and a petition drive asking that the Vienna conference 'incorporate women into the agenda in two ways: in relation to all the other topics; and by specifically addressing the question of violence against women'. By the time of Vienna, over 1000 sponsoring groups had gathered almost half a million signatures from 124 countries. Local action by women's groups included: holding dialogues with local human rights groups on women's rights issues; developing their own agendas for the regional conferences that were part of the preparatory process; documenting violence against women by holding local and regional hearings on the violation of women's human rights; drafting resolutions based on this material; and preparing a consensus document on integrating women's rights into human rights for consideration at the conference.

[36] Charlotte Bunch & Niamh Reilly, *Demanding Accountability: The Global Campaign and Vienna Tribunal for Women's Human Rights*, New Brunswick, NJ: Rutgers University Center for Women's Global Leadership and New York: UNIFEM, 1994, p 5.

[37] Ibid.

[38] Previous tribunals, such as the one at the World Women's Congress for a Healthy Planet in Miami in 1991 and the International Tribunal on Crimes against Women in Brussels in 1976, were sources of inspiration.

[39] Bunch & Reilly, *Demanding Accountability*, p 8.

[40] Ibid, p 16.

[41] Ibid, p 104.

[42] Claudia Gracia-Moreno, 'Introduction', in: *Reproductive Health and Justice: International Women's Health Conference for Cairo '94*, New York: International Women's Health Coalition [IWHC] and Rio de Janeiro: Citizenship, Studies, Information, Action [CEPIA], 1990.

[43] The bracketed portions of a draft document contain text on which no consensus has been reached and over which there were often heated debates.

[44] UNIFEM and UN/NGLS 1995, p 28.

[45] Adrienne Germain & Rachel Kyte, *The Cairo Consensus: The Right Agenda for the Right Time*, New York: International Women's Health Coalition, 1995, p 4.

[46] Joan Dunlop, 'Preface' in ibid, p i.

[47] Germain & Kyte, *The Cairo Consensus*, p 1. Out of the 184 countries, 167 countries agreed to the Cairo Document in its entirety. 'In the end, only 17 nations expressed reservations, each reservation being on a specific chapter or paragraph of the Programme of Action. No country reserved on the entire document.' Ibid, p 3.

[48] Early in the preparatory process for Cairo, Dr Sadik had been extremely resistant to including NGOs in the conference process. However, under pressure from the donor and NGO community, she conceded. By the third PrepCom, Sadik was encouraging all countries to include NGOs in their delegations to Cairo. By then, NGOs had proved their worthiness in the regional preparatory meetings and the expert group meetings.

[49] Germain & Kyte, *The Cairo Consensus*, p 6.

[50] From a speech by Joan Dunlop, president of the International Women's Health Coalition, at the New England Regional Conference 'Toward Beijing: Priorities '95' held at Harvard University, March 1995.

[51] Bunch & Reilly, *Demanding Accountability*, pp 110–111.

[52] InterAction's Commission on the Advancement of Women, *Mobilizing for Beijing '95*, 4, 1995.

[53] Bunch, 'Organizing for women's human rights', p 145.

■ Part 3 ■
Cross-Cutting
Themes and Processes

■ 8 ■

Scaling Up the Grassroots and Scaling Down the Summit: The Relations Between Third World NGOs and the UN

PETER UVIN

Two trends are slowly reshaping the international development system. They hold the promise of democratizing and reforming the international system and the international practice of development. One is the process of 'scaling up', in which grassroots organisations and local nongovernmental organisations (NGOs) seek to expand their impact and move beyond the local level. In doing so, they are becoming players, often reluctantly, at the national and international levels. 'Scaling down' refers to processes whereby international organisations (IOs) change their structures and modes of functioning to allow for meaningful interaction and cooperation with grassroots organisations and NGOs.

This essay analyses the nature of scaling up and scaling down, how extensively they have taken place, how that has been done, and the risks and difficulties associated with these processes. It will do so largely from the point of view of Third World NGOs and within the context of development.

Part one briefly defines terms. Part two deals with scaling up the grass roots. It first presents a typology of scaling up, and then discusses the reasons that motivate NGOs and IOs to collaborate. Afterwards, it puts forward a hierarchy of NGO participation in international regime creation and implementation. Finally, it discusses some of the dangers and risks that NGOs face when scaling up. Part three deals with scaling down the summit. It first presents various arguments in favour of scaling down the summit and then analyses how much such processes of scaling down have occurred.

The grass roots and the summit: some preliminary observations

In this paper, the generic term 'NGOs' will be used to refer to Third World, local organisations of civil society whose objective is to promote grassroots development in a participatory manner. This includes two main types of organisations: membership organisations composed of poor people who seek to advance their own interests, and support organisations that seek to create and strengthen membership organisations. The former have been called 'people's organisations' (POs), 'self-help organisations' (SHOs) and 'grassroots organisations' (GROs). The latter have been labelled 'intermediary organisations', 'self-help support organisations' (SHPOs) and 'grassroots support organisations' (GRSOs). We adopt here the terminology of GROs for membership organisations and GRSOs for support organisations.

The number of GROs is estimated to be in the millions, with new ones being added daily. They have come into being through the activities of GRSOs or foreign aid projects, through imitating neighbouring villagers' actions, or through internal learning processes. They are composed of farmers, women, neighbours, informal sector workers, youngsters, Muslims, Christians, or recent immigrants. Their size ranges from a handful of villagers to federated structures composed of tens of thousands of persons. Their budgets are small and hard to measure, for they largely depend on internally mobilised resources that are difficult to quantify: the time and energy of their members, the labour of volunteers, the financial contributions of villagers, the small savings of women and the materials of artisans.

GRSOs are organisations that seek to beget and support GROs. GRSOs currently number anywhere between 10 000 and 30 000, with heavy concentrations in some countries (for example, India, Bangladesh, Brazil, South Africa) and noticeable absences in other countries (for example, China, the Maghreb countries, Burundi). Although some may become very large over time, employing hundreds of staff and touching millions of people—the Bangladesh Rural Advancement Committee, Grameen Bank, Sarvodaya Shramadana, and Six-S immediately come to mind—they have usually started out small, often at the initiative of one visionary person. Most of them remain small ventures, with fewer than 20 employees. Their budgets are small (usually in the thousands of dollars) and they depend heavily on foreign aid.

This is the picture of the grass roots: millions of small organisations with extremely limited budgets apart from the internal resources of their members, and more or less supported by organisations that are small, localised, under-funded and often inefficient and elite-based. At the other end of the spectrum is 'the summit': the big, international development aid organisations, be they governmental, intergovernmental or nongovernmental. In between is a third entity, the state, which is not the subject of this essay, but is clearly a crucial actor.

The summit can be divided into three parts. The first consists of the 20 or so international organisations active in the field of development, almost all of them part of the UN system. These include the World Bank and the International Development Association (IDA), the UN Development Program (UNDP), the Food and Agriculture Organization (FAO), the World Food Programme (WFP), the International Fund for Agriculture and Development (IFAD), the World Health Organization (WHO), the UN Children's Fund (UNICEF), the UN High Commissioner for Refugees (UNHCR), and a host of other, smaller organisations dealing with women, habitat, population, the environment, and so on. The budgets of these organisations range from hundreds of millions of dollars for the smallest ones to more than $1 billion for WFP and UNDP, and more than $10 billion a year for the Washington-based institutions. All of them are active worldwide and have hundreds, if not thousands, of well-paid and highly qualified employees. Since they are IOs, their members are countries, and their decision-making systems are based on governments.

A second summit actor consists of 20 or so bilateral donors, with budgets even larger than those of the IOs. Although they are very differently organised, and hold divergent domestic political views of the rationale for foreign aid, all rich countries and some OPEC (Organization of Petroleum Exporting Countries) ones have development cooperation agencies. Except the smallest, all have budgets in the billions of dollars; then US Agency for International Development (USAID) and the Japanese International Cooperation Agency (JICA) have budgets above $11 billion. They have thousands of professional employees.

A third category in the summit is composed of international NGOs (INGOs), located in rich countries and the subject of most articles in this issue. They share with Southern GRSOs their nongovernmental nature and their attachment to participatory development. Yet they are on a different plane in their access to resources as well as in their structure; they are conduits of billions of dollars of aid to Southern NGOs. Worldwide, there are about 2000 of them, located in Europe and the USA, but maybe 50 of them represent up to 80% of total resources. These resources come from the public (some $5 billion) and from their own governments (around $2.2 billion).[1] They often have programmes in tens of countries, draw on highly capable and well-paid staffs, and have their offices in the same Western capitals as the other summit actors.

One reason for the above distinction is to remind the reader of the basic, qualitative differences between these two types of actors. On one hand, there are hundreds of thousands of small, usually localised, financially strapped, often volunteer-based organisations; on the other hand, there are 100 or so large, professional, billion-dollar worldwide multinationals of development. The differences become clearer still when one looks at the direction of the flows of resources: the hundreds of thousands of Third World NGOs are all competing for pieces of the roughly $50 billion of yearly development aid that is almost exclusively controlled by the 100 or so summit organisations. Some readers might object to the inclusion of Northern NGOs under the summit, and, indeed, this does injustice to a number of them. However, from the point of view of the local communities in the Third World, there is little organisational difference between most INGOs and the rest of the summit—although there might be some important programmatic differences. The large majority of the INGOs are located on the same 20 square miles of the world's surface as the other 'summiteers'; they employ people with the same backgrounds and incomes, with some individuals changing employment from bilateral agencies to INGOs to IOs; and they channel billions of dollars to the Third World.

Scaling up the grass roots

A definition and taxonomy of scaling up

Scaling up is the process by which Southern NGOs expand their impact, moving beyond being local and small. In doing so, they may eventually come to build relations with the summit. Almost all NGOs that interact with the United Nations do so as part of a process of scaling up, because few of them were born on that level and with that mandate.

Several definitions of scaling up exist in the literature. In a recent US AID evaluation of two innovative credit projects in Africa,[2] the term 'scaling up' is equated with expansion, or, more precisely, with the need to 'reach several times the actual number of members' in the countries concerned. This definition of scaling up as expansion of membership or target group is probably the most commonly used.

Social scientists propose more complicated definitions. Goran Hyden differentiates between scaling up organisationally and functionally.[3] 'Organizationally' is defined as 'serving larger constituencies', that is, the same meaning as expansion. 'Functionally' means that the same organisation increases or diversifies its range of activities, regardless of size. Howes and Sattar talk about 'intensification', referring to the addition of new activities to existing programmes.[4]

Clark discusses 'influencing policy reform' as one form of scaling up,[5] while Fisher defines scaling up as the process of influencing policy; she uses the term 'scaling out' to describe expansion.[6] Although Korten does not use the term scaling up in this context, he clearly discusses a similar process where he advocates so-called 'third generation' NGOs.[7] The latter are distinct from first- and second-generation ones by their concern for 'bridging the gap between micro and macro' (that is, moving beyond the local level), and their desire to deal with the root causes of underdevelopment and not merely its manifestations. Therefore, Korten, Clark, Fisher and many others consider influencing politics or policies to be an important form of scaling up.

Finally, and coming from a different tradition, Bernard Lecomte, a French grassroots specialist with decades of experience in Africa (and co-founder of the 'Six-S' movement) writes about different phases in the maturing of GROS— phases mainly characterised by increased capacity to innovate, generate local resources, and manage organizations.[8] His scaling up is a matter of autonomy, self-reliance, independence.[9]

This variety of definitions is important. It allows examination of the phenomenon in several ways, providing insight into the complexity of the NGO sector. It also suggests that there are different types of scaling up, which often go together but are not identical. The typology below distinguishes four types of scaling up, in terms of either structures, programmes, strategies, or resource base.[10]

The first type of scaling up is when a programme or an organisation expands its size, through increasing its membership base (for GROs) or constituency (for GRSOs) and, linked to that, its geographic working area or budget. This is the most evident type of scaling up, equivalent to 'growth' or 'expansion' in their basic meanings. This is quantitative scaling up.

A second type of scaling up occurs when a community-based programme or a grassroots organisation expands the number and the type of its activities. Starting in agricultural production, for example, it moves into health, nutrition, credit, training, literacy, etc. This is functional scaling up.

The third type of scaling up refers to participatory organisations moving beyond service delivery and towards empowerment and change in the structural causes of underdevelopment. This will usually imply active political involvement and developing relations with the state, or with international organisations. This is political scaling up.

Finally, community-based programmes or grassroots organisations can increase their organisational strength to improve the effectiveness, efficiency and sustainability of their activities. This can be done financially, by diversifying their sources of subsidies, by increasing the degree of self-financing through income-generating activities, or by assuring the enactment of public legislation earmarking entitlements within the annual budgets for the programme. It can also be done institutionally, by creating external links with other development actors, both public and private, and by improving the management capacity of the staff. This is organisational scaling up.

There is no hierarchy among these four types of scaling up. They can occur independently or jointly. Organisational scaling up, however, occupies a distinct position: it can occur alone, with NGOs improving their management structures while keeping their membership base and activities range stable, but it is also a prerequisite for all other types of scaling up. As Hodson states, 'There is no escaping the organizational reality that any attempt to scale up impact, whatever the strategy, has serious and difficult organizational implications'.[11]

Why do international organisations want to increase the participation of NGOs?

Schematically, IOs have five related reasons for seeking to collaborate with NGOs. These are increased funding, ideological preferences, programme effectiveness and sustainability, external pressure and the creation of constituencies.

No matter how important their financial resources, development IOs generally recognise that the development needs of the one billion or so poor people in this world are vastly beyond their financial capacities. Other sources of funding have to be found, including sources in the poor communities themselves. NGOs are seen as far better at mobilising local resources than are IOs. Hence, collaborating with NGOs may lower the cost of programmes, or provide community-based maintenance,[12] an important argument in times of budget distress.

A conservative ideology of state disengagement, privatisation, competition, self-help, and democratisation also reigns in most international organisations and development aid institutions. The dominant development ideology is predisposed towards the private sector. In this view, enterprises produce wealth, and NGOs redistribute it. Hence, one of the main reasons for the prominence of a discourse of participation, empowerment and self-help since the 1960s is the neoconservative forces behind structural adjustment and privatisation.[13]

Moreover, it is increasingly recognised that including NGOs in project management and design can entail major benefits in terms of project effectiveness and sustainability. Evaluation after evaluation has shown that projects financed and managed by the summit tend to lack sustainability, and that the prime cause for this is failure to involve local communities and to ensure participation.[14] NGOs are seen as having comparative advantages in precisely these fields: flexibility, community trust, capacity to work with the poorest of the poor, to work in remote areas and independence from governments.[15] It may be that NGOs are less good at using their so-called comparative advantages than their rhetoric suggests, but they are superior to IOs in these fields.[16] NGOs are also considered useful in adapting international programmes to local realities and informing specialised agency headquarters about local conditions.

IOs are under pressure to collaborate with NGOs. Part of this pressure emanates from the NGOs themselves, with thousands pushing for collaboration, proposing models, fighting projects that they consider against their interests, and generally imposing themselves as unavoidable partners. Another source of pressure can be found in donor governments that ideologically favour grassroots participation.[17]

Finally, NGOs can fulfill one more important function for IOs: they can help build local constituencies for IO policies and programmes. In fact, NGOs are obliged to do so by UN Resolution 1296, which states that 'the organization [NGO] shall undertake to support the work of the UN and to promote knowledge of its principles and activities'.[18] UNHCR, for example, recognises that support for refugees depends on the attitude of ordinary people, and NGOs can better and more freely campaign to change these attitudes than can the UNHCR, which seeks to minimise controversy or criticism with member governments.[19] Chatterjee and Finger offer a convincing argument that the main advantage of involving thousands of NGOs in the UN Conference on Environment and Development (UNCED) process has been to increase the visibility and legitimacy of UNCED and the UNDP.[20]

Why would NGOs want to work with the summit?

Most Third World NGOs came into being to work with and in local civil society to protect forests, increase agricultural wages, receive better prices for cash crops, build social infrastructure, provide credit to members, train women, and pressure local government to build clinics and schools: Why would they seek to move beyond that and interact with the United Nations system? There are three reasons: the availability of funds, the need to influence IO policies and programmes of direct concern, and the possibility of influencing national government through the IOs.

Grassroots initiatives that are funded solely by internally mobilised resources have a limited capacity to expand activities or touch more people. They need external resources for quantitative, functional and organisational scaling up. The Bangladesh Rural Action Committee (BRAC) could not provide oral rehydration therapy (ORT) to 11 million children without millions of dollars of UNICEF money, nor could the Grameen Bank extend its programme without frequent IFAD and World Bank grants. The summit has financial resources that dwarf GRO resources or anything that they could hope to mobilise from their own governments or local private sources. Getting access to resources drives Third World NGOs seeking to build relations with the summit. If NGOs were able to find funding elsewhere, most of them would no doubt drastically reduce their relations with the summit, including the INGOs.[21]

A new type of GRSO is coming into being that is much less negative towards IOs. These are a class of professional intermediaries, not motivated by strong ideology or anti-state feelings, but by a desire to get a well-paid job done. Under conditions of tight labour markets, and with large sums of money available for grassroots development, founding or joining GRSOs has become a viable career alternative for middle class professionals in Latin America, Africa and Asia.[22] These NGOs have no qualms about collaborating with the summit, especially in the field of service delivery.

A second reason for seeking collaboration with IOs is that some of the constraints on development emanate from the international policy level. Although NGOs might have purely local objectives, they need to 'go international' to address the causes of their local problems. This is an inversion of the famous WHO slogan: 'think locally, act globally'. Some local problems, such as water pollution or depletion of fish stocks, have international causes; only international action can provide solutions.[23] In other cases, the causes of a problem may not be international, but its solutions have attracted international interest. The international humanitarian and development aid system is omnipresent in the Third World. Even if a development issue is purely local, there is a strong likelihood that an international organisation is involved in addressing the issue. The poorer the country and the weaker its government, the more important the role and the power of international development organisations. In many African countries, for instance, development is basically managed by the UNDP resident representative and the World Bank delegation. For local communities, this international presence is often as much part of the problem as of the solution. As such, it is crucial for NGOs to influence the summit; it is a prime form of political scaling up required to change local conditions.

Third, NGOs may work with international organisations to change government policies, which are often by far the most important determinants of local outcomes.[24] External links also can help the NGOs gain greater recognition and freedom. Indeed, the World Bank sometimes puts pressure on national governments to establish more favourable public policies towards NGOs or to allow their participation in bank-funded projects.[25] NGOs lobby IFAD or the UNDP so that the latter 'advocates links with NGOs at the start of its dialogue with governments'.[26]

Types of participation by NGOs in international regime creation and implementation

Just as there are many different levels in which local communities and poor people participate in the programmes that affect them, the term 'NGO participation' covers a diverse set of roles played by NGOs at the international level. This section distinguishes five:

- Consultation/information: NGOs' points of view are surveyed.
- Surveillance/control: NGOs monitor implementation of IO policies and programmes.
- Implementation/management: NGOs are involved in implementing IO programmes.
- Decison-making/policy-making: NGOs are partners in the decision-making process of IOs.
- Lobbying is a case apart: depending on the effectiveness, it moves up or down on the hierarchy of participation between information and decision-making.

A particularity of the international system is that, although regime creation usually takes place at the global level, programme implementation is done by a myriad of individual international actors, including, but not limited to, IOs. NGOs can seek to have an impact at both levels: the global one at occasions where international regime creation is deliberately sought—international conferences, and, to a lesser extent, General Assembly, ECOSOC or World Bank Board of Governors sessions—and the level of individual international actors. In the field of development, the latter implies mostly 'low politics' regarding the design, selection and management of development projects by organisations such as the UNDP or the World Bank.

Consultation

Historically, most NGO participation in international regime creation and implementation is at the consultation level, and limited to accredited NGOs.[27] In the 1980s, IOs such as the UNHCR, UNDP and World Bank created institutional links for regular consultation with NGOs.[28] Since the 1992 Earth Summit, the number of Third World NGOs that participate in international conferences has greatly increased; the expenses of some Third World NGO leaders were even paid by the UNDP to attend the UNCED.[29]

NGOs are also increasingly being consulted on the level of individual projects and programmes, mainly during the design phase. USAID, for example, has a 'legal requirement for consultation with, and participation by the poor in the design and implementation of programs and projects' in Africa. Since 1987, the World Bank has an operational directive obliging project managers to consult, where possible, with local NGOs during the design phase.[30] In practice, this consultation is still weak and often unsuccessful from the point of view of the grass roots. A USAID analysis made clear that participation by local or international NGOs was very poor, with local people largely absent.[31] Similarly, in a World Bank study of 20 highly participatory projects, the author concluded that 'there is virtually no evidence from the 20 operations which highlights capacity of people, especially disadvantaged people, to actively and explicitly pressure the bank to develop interventions which empower them to make decisions'.[32]

Lobbying

It is not possible to include the act of lobbying in the hierarchy of participation as presented above. Depending on its degree of success, lobbying can range from playing an information role to actual participation in decision making. NGO documents routinely state that 'the themes addressed by the NGOs are reflected throughout the final draft version' or that 'the victory is that NGO language has become the basis for negotiations'.[33] Yet the concrete impact of lobbying efforts is much harder to measure than these statements suggest.

An important lobbying technique that NGOs have refined is the organisation of parallel conferences, whereby hundreds of non-accredited and often Third World NGOs come together at the same time and in the same city as the main intergovernmental meeting. They seek to draw on media presence to get worldwide exposure for their ideas and desires. At the UNCED, the NGO Summit, which brought together over 30 000 persons from the NGO sector, attempted not only to influence governments, but to create its own counter-regime. Participants adopted a series of 28 alternative citizens' treaties, including plans of action in all fields of the conference.[34]

But NGOs need not wait for international conferences to lobby IOs. At any moment, they can exert pressure on organisations' central headquarters or field offices. This pressure can be exercised to obtain the implementation of policies, develop new programmes, or modify specific project designs. Some of the most famous examples are NGO coalitions lobbying for the reconsideration of massive World Bank dam projects, but many such efforts take place throughout the world, in various fields.[35]

The grass roots does not have to be physically present at international conferences to influence their outcomes. Through direct government lobbying or public education, NGOs can and do exert domestic influence over the positions of their respective governments in these conferences. NGOs that manage to influence the governments of industrialised countries can have a great influence on international conferences. As a result, Third World NGOs increasingly attempt to link up with Northern INGOs in order to influence rich country governments. Haitian NGOs pass information about disappearances and torture to their Northern partners, who publish them to influence public opinion; Oxfam lobbies the World Bank to suspend a planned dam in Brazil; the Unitarian Universalist Service Committee (UUSC) pressures US senators to sponsor legislation for the clean-up of former military bases in the Philippines. Northern INGOs increasingly serve as lobbyists for their Southern partners, working with them to promote policy change at the summit.[36]

The role of the USA is central because it remains the most powerful state in the United Nations. Its contributions are still the largest, and its leadership role, although contested, is still a reality. Moreover, Washington is especially vulnerable to NGO lobbying. This is partly because US politics are imbued with a culture of lobbying and partly because the executive branch is dependent on Congress. INGOs from the USA are among the largest, best-funded and most professional in the world, especially well-versed in the art of advocacy and lobbying. As a result, Congressional policy-making provides the INGO community with regular opportunities for influencing the behaviour of the most powerful UN member state. Every two years, for example, Congress has to approve the IDA replenishment; environment and development INGOs use the occasion to lobby for stricter environmental standards and more participation. Through this, some critics charge, it is mainly US INGOs that set the policy of IDA.[37]

Surveillance

Over the years and without a formal invitation, NGOs have taken upon themselves the function of surveillance. They collect and disseminate information to hold governments accountable for the decisions to which they commit themselves internationally. By far the most successful field of NGO surveillance is human rights.[38] The NGO role in international surveillance is being increasingly recognised in General Assembly declarations, thus conferring upon it a certain enhanced international legitimacy.[39]

The surveillance function is one area where IOs and NGOs have parallel interests that are in conflict with those of governments. For the IOs in charge of the implementation of international declarations and treaties, NGOs are often the only source of information apart from official government reports. NGOs are capable of making sensitive or politically unpleasant information public—something international organisations have greater difficulties in doing, dependent as they are on their governmental members. Moreover, combined with their lobbying, NGOs can go one step further and pressure governments to change their policies, or they can attempt to influence public opinion for more vigilance on certain issues. It is hardly an overstatement when the secretary-general of the International Conference on Nutrition (ICN) states that 'when we all go home, it will be the NGOs that will continue the pressure on governments'.[40] For NGOs, the ability to refer to international declarations to justify and legitimise their work is important; these declarations provide points of pressure on governments and legitimacy to NGO actions. Thus, both IOs and NGOs have parallel interests in surveillance.

Implementation

Implementation is the role favoured by the summit in its relations with the grass roots. In the last decade or so, all UN resolutions urge governments to associate NGOs in the implementation of international programmes. The World Bank, for example, publishes a list of 'World Bank-financed projects with potential for NGO involvement'. This involvement is usually that of implementation rather than design.[41]

NGOs are increasingly involved in the implementation of projects financed by intergovernmental organisations. Between 1969 and 1986, for example, UNFPA spent about 10% of its funds on activities implemented by NGOs.[42] UNICEF, FAO, the UNHCR and UNDP have programmes in which NGOs are given operational, subcontracting roles. According to a recent brochure by the World Bank, 'more than 40 percent of the total number of the bank projects approved in 1993 involved NGOs'.[43] However, this is usually limited to using community workers for information, and in-kind or financial contributions by villagers. Only in three cases were villagers given major management and implementation roles.[44]

Decision making

Within the UN, at the level of regime creation, formal participation in decision making is impossible. Except for the International Labour Organisation (ILO), governments are the only decision makers in the United Nations system. However, on a few occasions, NGOs have managed to become internal and acknowledged participants in the regime creation.

One example is the Conference on Popular Participation in African Recovery and Development, which took place in Arusha in February 1990 and was organised jointly by the UN and the NGOs, at the initiative of the latter. At this conference, an 'African Charter in Popular Participation' was produced, which was later adopted by the UN General Assembly and the OAU.[45] Another case was the World Bank Hunger Conference, held in late 1993. The conference content and structure were organised by a steering committee on which four US NGOs were represented, to express NGO objectives and concerns. After the conference, the steering committee was reconstituted to include five Southern and one Northern NGO consortia. In its first follow-up meeting, and at NGO request, this group decided to organise a follow-up conference in Mali. The design of this conference involved NGO representatives of the steering committee, the World Bank, the Government of Mali, and the Federation of Malian NGOs. Its objective was to modify the planning and design of World Bank-supported interventions.[46]

NGOs are also increasingly involved in decision-making at the level of specific IO field programmes. This is basically the result of the experience and credibility NGOs gained as a result of their participation in implementation. The level of participation depends on individual personalities and the credibility of specific NGOs rather than on any formal status.[47] In many countries, the World Bank has created 'social funds' to compensate for the negative effects of structural adjustment on the poor by micro-lending. These social funds typically have NGOs on their boards of directors, sometimes even constituting as many as half the members.

Some problems in linking up to the summit

What are the problems and risks associated with this process of scaling up? At a practical level, NGO participation in international policy making is costly, and this has to be weighed against direct help to the poor and the hungry. Employing professional staff and procedures and the increased travel abroad that flow from participation in international policy-making pull the organisation's ideology and style of functioning in directions beyond the control of the grass roots. As they engage more of their time, energy, and personnel in policy influence, NGOs lose their contact with their grassroots base, and can end up promoting grassroots apathy.[48] As NGOs participate in national and international debates and learn how to be effective, they can lose sight of their goals of empowerment and structural change, and 'soften' their positions in order to be more acceptable to the summit. One observer has commented that NGOs may come to emphasise 'modernization goals' over 'empowerment'.[49]

Moreover, to the extent that states and international organisations remain top-down, or repressive, or disempowering, working with them risks supporting or legitimating these processes. As Fowler writes, 'increasingly, NGOs are required to fit into non-participatory systems of development administration'.[50]

Increased funding and the requirements attached to it, as well as the need to sustain it over time, creates a dynamic in favour of staying in business at any cost. It also can lead to adopting projects for which funding is available, rather than focusing on local needs.[51]

Fowler provides a fitting conclusion: 'maintaining accountability to its grass-roots constituency while simultaneously building competencies and credibility with decision-makers is perhaps the overriding challenge facing NGOs that would influence policy'.[52] The central issue remains how much NGOs can become effective actors at the level of the summit without losing their strengths—links to their communities, participatory methodology and pursuit of structural change. In other words, how can NGOs scale up without becoming like the summit?

Scaling down

Theoretical rationale for scaling down

It is generally believed that for the interaction between scaled up NGOs and the summit to be meaningful, the summit should also scale down—that is, it should adopt structures and modes of operation that allow local communities and NGOs to build their conceptual, operational and institutional capacities. In the words of one World Bank official: 'The Bank had to learn to scale down its operations in order to successfully scale up someone else's participatory effort: starting small, learning from doing, growing at a pace that is responsive to demand and capacity'.[53] This implies a coherent and shared vision of the goal in terms of grassroots development and empowerment. Further, it implies what Fowler calls 'management for withdrawal', that is, the development of structures and practices that are geared not at perpetuating or enhancing the hold of the summit over the grassroots, but rather towards beneficiary scaling up and autonomy. The summit 'should become less operational and work more through local structures'.[54] Until recently, the only part of the summit that has taken scaling down seriously has been the INGO sector, those whose organisational ideology resembles that of many NGOs, for example Oxfam and the Unitarian–Universalist Service Committee in the USA. The IOs and the UN have lagged behind.

Scaling down the summit is to a certain extent the mirror image of scaling up grassroots organisations and programmes. We could distinguish between scaling down quantitatively (decreasing budgets and geographical intervention levels), functionally (shedding activities to other actors), politically (working with decentralised government structures and civil society organisations), and organisationally (decentralising decision making and abandoning rigid project cycles).

Scaling down is an important element of the pressure the NGO community brings to bear on the summit. Indeed, there are hundreds of NGOs that in various ways seek to prod the World Bank and other UN institutions into adopting a more participatory, accountable and decentralised mode of functioning. In the next sections, we discuss changes underway and progress to date by some United Nations organisations.

Elements of scaling down

Scaling down covers a whole series of changes desired by NGO coalitions, which should be undertaken in parallel. They can be grouped in three categories: changes in the project cycle, changes in the profile of IO staff and changes in the structure of accountability of IOs.

There is general agreement that if the summit is serious about strengthening the grass roots it has to abandon the project cycle as the main mode of financing and replace it with funding for programmes and institutional development. Current project cycles are too short, take too long to start, and are too rigid and large (the average World Bank loan is $50 million). NGOs seek multiyear, flexible, more participatory 'institutional support' that builds on their existing efforts at the grass roots and strengthens them.[55] Such programmes should begin more quickly—the World Bank project cycle takes up to 12 years to complete— and last longer, while being open to renegotiation with the people concerned.

This will entail the adoption of a learning process instead of the usual 'blueprint model'.[56] Adams and Rietbergen-McCracken write about the Bank's need for 'a learning attitude, open to innovation, among those responsible for both lending and non-lending work'.[57] It also requires a decrease in the financial size of projects and the administrative conditions associated with them. Brodhead states that 'the size and the complexity of many bank-funded projects make it difficult to scale down or to escape a top-down approach to design, implementation, and monitoring'.[58]

The profile of IO staff should also better reflect a commitment to community participation and NGO scaling up. The number of staff persons with experience in participatory development as well as a knowledge of the sociocultural aspects of development should be increased.[59] Performance appraisal and criteria for career advancement should be shifted away from the quantity of resources that are disbursed towards the degree of successful community involvement and long-term project sustainability.[60]

Finally and most importantly, NGOs are calling for changes in the structure of accountability of IOs. This certainly implies decentralisation of decision making to the country level. As Cernea writes: 'more decentralized patterns of development work, particularly in regional and local planning, offer important opportunities both to governments and NGOs for "appropriate administration" and for organizational strategies for managing local-level development'.[61] But according to most NGOs, much more is needed. This includes improving access to project information for NGOs, regular NGO and beneficiary involvement in annual evaluation and programming exercises, and creating permanent project-level feedback structures and whistle-blowing opportunities.[62]

Experiences with scaling down

During the last decade, there has been an undeniable ideological change within the summit towards a greater acceptance of the need for grassroots participation and community involvement, and this has had operational implications. Most IOs created special facilities for small grants to NGOs. WFP local representatives can rapidly allocate small donations of food aid to local NGOs for specific actions.[63] The Special Facility of USAID allows its mission leaders to fund small grassroots actions. Since 1990 UNDP's Partners in Development Program has made small grants ($25 000 per country) to NGOs possibly in order to implement community-based initiatives.[64] All these mechanisms seek to allow NGOs to scale up on their own terms—a new phenomenon in international aid. They are also inexpensive and small crumbs from the summit table. They do not modify the mode of functioning of the summit or change the spending patterns of most activities, which is what scaling down is really about.

Other processes, however, hold greater promise for meaningful scaling down. Here, examples come from the World Bank and the UNDP. In 1984 the bank created its first mechanism for regular consultation with NGOs, and NGOs currently participate in 40% of its projects, albeit mostly at the 'junior implementation partner' level. There are three more recent changes, however, that move the bank in the direction of more substantial scaling down.

First, the bank has written into official operational directives consultations with affected groups and NGOs. This was done under pressure from Washington, and against the will of most Third World member states, which considered this a violation of their sovereignty. The language of this directive states that consultation shall be done by the borrowing government ('the Bank expects the borrower to consult with affected groups and local NGOs'), which is logical in the World Bank's language, because it always acts through governments.

Second, as a result of NGO pressure, and 'following a new policy of disclosure of operational information approved by the Executive Directors in August 1993', the World Bank has created a Public Information System, designed to 'make available to the public a range of operational documents that were previously restricted to official users'. Ordinary citizens now have access to more project information than before, but not all information.

Third, the World Bank created an independent inspection panel composed of three persons who can deal with complaints about violating its own procedures. Cases can be brought before the panel by any organisation representing the people affected. This is difficult, because it requires knowledge of a project and of the bank's procedural guidelines. In practice, that means Southern NGOs can launch complaints only with strong Northern NGO backing. Recently the first case, regarding the Arun dam project in Nepal, was presented to the panel.[65]

The UNDP created its own body for regular consultation with NGOs and developed innovative funding mechanisms for them. Among the latter are the Grassroots Initiatives Support Fund, which provides small grants to self-help initiatives in Africa, and the Africa 2000 Network (followed by similar initiatives in Asia and Latin America), which supplies grants and technical assistance to Southern GROs and GSROs active in ecologically sustainable development.[66] In November 1993 UNDP endorsed a strategy paper that emphasises the need to include NGOs in its policy dialogue with governments, and to develop new operational frameworks and procedures that allow for effective capacity building of NGOs. The latter category implies potentially important processes of UNDP scaling down: modification of operational procedures regarding contracting and procurement; reformulation of UNDP staff recruitment, training and performance criteria; increased freedom for national country representatives to speak with and collaborate with NGOs; and funding for dissemination of NGO publications. These innovations have the potential to create a new learning process whereby the UNDP and its staff, traditionally highly government-centred, learn to work in a meaningful manner with NGOs.[67]

Conclusion

The processes discussed above reflect and help promote profound changes in the structure and the nature of international development. NGOs are now routinely consulted during international conferences. They also lobby IOs at all levels, from the field offices to the headquarters. In this process of political scaling up, they have found partners in some of the Northern INGOs, which transmit their views to the most powerful capitals in the world. Together, Southern and Northern NGOs have assumed roles of surveillance and control of their own governments. Moreover, many NGOs have begun collaborating with IOs in implementation roles, motivated chiefly by a desire to obtain funding, but also to scale up quantitatively and spread the use of participatory methods and models. NGOs have even managed to make inroads into the level of decision making, although states clearly remain central at this level. All in all, there is no doubt that organisations emanating from civil society in the Third World have become actors in international politics, scaling up their impact beyond the local level. In doing so, NGOs are pushing IOs to scale down, to become more accountable to and supportive of grassroots organisations and initiatives.

The process of scaling down is clearly less advanced than that of scaling up. IOs remain highly centralised organisations that are attached to rigid and costly project habits. Most fundamentally, they remain under government control, which can successfully minimise NGO involvement within their borders. Yet, as NGOs scale up and also influence their own governments, the pressure on IOs to scale down necessarily increases.

The processes of scaling up and scaling down are mirror images. One process cannot advance without the other and can go only as far as the other. NGOs cannot scale up meaningfully if the summit does not scale down and develop procedures for interaction. For that matter, summit scaling down is largely the result of pressure emanating from grassroots organisations that as part of their process of political scaling up request changes in the structure and the mode of functioning by the summit. Similarly, summit scaling down makes little sense without a concomitant scaling up of the grassroots organisations. It is impossible for the summit to deal with millions of small, localised, heterogeneous organisations. Part of the impetus of NGO scaling up comes from the summit. Through its funding, the summit deliberately seeks to promote the emergence of large, professionalised NGOs. Consequently, both processes are dialectically linked, mutually influencing and enabling to each other.

The processes of scaling up and scaling down seem to suggest that the state is being caught in the middle, squeezed from both sides and pushed into irrelevance. What, if any, role is left for the state when the grass roots have scaled up and become large, efficient agents of development, interacting with a scaled-down summit? Do we not see this process of marginalisation of the state already taking place, as international and even bilateral cooperation agencies increasingly turn to direct NGO financing, bypassing the state and developing direct working relationships with NGOs? It is too early to predict the demise of the state, which still controls the production and distribution of wealth. It will remain for some time the sole actor capable of doing so on a national level. The state retains its capacity to regulate and control NGOs, using for that purpose not only legal but also repressive means. The state, finally, remains by far the most important instance of IO decision making and implementation. No wonder, then, that the state remains the focal point of much of the attention of both the summit and the grass roots. It is through the interplay between NGO and IO pressure on the state and state influence on NGOs and IOs that the dynamic of social and political change emerges.

Notes

The author wishes to thank Mary Anderson, David Brown, Tom Marchione, Ellen Messer, Robert Northrup, Paul Wapner and especially David Miller for their comments.

[1] OECD, *Development Cooperation 1993*, Paris: OECD, 1994 pp 154, 163. See also Donini & Natsios in this issue.

[2] Ashe *et al*, *Access to Credit for Poor Women: A Scale-Up Study of Projects Carried Out by Freedom from Hunger in Mali and Ghana*, Technical Report No 33, Bethesda, MD: GEMINI, 1992.

[3] G Hyden, *Some Notes on Scaling Up*, Gainesville, FL: unpublished paper, 1992.

[4] M Howes & M G Sattar, 'Bigger and better? Scaling-up strategies pursued by BRAC 1972–1991', in M Edwards & D Hulme (eds), *Making a difference: NGOs and Development in a Changing World*, London: Earthscan, 1992.

[5] J Clark, *Democratizing Development: The Role of Voluntary Organizations*, West Hartford, CT: Kummarian Press, 1991.

[6] J Fisher, *The Road from Rio: Sustainable Development and the Nongovernmental Movement in the Third World*, Westport, CT: Praeger, 1993.

[7] D Korten, *Getting to the 21st Century. Voluntary Action and the Global Agenda*, West Hartford, CT: Kummarian Press, 1990.

[8] B Lecomte, 'Processus d'autopromotion et formes d'appui adaptées', in Kwan Kai Hong (ed), *Jeux et enjeux de l'auto-promotion. Vers d'autres formes de coopération au développement*, Geneva and Paris: Institut Universitaire d'Etudes du Développement, Presses Universitaire de France, 1991.

[9] See Robert Berg on managerial scaling up, *Non-Governmental Organizations: New Force in Third World Development and Politics*, East Lansing, MI: Center for Advanced Study of International Development, 1987.

[10] For a more detailed treatment, see P Uvin & D Miller, 'Scaling up: thinking through the issues', (Providence, RI: World Hunger Program Research Report, 1994; and P Uvin, 'Fighting hunger at the grassroots: paths to scaling up', *World Development*, 23 (6), 1995.

[11] R Hodson, 'Small, medium or large? The rocky road to NGO growth', in Edwards & Hulme, *Making a difference*, p 129.

[12] Bhuvan Bhatnagar, 'Participatory development and the World Bank: opportunities and concerns', World Bank Discussion Papers no 183, 1992, p 29.

[13] J Clark, *The Relationship Between the State and the Voluntary Sector*, electronic message: International Development and Global Education List, intdev-l&uriacc.bitnet, 13 June 1994; A Bebbington & J Farrington, 'Governments, NGOs and agricultural development: perspectives on changing inter-organisational relationships', *The Journal of Developmental Studies*, 29 (2), 1993, p 202; and A Bebbington & G Thiele (eds), *Non-Governmental Organizations and the State in Latin America. Rethinking Roles in Sustainable Agricultural Development*, London: Routledge, 1994, p 200.

[14] For the World Bank, see M Cernea, *Nongovernmental Organization and Local Development*, Discussion Paper 40, Washington, DC: World Bank, 1988, p 28; and M Cernea, 'Nongovernmental organizations and local development', *Regional Development Dialogue*, 10 (2) 1989, p 12.

[15] Clark, *The Relationship Between*, pp 5–6; and 'Facts and feelings: the UNHCR/NGO relationship', *Refugee*, September 1989, p 29.

[16] A Fowler, *Non-Governmental Organizations in Africa: Achieving Comparative Advantage in Relief and Micro-Development*, Discussion Paper 249, Sussex: Institute of Development Studies, 1988; and J Tendler, *Turning Private Voluntary Organizations into Development Agencies: Questions for Evaluation AID Program Evaluation*, Discussion Paper 12, Washington, DC: USAID, 1982.

[17] Bhatnagar, 'Participatory development', p 24. See below for the case of the US Congress.

[18] M Ennals, *Relations between the United Nations (Intergovernmental Bodies and Secretariat) and Non-*

Governmental Organizations, London: a report prepared for the Director General for Development and International Economic Cooperation, 1986, p 14.

[19] 'Facts and feelings', p 29; 'High Commissioner calls for partnership with NGOS', *Monday Developments*, 30 September 1991, p 1.

[20] P Chatterjee & M Finger, *The Earth Brokers. Power, Politics and World Development*, London: Routledge, 1994, ch 5–6.

[21] M Nerfin, 'The relationship NGOs/UN agencies/governments: challenges, possibilities, prospects', in *Development, International Cooperation and the NGOs. First International Meeting of NGOs and the United Nations System Agencies*, pp 79–96; and IBASE-PNUD, Rio de Janiero: IBASE-UNDP, 1992, p 82.

[22] Bebbington & Thiele, *Non-Governmental Organizations and the State*, pp 201, 203, 213–214.

[23] International relations scholars have studied this in some detail: P Haas, R Keohane & M Levy (eds), *Institutions for the Earth. Sources of Effective Environmental Protection*, Cambridge, MA: MIT Press, 1994; and O Young, *International Cooperation: Building Regimes for Natural Resources and the Environment*, Ithaca, NY: Cornell University Press, 1989.

[24] Bebbington & Farrington, 'Governments, NGOs and agricultural development', p 211.

[25] Cernea, 'Nongovernmental organizations', pp 134–35: 'The Bank is actively encouraging national governments to consider structured NGO participation in Bank-financed projects, and to explore new forms of partnerships between governmental institutions and the growing number of NGOs'.

[26] 'IFAD, NGOs agree on measures to strengthen collaboration', *Monday Developments*, 9 July 1990, p 8. For the case of UNDP, personal communication from Sarah Timpson, UNDP Deputy Assistant Administrator, Bureau for Programmes and Policy.

[27] This section is brief, for it is dealt with excellently elsewhere in this issue; see the articles by Ritchie, Donini and Conca.

[28] Nerfin, 'The relationship NGOs', p 86. The NGO–World Bank Committee has 28 members, 16 of which are Third World NGOs. T Brodhead, 'Cooperation and discord towards collaboration among NGOs, aid donors and Third World governments', in *Development, International Cooperation and the NGOs*, pp 97–107; IBASE-PNUD, p 106. For the UNHCR, see 'Facts and feelings', p 20, and the Natsios and Donini articles in this volume.

[29] Chatterjee & Finger, *The Earth Brokers*, p 102.

[30] Brodhead, 'Cooperation and discord', p 107.

[31] 'INTERACTION and the Development GAP Meet AID's Africa Bureau to Discuss its Poor Record on Popular Participation', *Monday Developments*, 19 April 1993, p 18.

[32] Bhatnagar, 'Participatory development', p 24.

[33] In order of quote: M Leach, 'NGOs are playing key role in ICN preparations', *Monday Developments*, 12 October 1992, p 6; 'On the road to Brazil '92', *Monday Developments*, 20 April 1992, p 15, referring to UNCED; see also 'Keeping alive Cairo goals for women', *New York Times*, 25 September 1994, A4.

[34] P Padbry, 'Non-governmental organization alternative treaties at the '92 Global Forum', Transnational Associations, 1993/4 (July-August). See also, 'On the road to Brazil '92', pp 13–14. For a critical view, see Chatterjee & Finger, *The Earth Brokers*, p 99.

[35] This lobbying is not often successful. The above mentioned World Bank study of 20 participatory projects studied whether grassroots pressure accounted for these projects' adoption of a participatory approach. The answer was 'yes, sometimes, but not as a rule', but the author managed to identify only three cases: Bhatnagar, 'Participatory development', p 23.

[36] A Hall, 'From victims to victors: NGOs and empowerment at Itaparica', in Edwards & Hulme, *Making a difference*; I Smillie 'Changing partners: Northern NGOs, Northern governments', in I Smillie & H Henny (eds), *Non-governmental organizations and governments: stakeholders for development*, Paris: OECD, 1993; C Dolan, 'British development NGOs and advocacy in the 1990s', in Edwards & Hulme, *Making a difference*; and M Benjamin & A Freedman, *Bridging the Global Gap. A Handbook to Linking Citizens of the First and Third Worlds*, Cabin John, MD: Seven Locks Press, 1989.

[37] Robert Wade, lecture at Brown University, 18 November, 1994.

[38] See Baer's article in this issue.

[39] Yolanda Kakabudse & Sarah Burns, *Movers and Shapers: NGOs in International Affairs*, Washington, DC: World Resources Institute, May 1994, p 6. See Conca's article in this volume for the case of the Commission on Sustainable Development.

[40] 'NGOs seen as key to achieving nutrition conference goals', *Monday Developments*, 19 April 1993, p 21.

[41] See for example the World Bank, *List of World Bank-Financed Projects with Potential for NGO Involvement*, Washington, DC: International Economic Relations Division, September 1991.

[42] R Livernash, 'The growing influence of NGOs in the developing world', *Environment*, 34 (5), 1992, p 16.

[43] World Bank, *Working with NGOs*, Washington DC: World Bank, 1994, p 1; Brodhead, 'Cooperation and discord', p 107; increasingly, however, these are Southern NGOs.

[44] Cernea, 'Nongovernmental organizations', p 130.

[45] 'The Role of NGOs in African recovery', *Transnational Associations*, March-April 1992, p 106.

[46] 'PVOS influencing agenda for World Bank conference on reducing global hunger', *Monday Developments*, 13 September 1993, p 10; 'Southern NGOs to join in Bank hunger conference follow-up', *Monday Developments*, 14 February 1994, p 7; 'Mali workshop is opportunity for unique dialogue on hunger', *Monday Developments*, 22 August 1994, pp 1, 8.

[47] Ennals, *Relations between the UN and NGOs*, p 7; T Shaw, 'Popular participation in non-governmental structures in Africa: implications for democratic development', *Africa Today*, third quarter 1990, p 12.

[48] A Fowler, 'Building partnerships between Northern and Southern development NGOs: issues for the nineties', *Development, Journal of SID*, 1, 1992, p 2.

[49] Charles Elliott, 'Some aspects of relations between the North and the South in the NGO sector', *World Development*, 15, Supplement, 1987; Shaw, 'Popular participation', p 13; A Fowler, 'The role of NGOs in changing state–society relations: perspectives from Eastern and Southern Africa', *Development Policy Review*, 9 (1), 1991, pp 59, 70; and Nerfin, 'The relationship NGOs', p 90.

[50] Fowler, 'The role of NGOs in changing', p 67; Brodhead, 'Cooperation and discord', p 101.

[51] Nerfin, 'The relationship NGOs', p 84; P A Kiriwandeniya, 'The growth of the SANASA movement in Sri Lanka', and K Constantino-David, 'The Philippine experience in scaling-up', both in Edwards & Hulme, *Making a difference*

[52] Fowler, 'Building partnerships', p 5; Fowler, 'The role of NGOs in changing', pp 71, 73; Brodhead, 'Cooperation and discord', p 108.

[53] Bhatnagar, 'Participatory development', p 19.

[54] 'Facts and feelings', p 24.

[55] Bhatnagar, 'Participatory development', p 18.

[56] Ibid, pp 5, 7.

[57] J Adams & J Rietlander-McCracken, 'Participatory development: getting the key players involved', in *Finance and Development*, September 1994, pp 36–38.

[58] Brodhead, 'Cooperation and discord', p 106; see Adams & Rietlander-McCracken, 'Participatory development', p 37 for the Bank's view.

[59] Bhatnagar, 'Participatory development', pp 12, 13; M Racelis, *People's Participation: The UNICEF Experience*, Washington, DC: World Bank, Workshop on Popular Participation, 1992, p 10.

[60] Racelis, *People's Participation*, p 10; '1999: a vision for NGOs and AID in Africa', *Monday Developments*, 13 September 1993, p 4.

[61] Cernea, 'Nongovernmental organizations', p 136. See also A B Durning, *Action at the Grassroots: Fighting Poverty and Environmental Decline*, Washington DC: Worldwatch Paper 88, 1989, p 48.

[62] Durning, *Action at the Grassroots*, p 45; '1999: a vision for NGOs and AID in Africa', p 4.

[63] 'Le PAM renforce sa coopération avec les organisations non gouvernementales', *Transnational Associations*, 3, 1990, p 178.

[64] Livernash, 'The growing influence', p 16; Nerfin, 'The relationship NGOs', p 85. It exists currently in over 60 countries.

[65] 'World Bank panel will soon begin hearing complaints', *Monday Developments*, 9 May 1994, p 4; D B Bradlow, 'You can help hold the World Bank accountable', *Monday Developments*, 9 May 1994, p 8.

[66] Nerfin, 'The relationship NGOs', p 86; Brodhead, 'Cooperation and discord', pp 104–106.

[67] UNDP, *UNDP and Organizations of Civil Society: Building Sustainable Partnerships*, a strategy paper presented to, and endorsed by, the Strategy and Management Committee on 23 November 1993; UNDP, *Note to the Administrator on Progress in UNDP Cooperation with Institutions of the Civil Society*, 1994; and personal communication with Sarah Timpson, UNDP Deputy Assistant Administrator, Bureau for Programmes and Policy.

■ 9 ■

Coordinate? Cooperate? Harmonise?
NGO Policy and Operational Coalitions

CYRIL RITCHIE

The extreme diversity that characterises the nongovernmental world, which is both its greatest strength and its greatest weakness, carries through to the policy and operational coalitions that nongovernmental organisations create and in which they participate. Just as NGOs exist, even thrive, at every level of society, so do their coalitions. Almost every country, certainly every continent, has many NGOs and consequently constellations of NGO coalitions.

This essay will refer to some of these national and regional bodies, but it will primarily look at the birth, life and infrequent death of international NGO coalitions, notably those that have a bearing on the accomplishments of the United Nations system. In doing so, the author draws primarily on real-life examples of NGO coalitions, particularly on the actual or intended influence they exert collectively on governments and on organisations of the UN family.

Organisational dimensions

It is important to recall that there is a long history of NGO coalition building. Some coalitions were created over a century ago. They include World Alliance of Young Men's Christian Associations (founded in 1855), the International Veterinary Congress (1863), the International Federation of Metal Workers Organizations (1893), and the International Council of Nurses (1899). In this century, the list would include the World Middle Class Block (1922), the Unio Internationalis Catholica Foederationum Caritatis (1924), the Federation of International Institutions in Geneva (1929), the Conference of NGOs interested in Migration (1950), or the International Society for Labour Law and Social Legislation (1958).

The tide is not about to turn. The 1990s have witnessed the birth of such networks as El Taller, the Réseau International d'ONG sur la désertification, the Climate Action Network, the World Alliance for Citizen Participation, and the Peoples Alliance for Social Development. All these illustrations demonstrate the diversity of the NGO world and its coalitions, even as they bring to the forefront the question of what constitutes a coalition. Essentially we are dealing with organisations that are coalitions of organisations. And since nongovernmental organisations deal with the entire spectrum of human values, human aspirations, human needs and human antagonisms, it is natural that NGO coalitions similarly reflect the human condition through their complexities and defy simple definitions.

Definitions

The search for definitions is not simplified by looking at who may create or join NGO coalitions. National Red Cross and Red Crescent Societies are both NGOs and government auxiliaries, yet their International Federation places itself unambiguously among the world's leading NGOs. The defunct International Union for Child Welfare and the far-from-defunct International Union for the Conservation of Nature and Natural Resources (also known as the World Conservation Union) had or have government ministries or departments as voting members alongside national NGO voting members, but their international status was and is that of an NGO coalition. The various NGO conferences set up with bodies of the United Nations system are autonomous NGO coalitions, but they may admit to membership only NGOs selected by the relevant UN body for consultative status. Again we see the diversity and complexity of the real world reflected in the way that different NGO groupings organise to deal with that world.

Terminology is not of great help in the quest for organisational definitions. NGO coalitions use, seemingly interchangeably, a rainbow of titles: conference, association, federation, league, alliance, union, council, consortium and network. There are even such apparently limiting terms as 'committee' or 'working group'. The word 'coalition' itself appears rather infrequently in the titles of international NGO groupings, but seems to have more favour at the national and regional levels. There is no evident correlation between the types of bodies that constitute the membership of any coalition and its title.

NGO coalitions may bring together like-minded persons or organisations with deeply-shared goals (International Board on Books for young people, International Union against Cancer, for example) or persons and organisations with sharply contrasting views (the Inter-Parliamentary Union, for example, itself another example of an 'NGO-plus'). Sometimes both approaches may occur within one organisation. While the members of the International Cooperative Alliance, the International Chamber of Commerce, or the International Federation of Journalists undoubtedly share common values within their respective organisations, it would be utopian to assume that they would therefore be unanimous in a debate on solutions to the world's economic troubles. This aspect should be kept in mind with the discussion later of goals and tactics of coalitions.

Size is another element that conditions a coalition's outreach, effectiveness, professionalism and image. Although it is far from a determining factor, coalitions that directly or indirectly serve and represent hundreds or thousands of members have the capacity to invest in good management, thorough research, professionally-produced publications and comprehensive representation to the United Nations system. Examples of these can include the International Confederation of Free Trade Unions, Education International, the World Organization of the Scout Movement, and the International Tourism Alliance. At the same time, there are outstanding examples of coalitions that are permanently squeezed for funds but that nevertheless have significant impact on the UN system, such as the International Babyfood Action Network, the International Council of

Voluntary Agencies, the Environment Liaison Centre International and Health Action International. Nor should one overlook on a different plane the World Federation of United Nations Associations or the Women's International League for Peace and Freedom.

Funding and services

NGO coalitions rely for their financing mainly on fees paid by their members, but there are examples—including most of those cited in this essay—of substantial funds sometimes being raised from foundations and government agencies. The precariousness of NGO coalitions resides in the general reluctance or inability of nongovernmental organisations to invest much in coordination. This causes many coalitions to live a hand-to-mouth existence unless they are authorised to seek external funding. Even then, many members of NGO coalitions fear that the fund-raising efforts of the coalition may conflict with those of the NGO. Such issues have occasionally become acute when there has been inadequate openness and transparency on the part of coalition management. Where authorised by their members, NGO coalitions may seek external funds not only for their management costs—which should be the responsibility of members—but for events and programmes that it is most appropriate for a coalition to undertake. This could include conferences and seminars; training courses; publications for information and advocacy; research and other activities that affect the interests of coalition members and that benefit from the mix of expertise or cost-effectiveness brought about through the existence of the coalition.

Whether or not a coalition has many or few autonomous programmes or projects, the nature of most coalitions is to provide a service to their members and to a cause. Consequently, coalition costs are frequently heavily weighted towards personnel compensation and the core administrative budget items that are inseparable from coordination and representation (for example travel, communications, rentals). Many disputes have arisen within coalitions over the proper balance between administration costs, which are often seen as unproductive even by NGOs that face the same quandary in explaining their budgets to their own members and donors, and productive programming costs. No general solution has been found, although the many hours of debate that governing and executive bodies have spent on the issue have often been educational and sometimes cathartic. Practical experience would indicate that salary and benefits of coalition personnel should be similar to the standards prevailing among the coalition's constituents—with allowance for geographical cost-of-living expenses—otherwise trouble is bound to surface. Coalitions that have a close relationship with the UN system are often subject to particular scrutiny by their members to ensure that the mis-stated 'inflated UN salaries' do not become the norm in the NGO coalition. Misapprehensions are notoriously hard to dissipate, save through the most open and honest divulgence of facts.

Such openness—desirable in all NGO dealings—is greatly facilitated if the NGO coalition has a clear legal basis and rule book. In the absence of an international legal instrument governing nongovernmental organisations, their coalitions must conform to national legislation. Concepts and legal terminology vary greatly from one system to another (for example, non-profit corporation, public-benefit institution, voluntary association, foundation, trust); they have been discussed extensively in this issue and elsewhere. An NGO coalition will always need a legal status that raises no doubts about its capacity to manage its funds, engage its personnel, and conduct its business. Thereafter the internal regulations should emphasise the harmony that should reign among the coalition members in pursuit of their common goals, rather than emphasising such detailed written constraints that sooner or later the coalition's actions will be impeded. Of fundamental importance is the requirement that coalition members and leaders first determine what is wanted in policy and structural terms, and only then involve the lawyers in writing the legal texts; legal draftsmanship can never fill a policy-making role.

Governance dimensions

Contact with and influence on the United Nations system is the *raison d'être* of many NGO coalitions and a substantial part of the activity of many others. Conferences of NGOs have consultative or similar status with one or another UN body. The conferences exist to protect and enhance that status and to give procedural or substantive consideration to issues that come before—or should come before—the relevant UN body. The relationship between each conference or committee of NGOs and its mother UN organ varies widely. The NGO Conference and Standing Committee of the UN Educational Social and Cultural Organization (UNESCO) benefits from year-round financial and material support from the UNESCO budget. In return, the organisations elicit, foster and provide substantial and substantive input at many levels of the UNESCO secretariat. UNICEF also provides modest financial support to 'its' NGO committee while seeking from the committee both regular and *ad hoc* input into its deliberations and field work. The World Bank funds an NGO–Bank Committee whose main concern over the 14 years of its existence has increasingly been to criticise World Bank developmental concepts and practices, and more recently to offer alternative approaches. In this example, there are of course a great number of other NGOs outside the NGO–Bank Committee that have offered persistent and much more virulent criticism of the Bank; these are only loosely organised in floating and perpetually-renewing coalitions.

Other parts of the United Nations system work equally closely with self-generated NGO coalitions at the consultation level without the elaborate rules of consultative status. Examples include the UN High Commissioner for Refugees with the International Council of Voluntary Agencies, a relationship that has recently culminated in the widely-supported and useful Partnership-in-Action (PARinAC) initiative; the UN Centre for Human Settlements with the Habitat International Coalition, with exceptionally close collaboration leading toward HABITAT II in 1996; and the United Nations Environment Programme (UNEP) with the Environment Liaison Centre International, whose constructive criticism of UNEP's performance has not been muted over the 20 years of its existence, irrespective of the significant financial support provided throughout that time. Another variant is illustrated by the practices of the World Health Organization

(WHO) and the UN Development Program (UNDP) that do not have standing NGO conferences but often convene sectoral or technical consultations with NGOs. Recent sessions of the WHO have focused on alcohol abuse or AIDS, for example; UNDP has looked at poverty or the environment and development link.

Diverse UN–NGO coalition links

Consultations between a UN body and an NGO grouping, however, represent only a fraction of interactions. All the UN organs mentioned above work with and through standing and temporary NGO coalitions to promote or implement pro- grammes worldwide. Whether through formal contracts, standing agreements, or *ad hoc* arrangements, UN organisations collaborate with and often rely on NGOs to deliver services, test new ideas, and foster popular participation. By belonging to an NGO coalition that has systematic relations with UN organs, an NGO has a certain additional legitimacy and also has the opportunity to join the collective exercise of responsibility and to influence the decision making of that UN body. UN secretariats and NGOs are often confronted with a common problem, namely persuading governments to adopt a particular course of action, whether it be allowing food convoys to reach refugees or ratifying the convention on the elimination of all forms of discrimination against women. NGO coalitions are powerful allies of the UN in such matters, and vice versa. NGO coalitions are perhaps increasingly essential partners in the advocacy roles that are needed to ensure that governments make decisions in the global public interest and carry out the obligations that result from international conferences and conventions. These activities may not have the media attraction of disaster relief or massive human rights violations, but they lie at the root of remedying many of the situations that will call for short-term media attention.

These further examples of UN and NGO coalition links fall short of exhausting the forms of existing experience. The Committee for the Promotion and Advancement of Cooperatives (COPAC) is an interagency committee created in 1971. This committee takes part in deliberations on an equal footing with UN, the Food and Agriculture Organization (FAO) and the International labour office (ILO), together with four NGOs that are both associations and coalitions: the International Cooperative Alliance, the International Federation of Agricultural Producers, the International Union of Food, Agricultural and Allied Workers Associations and the World Council of Credit Unions. The members provide COPAC's funding, and external financial support is sought for services, research, seminars and the like. A similar vein of equal participation, along with equal rights and responsibilities, can be found in the Administrative Committee on Coordination's Sub-Committee on Nutrition, in the UN Children's Fund (UNICEF)/NGO Committee on Central and Eastern Europe, or in the Nansen-Medal Committee, which is serviced by the United Nations High Commission for Refugees (UNHCR). A remarkable case of fruitful and intense cooperation exists within the UN Department of Humanitarian Affairs (DHA), where the Inter- Agency Standing Committee (IASC) and Inter-Agency Support Unit give unpre- cedented access to particularly relevant and competent NGOs and have an officer named to their staff by the appropriate NGO coalition, the International Council of Voluntary Agencies (ICVA).

These examples show that when both sides see that the product will be enhanced by unrestricted collaboration, the doors open. NGO coalitions that are, to repeat the key term 'particularly relevant and competent' can and must find ways to pass through these doors. In terms of both effectiveness and credibility, the UN and NGOs both benefit, and the result is better. Since the result is so often the improvement of humanity's living conditions, notably in developing countries, what better reason could there be for governments to authorise and encourage 'their' UN to be more open and innovative in its structured and less-structured relations with NGO coalitions? In these times of financial strain, the cost benefits are also persuasive.

Special mention must be made of the ILO, though no other intergovernmental agency is rushing to emulate its unique tripartite structure, in which representatives of governments, employers and workers interact on every aspect of every decision. The employers' and workers' representatives are grouped in coalitions within coalitions. And 75 years of experience and tradition have brought the art of confrontation, negotiation and compromise to singular heights. Some echoes of ILO's successful functioning are occasionally heard in proposals to institute a People's Assembly or People's Chamber alongside the UN General Assembly, though the democratisation of global governance has not yet worked up the necessary head of steam.

World conferences

One area in which the democratisation of global governance is probably building momentum is the participation of NGOs and their coalitions in international conferences. As far back as the 1972 UN Conference on the Human Environment in Stockholm, the UN itself—particularly the secretary-general of the conference, the omnipresent Maurice Strong—created an NGO committee that was in effect a coalition to provide advice. For the conferences on population (Bucharest, 1974), food (Rome, 1974) and habitat (Vancouver, 1976), NGOs created their own coalitions, pushed the idea of producing an NGO conference newspaper and took on the arduous role of organising a parallel NGO forum. In the later 1970s and throughout the 1980s, UN conferences became inseparable from increasingly complex and expansive NGO participation, on topics like desertification in Nairobi (1977), science and technology for development in Vienna (1979), population in Mexico City (1984) and the first three world conferences on women. By the 1990s NGO participation in and NGO coalition-forming around world conferences seemed at times to have reached satiety, only to be surpassed anew with gatherings in environment and development in Rio (1992), human rights in Vienna (1993), population and development in Cairo (1994) and social development in Copenhagen (1995).

There may be disagreement on whether the very holding of UN world conferences, even world summits, has become counterproductive in terms of the time, money and energy invested in them. But since conferences on women (Beijing, 1995), HABITAT II (Istanbul, 1996) and probably both racism and migration in the immediately following years are already scheduled, there can be no diminution in the interest and attention that NGOs and their coalitions will give to these events. Two factors are particularly important in this consideration. In the first case, world conferences and summits are the occasions—not always fully seized—for a truly global airing of issues vital to humanity's future. They are the occasions for governments to make the decisions of principle that cannot sensibly be made only at the national level. They are the occasions for the setting of standards for governmental and human behaviour, and for a look at the longer-term needs of the planet, beyond the confines of national electoral or budgetary considerations.

These are utopian goals and reality falls far short of them. This reality in no way diminishes their fundamental importance, and it leads directly to the second factor to be discussed in this essay. World conferences and summits need the full-scale input and presence of NGOs and their coalitions to have any hope of achieving their goals. Governments must have available for these conferences— notably in the preparatory phases—the best expertise that civil society can provide: professional, technical, legal, political. Governments and civil society are partners in improving the human condition and NGO coalitions have an increasingly important responsibility to procure, mobilise and channel that expertise. Furthermore, governments must be made aware that civil society is listening and watching their moves, declarations, decisions, silences and compromises. The organised and increasingly massive presence of NGOs throughout all phases of world conferences is a manifestation of that role, which should be greatly reinforced during the implementation of declarations and plans of action. The heterogeneity of NGOs' input and interest has led to the creation of yet more coalitions—based on subject, geographic location, age, gender, language, even on enthusiasm or courage. There is no turning back from this path. These coalitions should increase their effectiveness through screening their members' relevance and competence, and securing some degree of financial autonomy. Governments, the United Nations and NGOs will all benefit from collaboration and interaction.

To improve the impact of NGOs on future world conferences, some practical questions should be addressed now. On many occasions in the 1970s and 1980s, NGOs' preparations for world conferences were stimulated or guided by a committee under the authority of the Conference of NGOs in Consultative Status with the Economic and Social Council (ECOSOC) (CONGO); there was considerable stability and transmission of experience from one event to another. There was also unremitting verbal sniping at the leaders of these CONGO committees; the NGO world is nothing if not independent-minded, which is a virtue because how else would even the most recondite human cause find a group to defend or attack it. The growth in the numbers of nongovernmental organisations appearing on the international scene, especially because so many have solely national or local bases, has somewhat overwhelmed the CONGO mechanism, and occasionally the UN mechanisms too. This has reduced its broad acceptability as a neutral focal point for harnessing NGO energies. Those who participated in the Rio (1992), Vienna (1993) or Copenhagen (1995) processes recall the initiatives, upheavals and chagrins that accompanied CONGO's efforts to play its central facilitating role. Whereas the conference planned for 1995 in Beijing has seen a more orderly planning process, the multiplicity of coordinating, cooperating and harmonising mechanisms now in place in the NGO world will need to find some platform for dialogue to achieve, as a strict minimum, the elimination of direct competition for funds, meeting space, speaking slots, big names, government delegates' ears, and even computers and typewriters.

That listing of minimum targets for augmented NGO coordination at conferences should be expanded to the physical running of NGO forums; the production of NGO newspapers (must there be five daily conference papers?); sponsorship of developing NGOs and orientation of first-time NGO participants; coherent production of common NGO position statements; and, above all, designation of an NGO coalition to mobilise follow-up and monitor implementation of the conference results. The democratization of global NGO governance of the future will make it all the more difficult to achieve such cooperation, but it would be unwise to delay making an effort.

No discussion of the world conferences 'map' and the place of NGOs on it can end without a specific reference to one unusual and commendable example of partnership, namely the World Conference on Education for All (WCEFA) in 1990. The executive heads of four agencies (UNDP, UNESCO, UNICEF, World Bank) invited governments, IGOs, and NGOs to participate in the preparatory process (including substantive regional meetings) and in the conference itself on the basis of complete equality of status and decision making. No one's self-love appears to have durably suffered and no insurmountable difficulties were encountered in reaching consensus. The follow-up to WCEFA was also intended to be innovative in that representatives of the four intergovernmental sponsoring agencies and of their four related NGO coalitions were to sit in partnership on a joint implementation committee. However, UNDP had not established a UNDP–NGO coalition, and the World Bank–NGO Committee had not been sufficiently involved in WCEFA to recognise the importance of joining the follow-up. Fortunately, the UNESCO- and UNICEF-related NGO committees have kept the flame alive. But this case history illustrates the danger of taking for granted the reactions of NGO coalition members when initiatives are perceived as coming from outside their ranks, and the parallel advantage of having as coalition leaders persons with sufficient international experience to know when and how to seize opportunities for new programmatic and governance methods.

UN conventions

UN conventions are yet another area where fruitful cooperation between the United Nations and NGOs offers lessons from the past and promises for the future. For the reasons given earlier, ILO conventions are a story in their own right, with representatives of governments, employers and workers responsible for drawing up, adopting and implementing such fundamentally important instruments as the 1948 Freedom of Association Convention, which guarantees workers and employers worldwide 'the right to establish and ... to join organizations of their own choosing without previous authorization', or the 1981 Collective Bargaining Convention, which 'applies to all branches of economic activity.' Beyond such ILO standard-setting are a host of other UN conventions, covenants and treaties. These are all of basic concern to one or more NGO coalitions, whether they deal with human rights, refugees, the law of the sea, civil and political rights, nuclear weapons or any of the multitude of other issues that are central to the purpose of both the United Nations and nongovernmental organisations. NGO participation in drafting some of these texts has been remarkably strong—for example in regard to the Convention against Torture and other Cruel, Inhuman and Degrading Treatment; the Convention on International Trade in Endangered Species; the Convention on the Rights of the Child; and the Conventions on Desertification and on Biological Diversity. Moreover, in the statement issued at the 1993 Vienna World Conference on Human Rights, the active cooperation of NGOs was described as essential to enable the treaty bodies to function effectively. For ample proof of the validity of that statement it is sufficient to look at the freedom of expression that prevails for NGOs and NGO coalitions in the sessions of the UN Commission on Human Rights. Although increasingly subject to curtailment because of repetitiousness and occasional abuse of speaking rights, freedom of expression is nonetheless significantly greater here than in other UN chambers. Further evidence of the role and responsibilities exercised by NGOs in this domain, which constitute precedents for future progress in governance, can be found in the UN Committee on the Rights of the Child. It provides access to NGOs by virtue of the convention that it monitors; and it has completely open sessions where NGO input constitutes the substance of the debate. A coalition of NGOs concerned with children's rights provides intersessional focus for these issues.

With so much testimony available on the positive results achieved through responsible UN–NGO cooperation on matters of programme and governance, one might be forgiven for assuming that states, as the political masters of the UN, would be only too ready to encourage and provide opportunities for such interactions. Yet in relation to some recent or forthcoming conferences or other UN events, statements have been put on record that NGOs shall have no negotiating role *vis-à-vis* governmental deliberations. This is a stipulation more honoured in the breach than the observance. Several examples throughout this essay of substantive actions and contributions by NGOs to UN conferences and conventions have been close to that of a 'negotiating role'. They have been so important to outcomes that it is difficult to see how governments can sensibly cut themselves off from such critical intellectual and specialist inputs. Depending on the circumstances, NGO coalitions have been important in stimulating, chan-nelling and managing such inputs. They should be ever more vigilant and entrepreneurial in defending and promoting the right of civil society to bring its professional competencies into the centre of international deliberations.

In his address to NGOs in September 1994, the UN Secretary-General Boutros Boutros-Ghali said, 'Nongovernmental organizations are a basic form of popular representation in the present-day world. Their participation in international organizations is, in a way, a guarantee of the political legitimacy of those international organizations ... NGOs are an essential part of the legitimacy without which no international activity can be meaningful.' The secretary-general renewed this declaration of faith when he spoke to the World Economic

Forum at Davos in January 1995. There he said, 'I should like nongovernmental organizations to occupy an increasingly significant place within the United Nations itself. From the standpoint of global democratization, we need the participation of international public opinion and of the mobilizing powers of nongovernmental organizations.'

Strategic dimensions

NGO coalitions are as varied as the world they reflect, respond to, occasionally define and constantly monitor. Many are single-issue on such matters as disarmament, whaling, philately, intellectual property, cardiology, pesticides, female circumcision, road transport, adult education, credit unions, ageing. This haphazard enumeration—based on the existence of real networks—shows that single issues are multifaceted and represent focal points of concern rather than narrow and exclusive tracks. It is the members of coalitions who define their specificity, frame their missions and policies and determine the broad links with other related coalitions, networks and alliances. Even single-issue coalitions (and there is virtually no such animal) will need to associate not only with NGOs working in their field but with many others whose economic or social work is relevant to theirs. How much more comprehensive therefore must be the strategic thinking and planning of multisectoral coalitions, and how much more broad their goals and outreach. The World Council of Churches, for example, touches in one way or another most facets of human existence. So too, though for different reasons, do the International Alliance of Women and the International Chamber of Commerce. These and similar bodies are both coalitions and associations, and the choice of term is not particularly relevant to the choice of a coalition's strategies or its mode of operations.

Variety of approach

Coalitions adopt many different stratagems and tactics to convey their messages. The coalitions that Greenpeace and The Development Gap assemble for meetings of the World Bank and International Monetary Fund adopt dramatic postures, with one eye on media coverage. Opinions are divided, including in the NGO community, about the value of this approach. Others prefer long-term lobbying of government delegates and of the media, whether it be in relation to the World Bank or FAO, for example, or to the UN regional commissions. Lobbying of national governments and officials at the country level is also a prominent tactic of NGOs and their coalitions. Trade and development issues have long been a priority for many networks for a long time, and the International Coalition for Development Action was specifically set up to ensure that knowledge, procedures, successes and failures at the national level would be shared and built on in other countries. Women's coalitions have blossomed in recent years and have had singular success at both national and international levels. They have built on the patient work of long-established women's associations in combating discrimination, exclusion, violence and arrogance.

On another level, the very first UN international year, World Refugee Year in

1959–1960, was proposed by individuals, lobbied for by NGOs and coalitions (notably the Standing Conference of Voluntary Agencies Working for Refugees, a predecessor of ICVA), and proclaimed by the United Nations. The world organisation then gave its formal recognition to an NGO coalition set up solely for the International Committee for World Refugee Year, which disbanded after a three-year life span, having been a trend-setting network in organising fund-raising and public advocacy.

More recently, a similar story can be told of the International Year of the Family (1994), which also owed its origins to NGO initiative. Virtually the only major international activities highlighting the year were in the hands of NGO coalitions, based in several 'UN cities', created to promote and propagate the year.

Only a few of the coalitions mentioned in this essay have gone out of existence. However, some have experienced, or are today experiencing, a period of quiescence for policy or financial reasons, or because one or more competing coalitions have come into existence and have eaten into the market. Until the 1970s or 1980s, most coalitions seemed to have been created as permanent coordinating mechanisms or federations. Coalitions created to relate to UN years or conferences have usually expired shortly after the specified time frame. Although nongovernmental organisations will always act independently and enthusiastically to achieve their goals, those contemplating setting up coalitions should reflect somewhat longer and inquire somewhat more deeply about whether or not there is a suitable coalition or network already in existence. For example, it is often asked whether there is indeed a need for so many networks serving women's rights, youth, sustainable development, children, education and so forth. Perhaps the answers will come from donors, who may begin to look askance at so many applications announcing that 'NGOs have, for the first time, acted to … '

Output dimensions

Many illustrations have been given of the variety of outputs that NGO coalitions expect to produce as they strive to serve their members and their causes. If it is assumed that a coalition has value only if it provides services that would not otherwise be available, then we again confront the issue of seeking a definition of a coalition. If one may define a group by describing outputs, we may note that coalitions have had both successes and failures in providing legal and fiscal defence or protection of their members and their members' interests; in obtaining or channelling funds for projects or contracts; in securing access to authorities or goods that would not be possible for the members to have individually; in analysing and distributing information; in recruiting, training and evaluating staff and consultants; in mobilising support, goodwill, enthusiasm and hope among members, supporters, donors, or clients; in establishing the parameters and mechanisms for interagency cooperation, whether among individual NGOs or among networks, or a combination of these; in advocating policies, educating publics, raising awareness and changing minds; in partly filling the gap in NGO collective or organisational memory; and last but not least in being available so that a coalition does not need to be created to respond to each new crisis.

The many examples of NGO coalitions cited have shown that coalitions span a wide range of organisational characteristics, professionalism, enthusiasms, policies, persistence, and of substantive and geographical scope. Only members can determine when a coalition has outlived its usefulness, sometimes manifesting their views not by formal legal action but simply by walking out. Indeed, starting and maintaining a coalition is surely more often a matter of shared vision and solidarity than a shared rulebook. Coalitions achieve results because members desire and commit themselves and their resources, not because a constitution is a well written guide to action. A coalition is a particular form of collective action; determination, inspiration and imagination are the essential glue holding its members together.

Civil society needs coordination, cooperation, harmonisation. Responsible policy and operational coalitions of nongovernmental organisations help provide for such accomplishments. International life and particularly the United Nations are the beneficiaries of such work and commitment.

Note

The author has drawn on a miscellany of official and informal documents of the United Nations Organization, its Specialized Agencies and other secretariat organs, and of the Union of International Associations. Background for this article also stems from reading a variety of publications from NGO and NGO coalitions, notably those associated with UN bodies and world conferences.

■ 10 ■

Partners in Development? The State, NGOs, and the UN in Central America

PETER SOLLIS

The number, size and type of nongovernmental organisations (NGOs) has grown rapidly in Central America over the past 20 years. Expansion was driven largely by increased international NGO aid during the political crisis and violent conflict of the 1980s. Inter-institutional relationships also evolved over this decade. Official donors, including specialist UN agencies, the United Nations Development Program (UNDP) and special UN programmes started to work with NGOs and grassroots groups. However, NGO and state relations remained weak and constrained by mutual distrust.

With Central America's war-torn societies now in the process of recovery, donors expect NGOs to have three positive impacts on future development. First, NGOs should help alleviate the effects of adjustment on poor and vulnerable groups. Second, NGOs should contribute to post-adjustment recovery policies that reduce poverty, develop human resources and protect the environment. Third, a thriving NGO sector should intensify democratisation processes by strengthening and pluralising civil society. This essay examines the growth of NGOs in Central America and the evolution of NGO and state relations, before looking at the UN's relationship with nongovernmental organisations and the role of UN agencies in realising the expectations placed on these organisations.

The political and economic context

The 1980s were the most turbulent years in Central America's recent history, as brutal conflicts in Nicaragua (1981–1990), El Salvador (1980–1992) and Guatemala (1962 to present) uprooted two million people and left 150 000 dead. Civil wars also deepened economic deterioration. Economies shrank and per capita incomes fell sharply under the combined effects of war, external shocks and adverse terms of trade movements. Even countries not directly affected by conflict suffered the side effects of refugee influxes, trade disruptions and investment destabilisation.[1]

Resolution of Nicaragua's and El Salvador's civil wars took place against the backcloth of communism's downfall, a factor that has not expedited an end to Guatemala's conflict. But negotiations and concessions have left the political landscape littered with incomplete processes of democratisation, demilitarisation and institutional reform.[2] Central America's emerging liberal democracies stand on shaky foundations. Although liberal democratic systems—with their periodic competitive elections, legalised leftist political parties and modicums of freedom of speech and association—represent a shift from pre-conflict military regimes, evolving political structures fall short of guaranteeing the essential elements of a functioning democracy, defined as 'effective participation by individuals and groups, a system of accountability, and political equality.'[3] With few civic traditions, and the memory of cruel war still fresh for large sectors of the population socialised by decades of oppression and overbearing officialdom, experience teaches that survival is best assured by silence, pretence and ignorance—behaviour that is the antithesis of political participation.[4]

The region's social fabric has been stretched to breaking point by orthodox stabilisation programmes designed to restore macroeconomic balances, cut inflation and steer vulnerable economies towards new, outward-orientated growth. With budget-cutting, private sector promotion and the privatisation of public sector enterprises, inflation has been checked and budget deficits cut, but GDP growth rates remain sluggish. Benefits from privatisation have accentuated the gulf between an affluent minority and the poverty-stricken masses. Indeed, recent improvements in basic indices—infant mortality, access to potable water, life expectancy at birth—disguise deeper impoverishment trends, and the large and increasing numbers, mainly in rural areas, who live below the poverty line.[5]

Under donor pressure to improve equity and transparency in resource allocation, institutional reforms to increase access to basic services include decentralisation policies. Both money and responsibility have been delegated to organisations closer to consumers. Constitutional amendments have increased the funding for municipal government throughout Central America. For example, Guatemala has now made it mandatory for 8% of ordinary government revenue to go to the municipalities for capital investment. Decentralised poverty programmes like the social investment funds count on municipal governments to identify priority social infrastructure. Decentralisation policies also depend on the reconstitution of associational life; the success of educational reforms in El Salvador is wholly attributed to the fact that Community Education Associations contract teachers directly and manage school properties.[6] The dilemma for urban elites who monopolise political and economic power is that organised beneficiary participation creates conditions for greater grassroots democracy and broader local autonomy at the same time that it facilitates smaller, cheaper and more cost-effective government. A consensual solution to this contradiction is the problem of governance in Central America today.

The growth of nongovernmental organisations

The growth of NGO activity in Central America dates to the 1960s and to two consonant processes. On the one hand, heightened Northern public interest in development—sparked by the UN Development Decade and the Food and Agricultural Organization's (FAO) Freedom from Hunger campaign—created conditions for enhanced NGO fundraising. On the other hand, credible Southern counterparts that were competent to request funds, execute projects and provide narrative and financial reports, began to emerge out of Catholic action groups and Christian base communities, as well as community development and self-help groups sponsored by external actors like Peace Corps volunteers and field-based agencies such as Catholic Relief Services (CRS). Local NGO numbers also increased thanks to massive international disaster relief programmes mounted to respond to the 1972 Managua earthquake, the 1975 Honduran hurricane and the 1976 Guatemalan earthquake. In Guatemala, for example, in 1976 and 1977, over 150 new associations were registered each year, a 50% increase on the pre-earthquake rate.[7]

When war engulfed the region, the rate of increase slowed. New spaces for association were created in the latter half of the 1980s, however, as the scale of repression and level of fighting diminished and concerted peace efforts were pursued through the Contadura and Esquipulas processes. By 1989 there were over 700 NGOs in Guatemala;[8] in 1990 there were 300 Nicaraguan development NGOs;[9] and by 1992 there were over 700 Salvadoran development institutions and association, over half founded after 1985.[10]

The 1980s also witnessed a new phenomenon as the numbers of international NGOs operating in Central America increased sharply. Many took unprecedented decisions to establish field offices, especially those traditionally operating programmes from headquarters offices. Nicaragua was the most favoured location, and by 1989 there were over 100 international NGOs represented there. After the Sandinista electoral defeat, significant numbers of solidarity-type groups left the region while some development NGOs relocated elsewhere, especially in El Salvador and Guatemala, to take advantage of opportunities offered by changing political conditions. The crisis also attracted conservative, often evangelical, agencies that worked in the United States Agency for International Development (USAID) funded emergency programmes in Guatemala, Honduras and El Salvador. Project Hope and World Vision were recruited to work in El Salvador. Other groups such as Family Foundation of America, Direct Relief International and the Knights of Malta worked closely with Salvadoran armed forces in civic action programmes.

The scale of NGO funding questions the stereotype of NGOs as small players in Central America's unfolding drama. Hard data on funding is difficult to gather because of the large number of funding sources, but estimates put the annual level of funding at over $200 million annually at the end of the 1980s.[11] NGO poverty-related spending in some countries outstrips government poverty efforts. In Honduras for example, NGO poverty spending in 1989 was estimated at $50 million, twice the annual budget of the social investment fund, the government's main poverty safety net.[12] Equally, NGOs managed large and significant amounts of humanitarian assistance. In El Salvador, DIACONIA, an ecumenical organisation, alone received about $6 million annually starting in 1981, peaking at nearly $10 million in 1986 and again in 1989; its $65 million total income approached the $75 million spent by USAID through the government's displaced persons programme between 1982 and 1992.[13]

The nature of the relations between donors and local NGOs developed beyond the purely financial. Throughout the 1980s many donors, including some bilaterals, preferred to channel humanitarian assistance through NGO groups, despite improvements in government programmes, largely because external support was intended to impart a political as well as a humanitarian message. The abundant funding through the Moravian Church on Nicaragua's Atlantic

Coast, DIACONIA in El Salvador and Guatemala Catholic Church organisations conveyed donor repugnance with bloody government counterinsurgency policies.

External NGOs also used their engagement with the region as a vehicle to explain the region's crisis to their respective constituencies. As resources flooded into the region, information flowed out—with added credibility afforded to eye-witness reports provided by field staff based in the region. The power of information and the importance of lobbying converged on the impact of the contra war on Nicaragua's health and education development; humanitarian space to meet the demands of uprooted people; and human rights violations against civilian conflict victims and humanitarian workers. For example, the collaboration created by FUNDASAL, the Low-Cost Housing Foundation, with support from the San Salvador Archdiocese, to promote the 1986 Tenancingo repopulation project shifted the terms of debate on humanitarian assistance for Salvadoran displaced persons. This high-profile project supported by a range of donors—including European governments and NGOs reflecting Protestant, Catholic and non-confessional constituencies in the USA and Europe—minimised human rights abuses, gave new legitimacy to the needs of the displaced and accelerated the resettlement process by establishing the fact that civilians lived in the conflict zones.[14]

The political view of NGOs

The philanthropic view of NGOs held by donor governments is not one generally shared by Central American governments. In fact, governments of every political stripe have taken a political view of NGOs. Two historical phases, collaboration on modernisation and confrontation over empowerment, characterise the evolution of government and NGO relations.

Collaboration on modernisation

The modernisation paradigm dominated development planning during the 1960s and advocated expansion in basic social services to maintain high growth rates. It implied a transformation in the state's role in welfare provision, most clearly expressed in El Salvador as the shift 'from a patron system to one where the state covers health and social welfare'.[15] International and local NGOs shared modernisation's basic premises and developed significant involvement in welfare activities like food distribution and nutrition projects. Typically, Public Law 480 was channelled by US NGOs—for example, CRS to CARITAS for distribution to mother's clubs, parent–teacher associations and farmers' clubs engaged in school lunch, mother–child health, and food-for-work programmes. Convinced by arguments that drop-out rates and children's health would improve as a result of school lunch programmes, international NGOs like Oxfam paid for vehicles to transport personnel and food. Governments encouraged welfare programmes. At minimal cost, they gained credit for high-profile, national initiatives; for example, at the height of the Honduran school-lunch programme in the 1960s, over 100 000 school children were fed daily. Equally important for governments, NGO welfare programmes did nothing to challenge the official view that beneficiaries should be passive recipients of development rather than active participants.

Confrontation over empowerment

NGO and government collaboration virtually ended by the early 1970s, with the failure of the modernisation paradigm. With revenues stagnating, governments proved less willing to assume additional welfare spending.[16] Increasingly, NGOs also understood development less as welfare provision than as a fundamental societal transformation.

A major factor was the content of the Catholic Church's pastoral work with poor and landless peasants, which increasingly focused on leadership training, raising consciousness, and the creation of representative organisations.[17] A broad informal education movement based on methods of liberation theology changed people's attitudes towards prevailing social and economic structures in ways not controlled by government.[18] Under church protection and with international NGOs furnishing funds, social justice was incorporated into development programmes; and significantly, the first local human rights organisations were created.

Faced with faltering economic growth, with political authority eroded by increasingly autonomous organisations and in the context of growing guerrilla activities, governments perceived all NGO activity, but especially NGO rural development programmes, as a direct threat to national security. During the 1970s and 1980s, governments devised four distinct, yet complementary, policies—legal restrictions, repression, cooptation and the creation of competing associations—to control NGO activity. The four policies provide the essential framework for an analysis of UN and NGO relations in postwar Central America.

Legal restrictions.   Normative frameworks to regulate the activities of not-for-profit associations are relatively underdeveloped compared to those applied to for-profit businesses. At various times in the 1970s, governments citing national security considerations justified legislation to control the activities of development organisations. For example, in 1976 the Salvadoran government passed the Law of Community Cooperation and Development to curb community development and leadership programmes through their inscription in a central register. In 1977 the Law of the Defense and Guarantee of Public Order was enacted, which determined that public order was disturbed by those 'maintaining relations with foreigners or foreign organizations in order to receive aid or instruction of any type'.[19] In Guatemala, the impressive post-earthquake growth of the cooperative movement was shackled by the 1978 New Cooperative Law that effectively placed the cooperative movement under military control.[20]

Elected civilian governments have applied legal instruments more deftly than their military predecessors. Legal registration (*personeria juridica*) has been removed from the national security framework and subjected to differentially applied procedures. The move away from high-profile blanket measures permits a more selective 'administrative' approach that allows expeditious processing for 'politically correct' organisations and obstructive handling for those considered politically dubious. For example, in El Salvador the Fundacion Oriental Salvadorena de Reconstruccion y Desarrollo Integral is an NGO created in 1992 to work with the National Reconstruction Plan. With the Salvadoran vice-president's father as the NGO's president, the application for legal registration was handled by the minister of the interior and approved two months after the NGO's foundation. In contrast, the Fundación para la Autogestión y Solídaridad de los Trabajadores Salvadoreños, (FASTRAS), created in 1987 to work with uprooted people, and considered an FMLN affiliated organisation,[21] found its application stuck in a two-year procedural labyrinth, despite top-level mediation from the United Nations Observer Mission in El Salvador (ONUSAL) and the vice-president of the National Assembly.[22]

The FASTRAS case is not an isolated example, and other NGOs working with civilian war victims have faced similar problems. These delays are significant because they hinder institutional development. While it was possible to survive without legal registration during wartime, the postwar context demands that NGOs normalise their affairs. Without legal registration NGOs cannot open their own corporate account, a prerequisite to meet new donor standards on transparency, accounting and accountability.

Repression.   Physical attacks on NGOs started in the 1970s and the most severe repression targeted NGO beneficiary groups. Governments responded violently to the growth of peasant groups in El Salvador and to the expanding Guatemalan Cooperative movement. Self-help farmers' organisations were also systematically destroyed.[23] In the 1980s uprooted populations were methodically subjected to harassment, army abuses, disappearances and assassinations.[24] Four NGO types—human rights, training humanitarian and representative organisations of the uprooted—have been persistently targeted.

Governments have tried to destroy human rights NGOs since their creation. They have endured because of personal courage, the mix of financial, technical and political support received from international NGOs and survival strategies crafted to suit local conditions. For example, the Catholic Justice and Peace Commission and El Salvador's Tutela Legal operated under the umbrella of church protection, CODEH (Committee for the Defence of Human Rights in Honduras) in Honduras maintained an office and duplicate files in Mexico, and the Guatemala Human Rights Commission operated clandestinely from Mexico.[25] Pressure on training NGOs increased as open conflict erupted in the late 1970s. Rural training centres closed first—for example, the Salvadoran Foundation for Cooperative Promotion (FUNPROCOOP) training school in Nueva Concepcion—followed by NGOs like the Labour Studies and Training Center, (CEDET) and the Education Support Institute, INDAE that focused on trade union education in El Salvador and Honduras, respectively.

Attention turned to representative organisations of uprooted populations once they formed in the late 1980s. For their advocacy of civilian rights and negotiated solutions to conflicts, members of the National Council of Displaced Guatemalans (CONDEG), the National Co-ordination of Guatemalan Widows

(CONAVIGUA) and the Christian Committee for the Displaced of El Salvador (CRIPDES) were subjected to telephone death threats, break-ins, the publication of newspaper death lists and assassination. In Guatemala, violent repression continues despite the election of civilian governments. During the 1990–1994 period, seven CONDEG members disappeared or were murdered and its offices ransacked.[26] Similarly, NGOs attending to uprooted populations were harassed throughout the 1980s in an attempt to curtail their activities. Most survived because of strong international links and small, low budget, decentralised administrative operations; some, such as the Solaridarity Committee with Central American Peoples, COSPUCA in Honduras, perished.[27] NGOs documenting and researching issues related to uprooted populations were also intimidated because of their infringement into policy areas considered the armed forces' preserve; the most infamous case was the murder of Myrna Mack, an NGO researcher in Guatemala.

Cooptation. The greater a government's application of repression, the more inconsequential the use of cooptation. Traditionally, Guatemalan and Salvadoran governments have not coopted NGOs to control them; an exception in El Salvador was an unsuccessful attempt led by USAID to bring CRS, the Mennonites and Save the Children USA into the government's emergency programme. Cooptation was most fruitfully used by the Sandinista government.

Two basic preconditions existed in 1980s Nicaragua. The first was a broad consonance between government, local and international NGOs about the meaning of development; and the second was the NGO willingness to subject institutional priorities to official ones by working through two coordinating agencies—one a government department, the other representing Sandinista affiliated popular organisations. With this precedent established over the first two years, NGOs subsequently collaborated easily with the Sandinista government's humanitarian programme as the country slid into conflict.

The NGO ability to appreciate the political implications of the humanitarian situation was quickly overwhelmed, and as their capacity to intercede with the government weakened, their ability to act independently was eroded. A close association with the Sandinista cause led some NGOs to refrain from relief work with Nicaraguans fleeing as refugees to neighbouring countries. Moreover, as NGOs became instruments of government policy, they failed to realise how much humanitarian assistance was part of the government's counterinsurgency and pacification strategy.

Competing NGOs. Two interrelated processes contributed to the growth in NGO numbers. A renaissance of grassroots organisations is evident, which was facilitated by donor focus on community-based development, a neoliberal ideology extolling self-help, and the advent of dynamic organisations of uprooted people that energised other marginal populations to reorganise. The process is most salient in El Salvador, where displaced groups accelerated the resettlement movement by their links with urban squatter and cooperative organisations, and in Guatemala, where refugee repatriation has led to the rejuvenation of production cooperatives, albeit as 'communal enterprises'. The grassroots revival has yet to reproduce the 1960s organisational density, but its significance clearly registered with Central American governments.

Mindful of the creative force represented by grass roots, political elites have devised a two-part strategy. While encouraging the arrival of US pentecostal church agencies, they have also organised their own NGOs. This process of elites forming NGOs is most developed in El Salvador and Guatemala. The Salvadoran business sector has created organisations through. Fortalecimiento de Associaciones FORTRAS, a USAID funded, the Salvadoran Foundation for Economic and Social Development FUSADES-located initiative.[28] In its first stage, FORTRAS supported the creation of organisations like the Business Fund for Educational Development, FEPADE, the Safety at Work Foundation, FIPRO, and Habitat, a housing foundation, capable of taking over government functions identified for privatisation. In its second stage, FORTRAS works with local business interests to create local development foundations as a counterweight to grassroots groups created bottom-up.[29] Private sector development foundations are closely connected to the governing National Republican Alliance (ARENA) party, facilitating movement of personnel into government and access to poverty funds from programmes like the social investment fund.

Guatemalan business interests have also created NGOs. But unlike El Salvador, where government's role was to encourage the private sector to create NGOs around the privatisation programme, the government in Guatemala has been directly involved in NGO creation, especially to execute micro-enterprise programmes.[30] The overall objective, however, is the same—the creation of enterprise culture NGOs to contest the associational space of those NGOs advocating empowerment.

As conflicts recede, the NGO community is characterised by fundamental contradictions. Though more numerous, the NGO community is more divided and heterogeneous. In many respects, its future is more uncertain than ever. A vibrant, initiative seizing sector of small, decentralised NGOs and grassroots groups, experienced in dealing with humanitarian issues, faces the challenge of acquiring skills to participate effectively in postwar reconstruction. Versed in human rights denunciation, human rights NGOs have to consider the strategies promoting a broader human rights agenda. Postwar political realignments within opposition forces test the ability of NGOs to achieve autonomy over policy, decision making and programming. It is precisely at this moment of transition that UN agencies identified NGO comparative advantage and began their efforts to get closer to them.

The evolving UN role in Central America

UN agencies traditionally provide technical assistance to line ministries. With few exceptions, notably UNHCR and UNICEF, UN agencies have lagged behind other official donors in their NGO relations. It was with the Partners in Development Program and the drafting of operational guidelines in 1988 that the UNDP created a framework for NGO relations. In the absence of a regional strategy, the regionwide evolution of UNDP–NGO relations has been patchy.[31] Similarly, it was only in 1991 that the Pan American Health Organization (PAHO) adopted a policy permitting programme relations with NGOs that 'possess local perspectives on health issues, embody indigenous knowledge and mobilize poor people in health related activities'.[32] Indeed, substantive NGO engagement was initiated by the UN's efforts outside the established agency system.

The UN's rapid task expansion in Central America into peacekeeping, peace-building and postwar reconstruction began in 1989.[33] The United Nations Observer Mission to verify the Electoral Process in Nicaragua (ONUVEN), the UN's first essay into verification of domestic elections in a sovereign state, was accompanied by the United Nations Observer Group in Central America (ONUCA), which was established to verify security aspects of the Esquipulas Agreements. The UN Observer Mission in El Salvador (ONUSAL) monitored human rights before the ceasefire—a significant advance over previous human rights reporting, which then served as the prototype in late 1994 for the UN's human rights verification mission in Guatemala (MINUGUA).

The UN's Special Economic Cooperation Plan (PEC) provided the framework for the International Conference on Central American Refugees (CIREFCA) and the Development Program for Refugees, Displaced and Repatriated Persons in Central America (PRODERE). Established to promote international assistance for refugees, repatriated and displaced persons in Mexico and Central America, CIREFCA evolved as a mechanism bringing together public agencies, national and international NGOs, official donors and beneficiary groups. With UNHCR as the lead agency, CIREFCA promoted projects and fundraising, disseminated information, and brought national refugee policies into line with accepted international standards.[34] PRODERE promoted the social and economic reintegration of more than two million uprooted people. The Italian government financed this five-year, $115 million relief, rehabilitation and development programme. PRODERE operated regionwide, but it emphasised conflict zones in refugee expulsion countries. Executed by the UNDP's Office for Project Services and with institutional collaboration from the International Labour Office (ILO), PAHO and UNHCR, PRODERE was originally part of CIREFCA but soon evolved into an independent programme.

With their involvement in human rights, humanitarian assistance for repatriated refugees, relief and development programmes with uprooted persons— already established key areas of NGO activity—ONUSAL, CIREFCA and PRODERE have closely involved nongovernmental organisations. This was all the more the case for ONUSAL's and PRODERE's decentralised programmes, backed by substantial human, financial and logistical resources, and armed with specific, short-term, operational mandates. Moreover, ONUSAL, CIREFCA and PRODERE critically redefined the context in which NGOs operate. The discussion of their impact on NGO development is organised around four themes: displacement, opportunity generation, capacity-building, and legalisation.

Displacement.   During the Salvadoran civil war, nongovernmental organisations were conspicuous as the only consistent reporters of human rights violations. The immediate effect of ONUSAL's human rights presence was to prevent further human rights violations. But the anticipated strengthening of national NGOs and institutions to monitor and protect human rights did not occur. ONUSAL's human rights work effectively sidelined the human rights work of NGOs and the Catholic Church, and it failed to collaborate with these organisations to redefine their role in a postwar situation.[35] Similarly, PRODERE acted with scant concern for NGOs, especially during the programme's initial emergency stage. Nongovernmental organisations were not involved in the selection of priority regions where PRODERE chose to focus its activities with the result that, rather than see complementarity between its own and NGO activities, PRODERE tended to ignore the contributions of nongovernmental organisations familiar with its priority regions. Initial NGO participation was largely confined to subcontracting as executing agents, but not as partners with a view to enhancing NGO capacity and establishing project sustainability.

Opportunity generation. CIREFCA created opportunities for local NGOs to participate in refugee policy discussions that were instrumental in bringing the NGOs 'from the shadows to center stage'.[36] By their participation at CIREFCA international meetings and their critical involvement in the definition of country refugee strategies, NGOs demonstrated a deep understanding of assistance. Increased access to official donors confirmed NGOs as legitimate counterparts. Activities around CIREFCA also initiated a process of institutional expansion with the formation of national associations of NGOs working with uprooted people and the creation of a regional association, Asociatión Regional para les Migraciones Forzadas, ARMIF. Joint activities served to strengthen communications between the UNHCR and NGOs, which had been strained earlier by differences over protection and repatriation policies.

The impact of PRODERE is more ambiguous. ARMIF is harshly critical of PRODERE, claiming it appropriated existing NGO structures and programmes.[37] Hyperbole notwithstanding, NGOs have a legitimate complaint about PRODERE's salary policy, which distorted local NGO salary scales and led to an exodus of NGO workers to better paid PRODERE jobs. However, over the short term, PRODERE has effectively helped to broker agreements between repatriated refugees in Guatemala and El Salvador and the respective education ministries to address long-standing grievances and incorporate teachers formed in the refugee camps into official education systems.

New spaces for participation also emerge from PRODERE's territorial planning approach. The creation, first of municipal planning committees to discuss community-level development priorities and subsequently departmental planning committees, has set in motion a series of processes permitting historically excluded populations to have a voice in setting priorities for community development. Similarly, the establishment of Local Health Systems (SILOS), Education Systems (SILED) and Human Rights Systems (SILPRODEH) with across-the-board representation of all interested parties has opened additional spaces for participation where historically polarised actors meet to discuss and decide upon sector-specific and human rights issues. Through their active engagement in these arenas, many popular sector grassroots organisations have gained unprecedented legitimacy. Yet institutional NGOs are circumspect about the new local participatory spaces. Though marginal to their creation, these NGOs are nevertheless key actors in their consolidation, which poses challenges to NGOs to assume new roles by working with municipal governments. This relationship had been anathema to NGOs and municipal governments alike; neither NGOs nor municipal governments were prepared for it.

Capacity building.   Creating opportunity is not always accompanied by building capacity support. The scaling up of NGOs that resulted from increased funding through CIREFCA was not matched by training for institutional strengthening. PRODERE's capacity-building activities have also tended to target agencies created by PRODERE rather than existing NGOs. Strategic thinking about priorities for capacity-building has been lacking within PRODERE. For example, municipal planning committees depend on strong NGO–municipal relations; but it was in early 1995, just four months before PRODERE's close that the first seminar on NGO and local government relations took place in El Salvador. Even then PRODERE figured more as a funder than as the initiator of the initiative.[38]

Capacity-building requires a long-term commitment of resources and sits uncomfortably within short-term operational interventions and their demand for immediate results. Institutions averse to risk also avoid capacity-building through 'learning by doing'. Thus, UNHCR selected an international NGO experienced with UNHCR accounting and reporting procedures to manage its Quick Impact Projects (QIPs) initiative in Nicaragua, thereby rejecting the alternative of investing in institutional training of local NGOs. UNHCR's practice of creating its own NGOs when it considers that there are no or too few reliable counterparts who can oversee opportunities for capacity-building. Furthermore, this practice can undermine existing NGOs already surviving with scarce legitimacy in a cash-strapped environment.

Faced with the problem of delivering assistance to repatriated Salvadoran refugees at a moment when existing NGOs had little credibility, UNHCR decided to create a dedicated NGO called the Salvadoran Integral Support Association (ASAI). Over the short term, existing NGOs were weakened, but over the longer term, as space opened up around the CIREFCA process, UNHCR began to work directly with NGOs representing the uprooted population, and ASAI itself became a respected, innovative and independent NGO.

Legalisation.   As noted earlier, PRODERE played an important role legitimising NGO activities, but it was also key in obtaining their legal papers. By taking advantage of decentralisation policies that extended municipal legal powers, PRODERE acted as the catalyst through which many local NGOs and representative organisations working in PRODERE-designated priority areas have been legalised. Paradoxically, this is an indication of evolving consensus and reconciliation. In El Salvador, ARENA mayors granted legal status to grassroots groups representing populations inhabiting former guerrilla zones. Despite attempts to broaden the impact through training programmes that advise mayors concerning their legal powers to grant legal status, the real constraint has been the absence of a strong external countervailing political force capable of mediating with mayors to exercise their authority in this area expeditiously, responsibly and prudently. Consequently, the significant efforts at normalising NGOs and associations institutionally have remained localised.

Collaboration over governance: an agenda for future action

As the special UN programmes end, UNDP will primarily be responsible for moving forward the UN–NGO partnership. It is sobering to recall here CIREFCA's lesson. The close NGO collaboration with UNHCR concerning humanitarian problems was not transferred to the UNDP's leadership of CIREFCA. Without smooth coordination among ONUSAL and UN organisations, there was a lack of synergy between ONUSAL's political, human rights and peace-building work and UN development efforts.[39] With little attention paid to working with national organisations that were capable of sustaining the progress made, ONUSAL may repeat the post-CIREFCA experience. Undoubtedly, there is a sustainability lesson here for MINUGUA.

PRODERE, however, leaves a solid framework for continued UN and NGO collaboration. The basis for future relations is the successful incorporation of social justice and human rights components into a recovery and rehabilitation programme. PRODERE has also prodded individual agencies into greater operational contact with NGOs. For example, PAHO has positioned itself to continue its work with SILOS and community-based health providers. In Guatemala specifically, full-time PAHO human resources have been relocated from Guatemala City to the departments as part of the institution's decentralisation policy.

Because of its close relations with Central American governments and its country offices and because the UNDP itself is rethinking its institutional mandate, it can position itself to play a significant role in bringing together governments and NGOs to discuss and exchange ideas about the promotion of participatory development. Prioritising NGO involvement in the development process is consistent not only with the UNDP's model of sustainable local human development, but also with the growing consensus about the importance of improved and broader stakeholder participation, which is understood as enhanced government ownership and beneficiary involvement in the design and execution of policies, programmes and projects. The pace and direction of progress will depend on the opportunities provided by a specific national context, but the vision and commitment of the UNDP resident representative in each country remains a key factor. In this respect, the first UNDP and NGO discussion on human development promotion in El Salvador was held in April 1994 and was a step towards creating greater mutual confidence and an opportunity to agree on work plans. Similarly, the UNDP has facilitated the first joint government, NGO and UNDP planning exercise in Honduras with the Human Development Program for Western Honduras, designed as the post-PRODERE programme.

However, with heightened attention paid to NGOs and as humanitarian NGOs adapt to different demands posed by postwar reconstruction, there is greater scrutiny of their comparative advantage. The small-scale nature of most NGO activities is dwarfed by the magnitude of existing development problems. Conditioned by the experience acquired during their formative wartime years, many NGOs have been slow to meet new development challenges. Although the process of decentralisation now underway in most Central American countries has created new opportunities, few NGOs have taken advantage by entering into new and innovative partnerships with public sector institutions, especially local municipal governments.

Moreover, NGOs have been unable to enter into national development dialogues on economic and social policy and poverty reduction with the institutional weight, clarity and vision that is necessary to influence policy formulation and decision making over resource allocation. Although national NGOs are significant counterparts for international NGO and bilateral cooperation, they have not convinced sceptical national governments of their potential. Given the recent history of state and NGO relations, it is not surprising that NGOs have failed to contribute to national legislative and development policy debates by promoting institutional reforms that foster participatory development. Also, NGOs and beneficiary organisations have not become important channels for public resources, even when the public sector has a recognised incapacity to spend money.

Donor policies are critical. Dependence on external sources of funds has acted as a disincentive to NGOs that seek access to national public resources. The deep insertion of local NGOs into the project and policy-making processes of bilateral donors and international NGOs contrasts with their marginal role in channelling public resources and gaining access to national policy-makers. Central American governments have not been convinced about potential NGO contributions to development. NGOs have also not been challenged about their reluctance to modify confrontational stances to seek negotiated changes in development practice. The resulting situation is as discrepant over the short term, as it is unsustainable over the long term.

A gap between government and nongovernmental organisations clearly exists that acts as a major constraint on sustainable development and effective democratic practice. Collaboration with government brings uncertainties, including the risk that NGOs will compromise themselves and lose their independence. To ensure effective partnership, the NGO sector must be strengthened. There are three areas where UNDP involvement could strengthen the NGO sector.

First, existing regulatory frameworks need an urgent overhaul. In the absence of well defined and fastidiously implemented frameworks to regulate nongovernmental organisations without compromising their activities, they are unable to develop institutionally. Ill defined and arbitrarily applied regulations also stifle initiative and act as a disincentive to forming new associations. Without attention to this critical issue, civic action is in danger of emasculation that results in the atrophy of local associations. There are dangers involved in any attempt at regulatory reform, as shown by experience in other parts of the world where amendments to normative frameworks are introduced as much to control NGOs as to enhance their development capacity. However, PRODERE's support for NGO legalisation in Central America has set a precedent in this delicate area. UNDP should take this work forward, implementing strategies to collaborate jointly with governments and nongovernmental organisations, and create fair and transparent NGO regulatory frameworks that afford equal priority to those developed for the profit sector.[40] Working collaboratively with government takes on particular importance in states that ascribe limited urgency to regulating associational economic and social activity. The work initiated by the Common-wealth Foundation is indicative of the type of process that could be applied in Central America.[41] Guidelines for good policy and practice were produced after a series of regional consultations, feedback on earlier drafts and workshops.[42] Apart from their ratification by Commonwealth NGOs, these guidelines hold the potential of being incorporated into mainstream government thinking and of becoming benchmarks for assessing NGO and governmental relations.

Second, the diversity and pluralism of NGOs in Central America, which have contributed to civil society's reawakening, must work in favour of good development. Donor agencies face a real dilemma. By equating the number of nongovernmental organisations with the deepening of democratisation, the result is a large and varied number of small, weak and under-resourced groups, whose contribution to development is often negligible and whose presence precipitates the erosion of necessary state development efforts when government responsibil-ities are jettisoned in favour of the NGO sector. The collective impact of small-scale NGO activities was demonstrated during the war years, when the proliferation of small NGOs and grassroots groups that emerged by guaranteeing the delivery of emergency assistance to communities of uprooted people eroded repressive state authority, as governments failed in their attempts to close the spaces for humanitarian action.

In postwar conditions, however, NGO fragmentation is a liability when it prevents the organisation of strong representative bodies to promote their collective interests and is a barrier to programme coordination. Fragmented NGO sectors hinder the effectiveness of resource-starved NGO associations. With their narrow membership base, NGO associations are unable to play an influential role in creating real commitment to greater coordination at the programme level. Individual NGO development efforts therefore have limited localised benefits at best, and are likely to be plagued by the competition between small-scale, socially and economically unsustainable projects.[43]

An important UNDP contribution therefore lies in mobilising donor support for strengthening NGO representational and advocacy capacity and in supporting the creation of frameworks for coordination between NGOs as well as between them and government. With its permanent in-country presence, UNDP could also play an important monitoring role reporting to donors on the broad trends affecting NGO evolution and advising donors on the wider development consequences of their specific NGO funding. Such roles would demand that UNDP builds adequate capacity with respect to its understanding of NGO roles in governance.

Third, NGOs have to democratise more by deepening their relations with their beneficiaries. Wartime conditions were not conducive to the organisation of time-consuming and expensive consultations. Difficult access was a barrier to quick and effective communication and information sharing. Benefits do accrue from involving beneficiaries, and organisations that give priority to this dimen-sion are strengthened.[44] Postwar conditions thus demand NGOs and donors reappraise policies. Funding for beneficiary meetings and newsletters can help create or improve NGO accountability. Whatever one's political views, the annual meeting of Nicaragua's Sandino Foundation (FACS) is a useful opportunity for beneficiaries to shape institutional policy, report on the impact of programmes and create beneficiary networks. Regular consultations further legitimise FACS as an institution able to speak for a wide constituency. In contrast, significant internal restructuring and policy changes without beneficiary consultation can seriously weaken NGO credibility. The numerous Salvadoran NGOs undergoing behind-the-scenes organisational changes as a result of the fallout from the political debates within the opposition set a poor example of transparency and democracy in practice. Consequently, nongovernmental organisations project themselves as party entities more concerned about politics than organisations dedicated to providing benefits to a constituency with a voice in determining organisational policies and programmes.

Conclusion

The NGO sector in Central America is at a critical juncture. Its ability to weather the conflicts of the 1980s as a robust and growing sector is a display of its versatility and durability. As the NGO sector manoeuvers to deal with the challenges of postwar recovery and democratisation, it must address critical shortcomings. After two decades of confrontation with the state, nongovernmental organisations are not fully prepared to deal with the processes that are inevitably propelling them into collaborative situations with governments. Without concerted support to strengthen NGO sectors through legalisation, enhanced technical capacity, effective coordination and greater accountability, there is a danger that NGOs will be unable to realise their potential contribution to development and democratisation.

The United Nations system plays a key role in supporting NGO institution-building and in helping to direct associational energies into policy making, and demands that the state perform better. But in assisting NGOs to meet these new challenges, the UN system and the UNDP specifically must also change. The UN's special programmes show how UN organisations can significantly affect NGOs, even when they are not directly working with them. If the UN system is to become an effective advocate for people's participation in the decisions that affect their lives and in government responsiveness, it will need to reposition itself with respect to the state. To play a role as arbiter successfully, the United Nations system should become less of an extension of government and more an extension of civil society within government; it should be less tied to the provision of sectoral technical assistance and more capable and adept at influencing the creation and shape of policy environments encouraging and guaranteeing the participation of all development actors. Unless these issues are addressed, a true partnership comprising equal members is unlikely to emerge.

Notes

The author would like to thank Mary Anderson, L David Brown and Caroline Moser as well as participants at the ACUNS workshop on Nongovernmental Organizations, the United Nations and Global Governance for their comments on an earlier draft. The author accepts the usual responsibilities.

[1] Sylvia Saborio, 'Central America', in John Williamson (ed), *Latin American Adjustment: How Much Has Happened?*, Washington: Institute for International Economics, 1991, pp 279–302.

[2] A fine survey of political developments is found in James Dunkerley, *The Pacification of Central America*, London: Verso, 1994.

[3] Richard Fagen, 'The politics of transition', in R Fagen, C Deere and J L Corragio (eds), *Transition and Development*, New York: Monthly Review Press, 1986.

[4] The concept of the 'rationality of distrust', developed by Gerrit Huizer to explain the motivation for peasants' lack of participation in community development projects in 1950s El Salvador is still relevant today. See Gerrit Huizer, *Peasant Rebellion in Latin America*, London: Penguin, 1973.

[5] According to the UN secretary-general's 1994 report on Nicaragua, 75% of Nicaraguan families live below the poverty line, with 44% in extreme poverty. See *International Assistance for the Rehabilitation and Reconstruction of Nicaragua: Aftermath of the War and Natural Disasters*, report of the secretary-general, 49th Session of the General Assembly, item 23. Nicaragua's acute situation is not unique; the number of Hondurans living in poverty increased from 67% to 73% between 1989 and 1992. See Dunkerley, *The Pacification of Central America*, p 18. Also see UNDP, *Human Development Report 1990*, New York: Oxford University Press, 1990 and; UNDP, *Human Development Report 1992*, New York: Oxford University Press, 1992.

[6] Under the EDUCO project, there are now 1700 community-managed schools with over 70 000 pre- and primary school children in the poorest municipalities. See World Bank, *El Salvador: The Challenge of Poverty Reduction*, Washington: World Bank, 1994.

[7] Avancso–IDESAC, *ONGS, Sociedad Civil y Estado en Guatemala: Elementos para el Debate*, Guatemala: mimeo, 1989.

[8] IDESAC, SERJUS & SOJUGMA, *El Fenomeno de las ONGs en Guatemala*, Guatemala: mimeo, 1990.

[9] CAPRI, *Directorio ONG de Nicaragua*, Managua: CAPRI, 1990.

[10] UNDP, *Directorio de Instituciones Privados de Desarrollo de El Salvador*, UNDP: San Salvador, 1992.

[11] In 1988 European and North American NGOs channelled between $200 and $250 million to Central America. See Eric Holt, *Las ONGs y la crisis centroamericana*, Managua: Cries, 1988; in 1992 European NGOs alone were spending an estimated $180 to $200 million in the region. See Kees Biekart, *La Cooperacion No-Gubernamental Europea hacia Centroamerica: La Experiencia de los Ochenta y las Tendencias en los Noventa*, San Salvador: PRISMA, 1994. These figures represent a two-fold increase from the early 1980s, when according to the author's own estimates, European funding was between $100 and $130 million.

[12] The figures on NGO poverty spending come from World Bank, BTOR *on Development NGOs in Honduras*, Washington: mimeo, 1989. The Honduran Social Fund is scheduled to spend $23 million annually over the 1995–1998 period.

[13] Cristina Equizabal, David Lewis, Larry Minear, Peter Sollis & Tom Weiss, *Humanitarian Challenges in Central America: Learning the Lessons of Recent Armed Conflicts*, Occasional Paper No 14, Providence, RI: Watson Institute, 1993.

[14] Peter Sollis, 'Displaced persons and human rights: the crisis in El Salvador', *Bulletin of Latin American Research*, 11(1), 1992, pp 49–67.

[15] H Blumstein, E Betters, J Cobb, J Leonard & C Townsend, *Area Handbook for El Salvador*, Washington DC: American University Press, 1971.

[16] Government commitment to welfare spending was always fragile. The Salvadoran government built health centres only under US pressure to comply with Alliance for Progress ideals, pressure that infuriated the oligarchy, who protested to the US Ambassador. See Walter LaFeber, *Inevitable Revolutions: The United States in Central America*, New York: Norton, 1984 p 174.

[17] Beyond its 'option for the poor', the critical issue of liberation theology was the activity it engendered to transform the poor from passive bystanders into active participants in their own development. See for example, Carlos Cabarrus, *Genesis de Una Revolucion: Analisis del Surgimiento y Desarrollo de la Organisacion Campesina en El Salvador*, Mexico DF: Ediciones de la Casa Chata, 1983.

[18] Between 1967 and 1974, 11 Christian-oriented rural training centres were established in El Salvador, espousing the 'training of pastoral agents of, and for, rural areas in the spirit of renovation outlined by Vatican II'. See Secretariado Social Interdioscesano, *Guia de Entidades de Ispiracion Cristiana que Promueven el Desarrollo*, San Salvador: mimeo, 1975. A similar expansion of training centres occurred elsewhere in Central America. See Philip Berryman, *The Religious Roots of Rebellion*, London: SCM Press, 1984.

[19] James Dunkerley, *The Long War: Dictatorship and Revolution in El Salvador*, London: Junction Books, 1982.

[20] Centro de Estudios e Investigaciones para Guatemala (CEIG), *Contrainsurgencia y Desarrollo Rural en Guatemala 1965–1985*, Mexico: CEIG, 1986.

[21] General Accounting Office (GAO), *El Salvador: Role of Nongovernment Organisations in Postwar Recon-struction*, Washington, DC: GAO, 1992.

[22] FASTRAS first applied for legalisation in April 1991. A routine procedure turned into a bureaucratic nightmare when a discretionary clause was used to send the application to seven government ministries and agencies

for their comments. The application was returned to FASTRAS by the Interior Ministry for modifications. A second application was submitted in February 1992. This time the Interior Ministry approved the papers and passed them to the Minister of the Presidency for final approval by the President of the Republic. The application then got stuck in the Minister of the Presidency's office for over a year with no explanation for the delay. See 'En busca de la Personeria Juridica', *Desarrollo Integral*, 5, June 1993, pp 32–33.

[23] Integrated rural development programmes that were a common feature of the development landscape in the 1970s had disappeared by 1980. Such programmes taught improved agricultural techniques, soil conservation, health, hygene and literacy. El Salvador was organised by the Catholic Church and funded by international NGOs. Participants abandoned the scheme over the 1979–1980 period when the National Guard began killing leaders, hacking them to death and leaving them as a warning. See Raymond Bonner, *Weakness and Deceit*, New York: Times Books, 1984, pp 83–84. The destruction of integrated development programmes in Guatemala is chronicled in CEIG, *Contrainsurgencia*, and Shelton Davis & Julie Hodgson, *Witness to Political Violence in Guatemala: The Destruction of a Rural Development Movement*, Boston, MA: Oxfam America, 1982.

[24] For example, see Iain Guest & Diane Orentlicher, *Honduras: A Crisis on the Border*, New York: Lawyers Committee for International Human Rights, 1985; and Lawyers Committee for International Human Rights, *El Salvador's Other Victims: The War on the Displaced*, New York: Americas Watch and Lawyers Committee for International Human Rights, 1984.

[25] The Guatemala Human Rights Commission operated underground, since previous attempts to start a Human Rights Commission had ended in the murder and disappearance of the organisers. A Guatemala office was finally opened in early 1995, some 15 years after the commission's foundation.

[26] Anne Manuel, Human Rights Watch/Americas & Greta Tovar Siebentritt, *Human Rights in Guatemala during President de Leon Carpio's First Year*, New York: Human Rights Watch, 1994, pp 80–85.

[27] Sollis, 'Displaced persons'; and Equizabal *et al*, *Humanitarian Challenges*.

[28] The USAID factor is important here since FUSADES itself is a USAID funded, private sector organisation that as the think tank of the ARENA party created the current neoliberal policy framework.

[29] The first was FUNDECOYO, the Development Foundation of Tepecoyo, founded by 55 members, the majority coffee producers. See Herman Rosa, *El Papel de la Asistencia de AID en el Fortalecimiento de Nuevas Instituciones del Sector Privado y en la Transformacion Global de la Economia Salvadorena: El caso de FUSADES*, paper delivered at the XVII LASA Congress, Los Angeles, September 1992.

[30] IDESAC *et al*, *El Fenomeno*.

[31] In 1991, even with the guidelines in place, the resident representative in El Salvador was mindful of the stricture about entering into relations with NGOs not approved by the government. Before the peace accords, the UNDP did not have good contacts with one of the most important development actors. The responsibility for NGO liaison was given to a junior official who also dealt half-time with Belize. The error of this policy still cuts across UNDP and NGO relations today.

[32] PAHO, *Collaboration between Governments and Non-Governmental Organizations: A Proposal to Establish New Precedents for Health Care in the Americas*, Washington DC: mimeo, 1991.

[33] S Neil MacFarlane & Thomas G Weiss, 'The United Nations, regional organisations and human security: building theory in Central America', *Third World Quarterly*, 2, 1994, pp 277–295.

[34] Adolfo Aguilar Zinzer, CIREFCA, The Promises and Reality of the International Conference on Central American Refugees, Washington, DC: Hemispheric Migration Project, 1991.

[35] David Holiday & William Stanley, 'Building the peace: preliminary lessons from El Salvador', *Journal of International Affairs*, 46(2), 1993, pp 415–438.

[36] Sergio Aguayo, *From the Shadows to Center Stage: NGOs and Central America Refugee Assistance*, Washington, DC: Hemispheric Migration Project, 1991.

[37] ARMIF, *Reflexiones Generales del Proceso PRODERE en Centroamerica desde La Perspectiva de las ONGS*, mimeo, Managua 1994.

[38] PRODERE was only one of four donors and the seminar was organised by the Fundacion Salvadorean de Apoyo Integral (FUSAI), with technical support from CELCADEL.

[39] Equizabal *et al*, *Humanitarian Challenges*, p 51.

[40] To date, most multilateral activity concerning legal reform has focused on legal and regulatory frameworks governing economic life. The World Bank, for example, has focused on countries in transition from command to market economies with support for enactment of privatisation, banking, bankruptcy and commercial laws, etc. With attention focused on the private for-profit sector, little, if any, concern has been paid to the framework governing NGO activity despite the expressions of support for the NGO sector. The stark imbalance between efforts supporting private business and the absence of activities supporting NGO development, despite protestations about NGO importance in development, is found in World Bank, *Governance: The World Bank's Experience*, Washington DC: World Bank, 1994.

[41] Personal communication from Ian Smillie.

[42] Commonwealth Foundation, *Non-Governmental Organisations: Guidelines for Good Policy and Practice*, London: Commonwealth Foundation, 1995.

[43] An example from El Salvador illustrates the general problems faced. It concerns an NGO-organised project to renovate coffee plantations with the potential to produce organic coffee for export. The beneficiaries are squatters awaiting land title, so uncertainty clouds their future. Despite agreements on areas apt for renovation and those most suited to subsistence crop cultivation, large areas of steep mountainside have been cleared of coffee bushes for maize cultivation. The decision to break the coffee agreement was made after a second NGO approached the farmers with an offer of subsidised credit for maize and beans cultivation. Unable to think long-term, the farmers took advantage of short-term opportunities. The future of organic coffee production is now uncertain. The only certainty is that there will be four or five good maize harvests until the topsoil is completely washed away.

[44] The Community Development Councils of Morazan and San Miguel enjoyed a strong mandate because of its foundation in 1988 at a meeting of 156 delegates representing 25 000 uprooted people.

■ Part 4 ■
Conclusions

▪ 11 ▪

NGO Participation in the International Policy Process

LEON GORDENKER AND THOMAS G WEISS

When viewed from the central vantage point of the United Nations (UN), each of the case studies above produces significant evidence that nongovernmental organisations (NGOs) have joined states as participants in organised international relations. At the same time, the principal participants in making policies and executing programmes in the international institutions in the UN realm remain government representatives. In each of the case studies, a complex set of equations emerges in which the variables are NGOs, intergovernmental organisations (IGOs) and governments.

Simple reference to these three categories of participants has a superficial and misleading quality. Day-to-day work is accomplished by people who, it can be assumed, have a variety of instructions or none at all from their governments or organisations. Relationships between NGOs and the United Nations vary from distant and indirect in the case of grassroots organisations to virtual equality in some human rights activities. In some instances, as in Partners in Action (PARinAC), mentioned by Cyril Ritchie in his essay on coalitions of organisations, the participation of NGOs as executing agencies is eagerly sought by an IGO, in this case the UN High Commission for Refugees (UNHCR), acting on behalf of governments. In other cases, as in the creation of environmental policies, as illustrated by Ken Conca, NGO participation has barely begun. Similarly, in the case of AIDS, described by Christer Jönsson and Peter Söderholm, NGOs participated in framing the epidemic as an international issue but had little direct role at the global level in managing programmes.

At the same time, in quantitative terms without reference to the character and aims of NGOs associated with the UN complex, the sheer numbers have mounted steadily and will likely stay at a high level. Moreover, the fact of mounting numbers has led—as suggested in the essay on coalitions, and in the case of Central America examined by Peter Sollis—to the creation of specialized meta-organisations. Yet the precise purposes of such coalitions, their membership and their relationships with IGOs and governments vary widely.

Reflections on theoretical approaches

Such descriptive conclusions only strengthen the scepticism expressed at the outset of this volume on the usefulness of conventional theoretical approaches to NGOs. The case studies describe nongovernmental organisations that challenge governments and their intergovernmental creations, even as these NGOs work parallel with governments and other NGOs that, in some respects, operate almost seamlessly with governments. Moreover, the attitude and actions of governments with respect to NGOs are hardly amenable to conventional strategic, zero-sum-based analyses that emphasise the power of competing states. It would make little sense, for instance, to attribute the activities of NGOs in Central America to the presumably overwhelming power of the United States. Nor would it explain much about human rights organisations to insist that their role is ultimately explained in the same manner.

Yet in varying magnitudes, states dispose of the most effective and far-reaching administrative apparatuses on earth. Both IGOs and NGOs, which for the sake of argument are assumed to be independent, usually need at least acquiescence from the state apparatus to operate effectively and reach goals. Governments engage IGOs to organise some of their cooperative common ventures, contributing funds as well as administrative capacities. Usually governments can ultimately open the way to, or suppress, NGO and IGO activities. Consequently, much activity attempts to convince governmental representatives at home and in IGO settings to take seriously, defer to, or follow NGO propositions.

In fact, all the case studies touch on a range of relationships between governments and NGOs. These are sometimes hierarchical, where governments exercise control over NGOs. As for IGOs, the fundamental effect on nongovernmental organisations has to do with access, which has become progressively broader and deeper. IGOs can also employ control by denial of, for instance, information or sometimes finances. Thus, many collaborative and cooperative relationships that mute conflicts between NGOs, governments and IGOs emerge from the case studies.

These findings support the proposition that a social approach and in particular interorganisation theory offers a promising way to understand the NGO phenomenon better. Further work would develop deeper information on how NGOs are constructed and how they operate. Interorganisation theory emphasises the quality of contact among NGOs through their personnel and among distinct policy and activity sectors; it does not assume a monolithic character of governments and IGOs. It makes identification of leaders and their organisational roles easier. In discussing NGO activity on AIDS, Jönsson and Söderholm explicitly use this approach to disclose the complexity and dynamism of relationships between NGOs and global IGO activity.

However, much remains to be done to approach a comprehensive theory of NGOs, either along social lines or from some other direction. The case studies here provide information and insights in that direction but, as anticipated, fall short of full explanation or observation of this tangled web of transnational relationships.

Dimensions

However remote, any general, testable theoretical approaches to NGOs may be, the case studies have developed much information that fills out the scheme of organisational dimensions set out in the introductory essay. At the same time, the studies show that much is still obscure and that some glaring gaps remain. The following pages point out some of the main findings.

Organisational dimensions

Nongovernmental organisations clearly operate in every geographic range from the community to the transnational. In discussing scaling up and scaling down, Peter Uvin calls attention to the impulses among NGOs to bridge several ranges. To a considerable degree, this bridging is related to the governmental contacts that NGOs seek and employ. Some NGOs, as Sollis's article on Central America suggests, have a regional range and connect with those at national and subnational levels. Conca points out, however, that few environmental organisations relevant to UN activities are truly transnational.

Data on the support base of NGOs is not highly developed in the case studies. Whether and how differences in organisational membership influence policy activities remains unclear. Democratic government of NGOs is an issue referred to in several case studies, but its effect is far from defined. In her essay on the women's movement, Martha Chen calls attention to the increasing number of women who attend the international conferences on women, although individual voluntary attendance and organisational representation are not quantified separately.

On the related subject of finances, Andrew Natsios identifies in his essay on humanitarian work a wide variation among NGOs, some of which refuse governmental funds, while others, including the new breed of 'super' NGOs, may be almost totally financed from public funds from governments and intergovernmental organisations. In the USA, legal rules provide that a nongovernmental organisation must raise 20% of its finances from private sources to be eligible for public funding. Nevertheless, some have grown to mega-proportions for this universe. Some NGO coalitions, as Ritchie describes in his essay on coordination, depend on IGOs for financing. Brief notice in several essays to philanthropic foundations implies the presence of endowment income, but few NGOs other than those mentioned appear to draw much from this source. Many of the essays mention contracting with governments and IGOs in the UN cluster as sources of finances for a set of nongovernmental organisations that deliver specific services.

Legal relationships affect NGOs in many ways. IGO regulations, dealt with by Antonio Donini in his essay on the UN bureaucracy, and by Ritchie, clearly affect access by NGOs. This relationship is especially highlighted in the case study by Conca on environmental organisations. Moreover, nongovernmental organisations can be inhibited or encouraged in their work at the community and national levels by the nature of local laws, as is noted by Sollis in his essay on state–UN–NGO relationships in Central America. The character of legal relationships between NGOs and other organisations clearly can be a focus of activity, as for example in the case of the environment, the status of women, and in the economic development field.

Several of the essays agree that the professionalism of personnel serving NGOs, especially those that have close relationships with the headquarters activities of IGOs, has risen markedly. This is also supported by the attention given by IGO personnel to NGOs in dealing with AIDS and with women's issues. Donini's examples of 'revolving door' personnel—people who move between intergovernmental and nongovernmental staffs—argue that professional standards in some NGOs and IGOs are equivalent.

Other findings related to personnel remain fragmentary. Although the use of research personnel in NGOs with technical, scientific or legal interests would seem indispensable, it remains hard to estimate either quantity or quality. Felice Gaer's essay on human rights, and the treatment of environmental organisations by Conca, give evidence of the payoff from high quality advance preparation for participation by NGOs in UN system meetings. The creation of intermediary organisations in Central America and in scaling up operations examined by Sollis and Uvin would appear to aim directly at employment of skilled personnel, either of a research or operational character.

Precisely how volunteers fit into NGOs in touch with the UN system remains rather obscure, even in the essays that speak of grassroots organisations and movements that go beyond defined NGO boundaries. By definition, grassroots organisations depend on voluntary participation. Such participation may extend to more upscale NGOs, at least in terms of boards of trustees. Membership organisations presumably have devices for representation of members, suggesting voluntary participation. Voluntary participation, moreover, has a close relationship with processes within NGOs. This is supposedly a precondition for accreditation to the Economic and Social Council of the UN (ECOSOC). Any generalisation about these issues, however, would depend on examination of NGO internal operations, and is beyond the scope of these essays.

Financing has a fundamental importance in the development of the mega-NGOs referred to by Natsios that operate in humanitarian emergencies. Much of this comes directly from governments and some comes via IGOs. Similar financing sources are evident in the Central American NGO picture developed by Sollis. In the AIDS field analysed by Jönsson and Söderholm, governments are the overwhelming source of funding for IGO programmes, but NGOs appear to operate to some extent on other financial bases. The women's movement, described by Chen, seems to be largely privately financed. How or whether endowments, except in the case of philanthropic foundations, figure in NGO financing is also not clear. As for income derived as compensation, with the spread of contracting for NGO services, this can be taken as an important channel for the specific transfer of financial resources.

Governance dimensions

Most NGOs probably exist to influence, to set direction for, or to maintain functions of governance or to operate where government authority does not. Consequently governance dimensions would be a strong presence in any inquiry about them. This is, in fact, the case in all of the studies. Donini points out that NGOs have even developed some roles in regard to the former diplomatic preserve of maintaining international peace and security.

In any case, NGOs are a strong presence at every contact point for transnational governance. Their presence differs, however, in specific areas. International conferences, as is shown in the cases of AIDS, the environment, human rights, women and humanitarian assistance, offer an entrance to deeper contacts between NGOs and the UN organisations. Some NGOs, equipped with expert knowledge and professional leadership, participate with special zeal and effect in the preparatory phases of such conferences. To some degree, NGO efforts at every stage shape the outcomes.

The global conferences both affect the agendas of intergovernmental agencies and are convened by them. The NGO presence and activity around the conferences convened by the United Nations and associated agencies is reconfirmed by the case studies. Donini calls attention to the changing environment for such association, while Ritchie makes it clear that many coalitions form and continue for the specific purpose of clamping NGOs and IGOs into a relationship with a set agenda.

Although the case studies focus on the UN agencies, national governments are never allowed to drift far from view. Gaer shows how the UN human rights organs provide a way for NGOs to embellish a critical and often adversarial relationship with national governments. Sollis discloses how NGOs working with IGOs have a virtually integral role in national governments in some instances in Central America, where a regional concept is also important. NGOs also seek contact, or cannot avoid it, with subnational governmental units, a point that is clear from both Natsios's and Uvin's discussions. In failed states, moreover, as Natsios's essay makes clear, NGOs take on some normal governmental programmes but not without misgivings about the propriety and result of such lack of normal contact with local authority. The frequent mention of grassroots organisation points to a community-level relationship for some NGOs.

Informal transnational relationships between NGO personnel and that of governments and IGOs is implicitly or explicitly demonstrated in all the case studies. It is especially emphasised in the case of the women's movement and AIDS. Since the governance dimensions are intended to highlight the variety of relationships between NGOs and authority, a variety of activities engaging the latter were set out. These include norm and policy setting, policy execution, contracting and inter-level mediation. In none of these are NGOs missing, although the depth and temporal extent of the contact vary greatly. For instance, Gaer and Chen show the constant and growing presence of NGOs in setting norms related to human and women's rights, while Conca's discussion of environmental agencies demonstrates a special density of contact during the norm-setting global conferences. Sollis reveals the involvement of NGOs in execution of policy. NGOs serving as contractors are engaged in the humanitarian activities discussed by Natsios. Ritchie's comments on coalitions and Uvin's analysis of scaling up and scaling down both have to do with NGOs related to interlevel mediation.

Strategic dimensions

Strategic dimensions supplement the data about governance dimensions by emphasising what is sought and what techniques are employed by NGOs in their relationships with various authorities engaged in governance processes.

As for goals, many and probably most of the NGOs in the case studies either concentrate on a single issue or a set of issues grouped around a particular topic. Gaer, for example, takes up some transnational human rights organisations that deal with no other subjects. At the same time, Gaer mentions representatives at the Vienna human rights conference with wider, multisectoral or broad social goals. In international cooperation on AIDS, Jönsson and Söderholm observe that some participating NGOs concentrate on persons with AIDS, while others aim at the position of homosexuals in society generally. In humanitarian emergencies, Natsios points to NGOs that aim narrowly at humanitarian relief or refugee issues in the short term, while others emphasise the continuum from relief to economic development that involves multisectoral approaches. Some of these organisations are church-related, and they define their aims in that light.

Both on women's issues, dealt with by Chen, and on arrangements for economic development, taken up by Uvin, some NGOs define their goals in terms of social ideology. For some feminists, wholesale changes in society are the goal, while some of the NGOs sponsoring grassroots development groups seek substantial changes in dominant economic structures.

Organisations that oppose the United Nations or the treatment of global issues by means of intergovernmental cooperation are unlikely to be visible in case studies focused on topics on the UN agenda. Yet it may be assumed that such organisations exist or that some NGO experience would lead to deep disillusion and therefore general opposition. These would be covered in a revolutionary/ rejectionist dimension. Some hints of such NGO aims occur in Uvin's essay, and by implication in Sollis's queries about the future of NGO programmes in Central America. Jönsson and Söderholm note that some AIDS activist NGOs find it difficult to cope with the UN milieu; they may well come to oppose both international programmes and policy making.

The case studies provide examples of every type of tactical mode in NGO strategy with regard to the United Nations and other authority. Probably a fair estimate would be that around UN headquarters and those of associated agencies advocacy/lobbying are the primary modes. Human rights activities analysed by Gaer provide a clear and familiar example. The coalitions described by Ritchie adopt a similar tactical mode, which also characterises NGO tactics at the global conferences on women and on the environment analysed by Chen and Conca.

The more passive monitoring mode is less visible than the positive tactic of advocacy/lobbying. It means following in an expert or at least informed manner the developments related to topics of particular interest to an NGO. All NGOs that concentrate on intergovernmental contacts and international conferences sponsored by the United Nations and associated agencies use the monitoring mode. Although the essays here provide little direct data on monitoring, it can be taken for granted in combination with the activities reported. In fact, Gaer's discussion of human rights indicates that intergovernmental organisations rely on the monitoring capacities of such independent NGOs as Amnesty International and Human Rights Watch. It is clearly also implied with regard to women's NGOs and coalitions described by Chen and Ritchie. On other governance lines, the frequency of monitoring is less certain, but the Sollis and Uvin essays give attention to intermediary organisations that could monitor UN activities on behalf of NGOs, but are unequipped to do so.

Mass propaganda and its specialised form, mass demonstrations, do not figure prominently in many of the case studies. Public reporting of human rights violations by NGOs may reach a wide audience and could be part of a mass propaganda programme, as hinted by Gaer, while reporting by environmental organisations, according to Conca, has a similar character. Women's organisations, too, have used such devices as the international tribunal reported by Chen. In these cases, mass communications media constitute an intervening organisational factor. This is not treated in the essays and in general poses difficult problems of description and analysis, which could be the nucleus of further specialised research.

A few single-issue NGOs concentrating on AIDS have used mass demonstrations to attempt to affect international conferences. The large presence of NGOs at the UN Conference on Environment and Development and at the women's conference could be viewed as mild mass demonstrations. In fact, showy mass demonstrations may only rarely be possible in international meetings; they could be easier to mount for local and national authorities, although this too is more a hypothesis than a finding.

Output dimensions

If strategic dimensions help disclose NGO relationships with authority, the output dimensions point in the direction of receivers of ultimate products, beneficiaries or end users. These dimensions tend markedly to reinforce each other and to overlap. One of the output dimensions, political feedback among governmental units, refers to the sometimes circuitous routes whereby the results of monitoring efforts and advocacy/lobbying are put before NGO membership and used in attempts to affect the policies of local or national authorities. This feedback process connects the decision-making in the UN system with that of national and local governments.

Because of its circuitousness, the process is difficult to trace, but the belief in its existence is manifest in the activities of NGOs in the human rights, women's movement and AIDS fields. Sollis provides data on how regional intermediary organisations in Central America affect governmental decisions in the region. Similar incidents are reported by Donini and Natsios.

Information, developed by NGOs of every persuasion, is stock in trade for them in looking towards ultimate consumers. It is a basic tool of political feedback in, for instance, the promotion of human rights as described by Gaer. A specialised use of information is in providing expert advice, noted in Chen's essay on women's movements, and is a standby of development NGOs at country sites. Other NGOs offer expert advice on the formation of grassroots organisations.

The case studies illustrate many instances of attempts to mobilise opinion by encouraging leadership. This is a significant function of intermediary organisations and an outcome sought by NGO participation in international conferences. The NGO activity in Central America, referred to by Sollis, in part had this aim. It is also a possible spin-off from the humanitarian activities analysed by Natsios, and is closely related to coalition-formation among NGOs described by Ritchie.

Nongovernmental organisations furnish material goods in humanitarian relief situations and in development activities, as illustrated in the studies by Natsios,

Sollis and Uvin. As mentioned earlier, this output is the mainstay of most NGO budgets. In humanitarian relief, large-scale distribution of material goods may occur, while in economic development the amounts are likely to be limited by the scale of projects, particularly by NGOs that tend to work in communities and on a small scale. NGOs also furnish material goods to each other in small amounts in the course of encouragement of networks and education of specific publics. Although the case studies do not take up this activity specifically, it is known that much trading of published materials among NGOs takes place, especially during intermediary functions and large gatherings. This was certainly the case with the women's movement and with human rights NGOs during the major gatherings documented by Chen and Gaer.

All NGOs implicitly encourage the creation of networks. This is quite explicit in the formation of the coalitions described by Ritchie and others. It was a by-product of the formal organising in Central America described by Sollis. Participation in global conferences, described by Conca and Chen, has this same effect. The human rights NGOs are old hands at trading information, a defining function of networks. Similar network-building was a prominent feature of NGO participation in transnational AIDS cooperation analysed by Jönsson and Söderholm.

Networking may link to education of specific publics. In this activity, NGOs seek to put before selected persons, such as senior officials of a bureaucracy, or business leaders in a country or a community, basic information about the subjects with which they are concerned. The implicit goal is to raise the level knowledge so that informed discourse can follow. Gaer and Chen demonstrate how well human rights NGOs and those involved with women's rights use this technique. Some NGOs are known deliberately to seek to inform academic audiences, although little evidence emerges from the case studies. With the education of members of a specific public, the possibility of further informal contact is heightened.

Negative potentials

The case studies as a whole suggest a vast range of energetic activities by nongovernmental organisations in many sectors of human life, whether dominated by the state apparatus or left to civil society. NGOs keep in touch with each activity by attenuated lines of communication and informal networks, some of which extend into governments and intergovernmental agencies. In international cooperation around the UN system, the case studies distinguish a large variety of dynamic practices and relationships. None of the case studies suggests anything approaching a static situation, although the direction of change can hardly be confidently discerned. Nor would it be accurate to think of this vast and highly pluralistic set of relationships as a substitute for the state.

Although the growth of NGOs may indicate vibrant participation in a civil society, it also suggests a potential difficulty. A modicum of state power remains necessary to support the essential order underpinning a society and to avoid civil war. The phenomenon of failed states suggests that 'inadequate stateness' may partly explain collapse. Moreover, nongovernmental organisations may compete for scarce resources. Without fungible resources, those going to NGOs from the United Nations Development Program's (UNDP) country allocations, for example, are unavailable for governments. Pluralism may have unintended costs if NGOs exacerbate the problem of inadequate central government capacity.

Yet, both international and local NGOs have become an unavoidable reality in the efforts by a rudimentary international community to respond to global problems. Because NGOs are increasingly important in world politics, theoretical and practical understandings of their activities are essential in comprehending the problems and prospects of the UN system. If the case studies open a window on this understanding, a great deal more needs to be done to approach a satisfactory and satisfying level of knowledge.

Both IGOs and NGOs thus have an intimate connection to the more general problem of global governance. The culture and character of nongovernmental organisations inclines them to act, rather than to contemplate and reflect. That adds yet more poignancy to exploring the relationships between IGOs, governments and NGOs in the context of global governance.

Ambiguities and dilemmas of NGO and UN interactions

In addition to the lessons and the consensus observations that resulted from the analyses in the preceding case studies, their discussion in Toronto, and our own research, several ambiguities also emerge, and present dilemmas facing policy makers. As such, they also constitute the skeleton of a future research agenda for scholars and policy analysts.

- The naïve and exaggerated notion that the outcome of NGO efforts is universally worthwhile is, in fact, contradicted by experience and analysis. There is no shortage of achievements, for example ranging from framing the agenda for human rights, women and the environment to delivery of technical assistance and humanitarian relief. At the same time, some activities that originally seemed justified by an implementing nongovernmental organisation have backfired in the longer run. Prominent examples can be drawn from the humanitarian arena, where the well-intentioned facilitation of the movement of refugees contributed to 'ethnic cleansing' and to the erosion of international norms. The development arena, too, is laden with examples of projects that were designed to introduce new technologies and production schemes, but that helped to destroy local capacities and the fabric of social structures. In short, any responsible NGO must try to anticipate negative externalities.
- Following this ambiguity is another one related to the mixture of conflict, competition, cooperation and cooptation as nongovernmental organisations determine how close their links should be with states or organisations of the UN system. These four 'Cs' could be viewed as a spectrum along which there are rather unclear boundaries; probably most would aim at the middle two categories on competition and cooperation. Even the extremes of conflict and cooptation can bring benefits, as several NGOs have demonstrated by using confrontational or rejectionist strategies (within the AIDS and environmental movements, for instance), or by becoming well integrated into UN program-

ming exercises for humanitarian emergencies. Moreover, as the examinations of cooperation in Central America or the coalition-building efforts within InterAction or the International Council of Voluntary Agencies (ICVA) suggest, there are few zero-sum outcomes. Policy makers and analysts are left with trying to determine the advantages and disadvantages of any partnership, at least for the present, on a case-by-case basis.

- The outcome that particular NGOs seek determines whether NGOs are better served by trying to define an issue narrowly (for example women and the environment) at the grassroots level and to concentrate efforts on well-circumscribed targets within logical organisational targets (for example the forthcoming Women's Conference in Beijing or the UN Environmental Programme) or, alternatively, whether it is better to 'mainstream' such issues into wider global concerns. To continue with these examples, it may be that both the causes of women's rights and sustainable development are better served by focusing educational efforts and advocacy upon more general issues of investment and development within the World Bank. The potential payoff from a change in policy by a major mainstream actor may dwarf more spectacular rhetorical gains in more narrowly focused institutional settings with ambitious agendas. Once again, generalising about the desired nature of a response depends on better data and analyses than we possess now. In fact, it may be that progress requires simultaneous efforts at both levels.

- The growth in NGO activity has had an impact at both ends of the spectrum of organisational size. On the one hand, a handful of 'super' nongovernmental organisations is emerging. In the humanitarian arena this means that eight to ten large conglomerates of international NGOs account for what may be 80% of the financial value of assistance in complex emergencies. Some of these are also involved in other operational areas with the UN system; but the same generalisations about human rights, the environment and women do not apply because there are no 'super' NGOs in these areas. With diminishing real public resources for development assistance, of which very little (perhaps 4% to 5%) has been devoted to education and advocacy, there are few 'super' agencies. At the other end of the spectrum—the community and local levels—the erosion and sometimes failure of state authority has permitted the emergence of an ever-increasing number of NGOs. Moreover, small and even minuscule international NGOs are also increasingly involved in the entire range of activities undertaken by the UN system. An evaluation of the advantages and disadvantages of the growth at both ends of the spectrum depends upon the issue area and may even depend upon the observer's evaluation of the necessity for enhancing the state capacity to provide at least a modicum of services. Although there is no nostalgia for the national security state of the past, clearly there is a downside to inadequate stateness.

- NGOs exist at the community, local, national, regional and international levels. These levels are obvious ones for analysis, but too little is known about links among them and about the direct and indirect feedback among the various levels. For example, powerful and influential international NGOs working on the AIDS pandemic can avoid the regulatory power of local and national authorities by linking directly with grassroots nongovernmental organisations.

Rather than direct confrontation, community-based and local NGOs working on human rights or the environment may decide to embarrass their state author-ities indirectly through an international conference or a communication from an intergovernmental governing body. The relative merits of various tactics depend upon evaluations, yet to be accomplished, detailing and comparing the results of previous efforts.

• The nature of representation within nongovernmental organisations as well as within their coalitions, and by NGOs within international gatherings, is a source of some perplexity if not ambiguity for analysts. NGOs themselves are not necessarily democratic, which raises the question of who represents what to whom. Elections are hardly frequent occurrences within NGOs, which do not function the way representative governments do. And the elites of large NGOs at the summit or even at lower levels of expenditures may hardly be different from those of IGOs or the governments that they supposedly confront. NGO leaders may push their own personal agendas rather than those of constituents. Nevertheless, the introduction of nongovernmental concerns into international dialogue is healthy. Perhaps the best that can be hoped for may be a kind of crude balance at the local, national and international levels in which a mixture of governmental, intergovernmental and nongovernmental voices more closely reflects reality than a state-dominated framework with only a smattering of intergovernmental input.

On a related issue, the previous essays suggest that the demand by local and international NGOs for the right to be represented in international forums has not been matched with an adequate effort to define concomitant responsibilities to accompany such rights. Within certain NGO families, efforts to formulate codes of conduct that move in the direction of defining minimal obligations have been made. Numerous dilemmas are associated with the various forms of representa-tion. Few unambiguous guidelines orient managers and decision-makers who seek to improve democratisation of the nongovernmental sector.

• The terms 'cooperation', 'collaboration', and 'coordination' are sprinkled liberally throughout international discourse and in the preceding essays. These concepts suggest a dilemma: cooperation and collaboration may be good, but on whose terms? Everyone favours coordination, but no one wishes to be coordinated. Joint ventures among NGOs and between them and members of the UN system involve unexpected as well as expected costs—human, temporal, financial, and lost autonomy—as well as benefits. Some experts argue that greater cooperation, coherence and centralisation are essential, especially during acute humanitarian emergencies. Others argue that the positive impact emanating from the diversity of NGOs and from competition among themselves and between this sector and the UN system outweighs purported benefits from pooling efforts. In any case, the different values and operating styles between NGOs and intergovernmental organisations, along with the NGOs' ferocious insistence on maintaining independence, probably preclude any far-reaching harmonisation of efforts.

• Independent statistical data from the Organization of Economic Cooperation and Development (OECD) and other institutions and the case studies here indicate that NGOs are receiving greater resources from both private and public sources. Both governments and UN organisations increasingly rely on NGOs to deliver services. Nongovernmental organisations collectively now disperse more official development assistance (ODA) than does the entire UN system (excluding the Washington-based financial institutions). Moreover, in many countries they are powerful sources of employment and foreign exchange. This development is strikingly evident in complex emergencies where state authority is extremely weak and sometimes nonexistent. This trend calls for deeper analysis on the basis of more complete data. At a time of diminishing and fungible resources, financing local and international NGOs is sometimes simply subtracted from that originally intended for governments. Moreover, some NGOs employ dramatic images to elicit contributions from individuals and from bilateral donors and intergovernmental secretariats. This public relations technique often works against the more nuanced messages intended to educate donor constituencies about the root causes of conflict and poverty.

- The quality and characteristics of particular UN institutions can help or hinder the development of an effective partnership between local and international NGOs. Virtually nothing is known about the sociology and anthropology of the cultures within the UN family, except that they are clearly not monolithic. UNHCR and UNICEF not only contract for services from NGOs but also endeavour to involve them more intimately in project formulation and policy consultations. This may reflect the fact that these institutions have a relatively high number of staff members who themselves have previously worked in NGOs or are at least sympathetic to many of their values and programmatic emphases. This is very different from the relationships between the World Bank and nongovernmental organisations. Part of the explanation may, no doubt, lie in the possibility that the staff and managers in Washington know less about the strengths of both local and international NGOs. Moreover, the dimensions of the World Bank's projects and the incentives to its managers for large-scale implementation would seem to impede closer working relations with NGOs. Yet such comments are merely speculative, since too few resources have been devoted to analysing the composition and behaviour of international secretariats.

- Beginning with the establishment of the United Nations, and especially since the General Assembly adopted Resolution 1296 in 1968, officials from governmental, intergovernmental, and nongovernmental organisations have invested a seemingly disproportionate amount of energy in determining which NGOs qualify for official consultative status. Our own observations and virtually all of the case studies suggest that formal relationships may not be the most essential element in determining the efficacy, power and overall impact of NGO efforts, even efforts to influence opinion and help set international standards. In fact, the superficial characterisation of informality as marginal or weak does not appear to apply to the efforts to foster women's rights or appropriate policy reactions to the threat of AIDS. Moreover, other types of informal relationships, such as those that characterise efforts by knowledgeable technicians and are often labelled epistemic communities within the environmental and other arenas, may be every bit as influential as NGOs that enjoy consultative status.

Some concluding thoughts

Three overall conclusions, which may not be surprising but which are hardly trivial, may be set out with some confidence. First and most evident, far too little useful statistical information or even basic descriptive information exists about the phenomenon of NGOs that are active in the milieu surrounding the United Nations system. This makes theory-building and policy recommendations a hazardous, if not totally nonfeasible, undertaking. We have no convincing or well-tested models. This reflects the difficulties of groping in a rapidly evolving, uncertain global society.

Second, the age of innocence is over for NGOs as they relate to the UN system. There is a need to understand better and to contextualise fully any programmatic activity before taking action. The staff and constituencies of NGOs have generally believed that human and financial resources devoted to policy analysis and evaluation were irrelevant and even wasteful. They have preferred action to reflection. However, visceral reactions are no longer an adequate basis on which to base projects and programmes. The wrong kind of assistance to displaced persons, for instance, can worsen their situation and respect for international norms, and perhaps even prolong conflicts. Inappropriate development—involving the continued treatment of women as second-class citizens or the destruction of non-sustainable resources—may not necessarily be better than none at all. Fundraising of a sensational nature, even if effective, can undermine longer-run efforts to improve public knowledge about issues of direct consequence. Disarmament efforts occasionally may work against the type of security required to conduct normal activities. All of this is by way of saying that more reflection and less action is sometimes in order, and that NGO resources can and should legitimately be spent on analysis.

Third, we return to the point of departure and the final part of this volume's title, 'global governance'. Several prominent intellectuals, as well as august commissions, have struggled with this notion. We, however, posited the straightforward idea that it consists of more ordered and more reliable responses to problems that go beyond the individual and even collective capacities of states. The agreed and proverbial bottom line for all definitions of global governance, however, consists of enhanced transparency, accountability and participation. Under the right conditions, the growth in the number of local and international NGOs and in their roles and responsibilities at all levels, along with their increasing relevance to the operational and normative activities of the UN system, provides more opportunities to satisfy the requirements for improved transparency, accountability and participation.

Acronyms

ACBAR	Agency Coordination Body for Afghan Relief
ACT-UP	AIDS Coalition to Unleash Power
ACUNS	Academic Council on the United Nations System
AI	Amnesty International
AID	United States Agency for International Development
AIDS	acquired immunodeficiency syndrome
ANGOC	Asian NGO Coalition for Agrarian Reform and Rural Development
APRODEV	Association of Protestant Development Organizations in Europe
ARENA	National Republican Alliance
ASAI	Salvadoran Integral Support Association
ASO	AIDS service organization
BRAC	Bangladesh Rural Action Committee
CAS	Canadian AIDS Society
CDC	Centers for Disease Control
CIDSE	Coopération internationale pour le développment et la solidarité
CIREFCA	International Conference on Refugees in Central America
CONAVIGUA	National Co-ordination of Guatemalan Widows
CONDEG	National Council of Displaced Guatemalans
CONGO	Conference of NGOs in Consultative Status with ECOSOC
COPAC	Committee for the Promotion and Advancement of Cooperatives
CRIPDES	Christian Committee for the Displaced of El Salvador
CRS	Catholic Relief Services
CSD	Commission on Sustainable Development
CUD	Coalition of Earthquake Victims
DAC	Development Assistance Committee
DAWN	Development Alternatives with Women for a New Era
DHA	Department of Humanitarian Affairs

DONGO	donor-organized NGO
DPI	Department of Public Information
DPKO	Department of Peace-keeping Operations
EC	European Community
ECHO	European Community Humanitarian Office
ECOSOC	Economic and Social Council
EFTA	European Free Trade Association
ELC	Environmental Liaison Centre
ERC	External Review Committee
EU	European Union
FACS	Augusto César Sandino Foundation
FAO	Food and Agriculture Organization
FFP	Food for Peace
FRELIMO	Front for the Liberation of Mozambique
FUNPROCOOP	Salvadoran Foundation for Cooperative Promotion
GAPC	Global AIDS Policy Coalition
GMC	Global Management Committee
GONGO	government-organized nongovernmental organization
GPA	Global Programme on AIDS
GRO	grassroots organization
GRSO	grassroots support organization
GSCO	global social change organization
IASC	Inter-Agency Standing Committee
IBRD	International Bank for Reconstruction and Development
ICASO	International Council of ASOs
ICG	International Crisis Group
ICN	International Conference on Nutrition
ICPD	International Conference on Population and Development
ICRC	International Committee of the Red Cross
ICVA	International Council of Voluntary Agencies
IDA	International Development Association
IFAD	International Fund for Agriculture and Development
IFRC	International Federation of Red Cross and Red Crescent Societies
IGO	intergovernmental organization
ILO	International Labour Organisation
IMF	International Monetary Fund
INGO	international nongovernmental organization
IO	International Organization
IOM	International Organization for Migration
IPF	Indicative Planning Figure
IRC	International Rescue Committee
IUCN	International Union for the Conservation of Nature
JICA	Japanese International Cooperation Agency

MINUGUA	United Nations Human Rights Verification Mission in Guatemala
MSF	Médecins Sans Frontières
MUP	urban popular movement
NAFTA	North American Free Trade Association
NAP	National AIDS Program
NGO	nongovernmental organization
NIEO	New International Economic Order
NIH	National Institutes of Health
OAS	Organization of American States
ODA	official development assistance
OECD	Organization of Economic Co-operation and Development
OFDA	Office of Foreign Disaster Assistance
ONUCA	United Nations Observer Group in Central America
ONUSAL	United Nations Observer Mission in El Salvador
ONUVEN	United Nations Observer Mission to Verify the Electoral Process in Nicaragua
OPEC	Organization of Petroleum Exporting Countries
ORT	oral rehydration therapy
PAHO	Panamerican Health Organization
PARinAC	Partners in Action
PEC	Special Economic Cooperation Plan
PGA	Parliamentarians for Global Action
PO	people's organization
PRIA	Society for Participatory Research in Asia
PRODERE	Development Program for Refugees, Displaced and Repatriated Persons in Central America
PWAs	People with AIDS
QuaNGO	quasi-nongovernmental organization
QIP	Quick Impact Project
RENAMO	Mozambique National Resistance
SCF	Save the Children Federation
SDM	savings development movement
SHO	self-help organization
SHPO	self-help support organization
SIDA	Swedish International Development Agency
SILED	local education systems
SILOS	local health systems
SILPRODEH	local human rights systems
SWABAC	South-Western Afghanistan and Baluchistan Agency Coordination
TFAP	Tropical Forestry Action Plan
UNAMIR	United Nations Assistance Mission in Rwanda

UNCED	United Nations Conference on Environment and Development
UNCTAD	United Nations Conference on Trade and Development
UNDP	United Nations Development Programme
UNEP	United Nations Environment Programme
UNESCO	United Nations Educational, Scientific, and Cultural Organization
UNFPA	United Nations Fund for Population Activities
UNHCR	United Nations High Commissioner for Refugees
UNICEF	United Nations International Children's Emergency Fund
UNIFEM	United Nations Development Fund for Women
UNOCA	United Nations Office for the Coordination of Humanitarian Assistance to Afghanistan
UNREO	United Nations Rwanda Emergency Office
UNTAC	United Nations Transition Authority in Cambodia
UUSC	Unitarian Universalist Service Committee
WCEFA	World Conference on Education for All
WEDO	Women's Environment and Development Organization
WFP	World Food Programme
WHO	World Health Organization
WRI	World Resources Institute
WTO	World Trade Organization
WWF	World Wildlife Fund

Annotated Bibliography

Overview, 227
Operations and Work, 229
Government Relations, 232
Networking and Scaling Up, 233
NGOs in the International System, Overview, 235
NGOs in the International System, World Bank Relations, 237
NGOs in the International System, UN Relations, 237

Overview

Anheier, Helmut K. "Private Voluntary Organizations and Development in West Africa: Comparative Perspectives." In Estelle James (ed.), *The Nonprofit Sector in International Perspective*. New York: Oxford University Press, 1989, 339–357. Offers a compendium of two theories of NGOs' existence and impact: the categorical constraint theory and the heterogeneity theory.

Boulding, Elise. "The Old and New Transnationalism: An Evolutionary Perspective." *Human Relations* 44, no. 8 (1991): 789–805. Traces the history of international NGOs, positing that their advent marks one of the most important innovations of our time.

Cernea, Michael M. *Nongovernmental Organizations and Local Development*. World Bank Discussion Papers, no. 40. Washington, D.C.: The World Bank, 1988. In addition to discussing local development efforts, this paper studies financial movements and the interaction between local NGOs and the World Bank. Even as financial resources are increasingly channeled through NGOs, the mainstay of NGOs' contribution to development is "not to financially induce development, but to organize people into structures for group action."

Drabek, Anne Gordon (ed.). "Development Alternatives: The Challenge for NGOs." *World Development* 15: Supplement (1987). A collection of contrasting views by Northern and Southern writers on international and local NGOs, NGO relations, and development strategies. The introduction summarizes the major issues confronting NGOs.

Edwards, Michael, and David Hulme (eds.). *Making a Difference: NGOs and Development in a Changing World*. London: Earthscan Publications, 1992. Though this volume does not examine the UN system, it contains many articles on the changing international role of NGOs. Anthony Bebbington and John Farrington posit that governments must view NGOs as more than simple vehicles for program implementation. John Clark and Chris Dolan study advocacy and lobbying as a means of scaling up NGOs' impact.

Edwards, Mike. "NGOs in the Age of Information." *IDS Bulletin* 25, no. 2 (1994): 117–124. Examines the comparative advantages and disadvantages of NGOs and other organizations in their use of information.

Fowler, Alan. "Distant Obligations: Speculations on NGO Funding and the Global Market." *Review of African Political Economy* 55 (1992): 9–29. Identifying the late 1980s phenomenon of direct official aid to Southern NGOs, Fowler predicts a continuing growth of funding to these organizations.

———. "Capacity Building and NGOs: A Case of Strengthening Ladles for the Global Soup Kitchen?" *Institutional Development* 1, no. 1 (1994): 18–25. PRIA, New Delhi. Looks at the implications of government funding on NGOs' institutional and organizational development. Echoing Brian Smith's thesis that governments are motivated by more than altruism, Fowler posits that official aid will steer NGOs toward providing socioeconomic services instead of promoting civil society.

Haas, Ernst B. *When Knowledge Is Power: Three Models of Change in International Organizations.* Los Angeles: University of California Press, 1990. A theoretical analysis offering three models of institutional change for international organizations: incremental growth, turbulent nongrowth, and managed interdependence. The book also compares and contrasts the organizational structures of NGOs, the UN, and the World Bank.

Haas, Peter M. "Do Regimes Matter? Epistemic Communities and Mediterranean Pollution Control." *International Organization* 43, no. 3 (1989): 377–403. Discussing the role of an "epistemic community" in the success of the Mediterranean Action Plan, Haas attributes the effective negotiation of this regime to a community of UN officials, midlevel government officials, diplomats, and scientists from various countries.

Korten, David. *Getting to the 21st Century: Voluntary Action and the Global Agenda.* West Hartford, Conn.: Kumarian Press, 1990. Comparable to a reference guide on NGOs, discussing everything from democratization to empowerment to structural adjustment. Korten also presents his theory of "four generations," a model of NGO evolution.

McCarthy, Kathleen D., Virginia A. Hodgkinson, Russy D. Sumariwalla, et al. *The Nonprofit Sector in the Global Community: Voices from Many Nations.* San Francisco: Jossey-Bass Publishers, 1992. Describes differing conceptions and goals of the nonprofit sector across borders and contains a variety of case studies on NGOs.

Meyer, Carrie. "Environmental NGOs in Ecuador: An Economic Analysis of Institutional Change." *The Journal of Developing Areas* 27 (1993): 191–210. Looking at a few case studies, Meyer concludes that the burgeoning of Latin America's environmental NGOs is a function of the availability of international finance. The article also raises concerns over free-rider problems, inefficiencies in the administration of funds, and the contentious relations between donors and NGOs.

Powell, Walter W. (ed.). *The Nonprofit Sector: A Research Handbook.* New Haven: Yale University Press, 1987. A collection of political, legal, and economic analyses. The volume does not deal with international NGOs specifically but with NGOs in general.

Salamon, Lester. "The Rise of the Nonprofit Sector." *Foreign Affairs* 73, no. 4 (1994): 109–122. Discusses the proliferation of NGOs as a phenomenon that may parallel the rise of the nation-state. Salamon identifies pressures that have led to this growth: from below (grass roots), outside (public and private institutions), and above (government policies).

Salamon, Lester, and Helmut Anheier. *The Emerging Sector: An Overview.* Baltimore, Md.: The Johns Hopkins University Institute for Policy Studies, 1994. Vaguely touches on a variety of topics such as definition, legitimacy, and globalization; however, it possesses a treasure of data not readily available elsewhere.

Schneider, Bertrand. *The Barefoot Revolution: A Report to the Club of Rome.* London: Intermediate Technology Publications, 1988. Remains one of the best introductions to the study of NGOs and development. Part 3 concisely states the definitions and history of NGOs, contending that the NGO phenomenon is a fairly recent occurrence. Parts 3, 4, and 5 collectively broach several issues such as accountability, funding, relations with international and national actors, obstacles, and economic and social achievements. In raising so many important topics, the book does not deal with each one in great depth, but it is nevertheless impressive in its breadth of issues.

Smillie, Ian. *Mastering the Machine: Poverty, Aid and Technology.* Boulder, Colo.: Westview Press, 1991. Chapter 4 broaches concerns over NGOs' proliferation and the new trend in financing. Observing that the growing friendship between bilateral donors and Southern NGOs coincided with a decline in funding from Northern to Southern NGOs, Smillie raises the possibility that Northern NGOs fear losing their raison d'être as Third World organizations acquire competency, management skills, and funding from multilateral agencies.

Smith, Jackie, Ron Pagnucco, and Winnie Romeril. "Transnational Social Movement Organizations in the Global Political Arena." *Voluntas* 5, no. 2 (1994): 121–154. Details the organizational structures of NGOs that attempt to influence national and international institutions. Looking at seven organizations, the authors also discuss NGOs' relations with IGOs and governments.

Young, Dennis R. "The Structural Imperatives of International Advocacy Associations." *Human Relations* 44, no. 9 (1991): 921–941. Contends that decentralized and federated structures are viable forms for NGOs in international advocacy and also briefly reviews the literature on institutional forms.

Operations and Work

Borton, John. "Recent Trends in the International Relief System." *Disasters* 17, no. 3 (1993): 187–201. This article assesses the changes in the international relief system since the Cold War's conclusion and highlights the participation of NGOs.

Bramble, Barbara J., and Gareth Porter. "Non-Governmental Organizations and the Making of US International Environment Policy." In Andrew Hurrell and Benedict Kingsbury (eds.), *The International Politics of the Environment.* Oxford: Clarendon Press, 1992, 313–353. Illustrates the strategies of internationally oriented environmental NGOs in the U.S., divides them into three types, and discusses NGOs' relations with the World Bank and governments.

Bush, Kenneth D. "The Role of NGOs in Peacebuilding." Paper prepared for the NGO Division of the Canadian International Development Agency, 1993. Examines the present and the potential roles of NGOs in the peace process. Of particular interest is the short discussion on the Gal Oya project as an example of participatory peacebuilding.

———. "When Two Anarchies Meet: International Intervention in Somalia." In Robert Miller (ed.), *Missions for Peace: Canadian Experience and Future Roles* (forthcoming). In examining the Canadian experience in the Somalia crisis, Bush discusses the interaction of the NGOs' peacebuilding role with the military's peacekeeping operations.

Caldwell, Lynton K. "Beyond Environmental Diplomacy: The Changing Institutional Structure of International Cooperation." In John E. Carroll (ed.), *International Environmental Diplomacy: The Management and Resolution of Transfrontier Environmental Problems.* Cambridge: Cambridge University Press, 1988, 13–27. In studying the direction of international environmental diplomacy, Caldwell discusses the various strategies NGOs use to ensure government compliance with international conventions.

Clark, John. *Democratizing Development: The Role of Voluntary Organizations.* West Hartford, Conn.: Kumarian Press, 1991. A thorough compendium of issues for NGOs in development. Clark highlights the trends in scaling up and lobbying, underlying the growing recognition that pressure for international policy change can be a more precious development resource than money. Yet these trends should not be interpreted as a present or a future main feature of NGOs' activities since NGOs still place greater emphasis on "doing" rather than "influencing."

Clayton, Andrew (ed.). *Governance, Democracy and Conditionality: What Role for NGOs?* Oxford: INTRAC, 1995. Reviewing case studies around the world, this publication analyzes the role of NGOs in democratic movements and governance.

Dichter, T. W. "The Changing World of Northern NGOs: Problems, Paradoxes and Possibilities." In John P. Lewis (ed.), *Strengthening the Poor: What Have We Learned?* New Brunswick, N.J.: Transaction Books, 1988, 177–188. Though NGOs have more responsibilities to implement projects, international donors realize that NGOs are somewhat deficient in their capabilities.

Duffield, Mark. "NGOs, Disaster Relief and Asset Transfer in the Horn: Political Survival in a Permanent Emergency." *Development and Change* 24 (1993): 131–157. Many NGOs, collectively transferring substantial resources to the South, receive considerable official funding and may be viewed as agents of donor policy. Moreover, international NGOs' relief efforts have often produced undesirable consequences such as weakened indigenous structures and a population's increased external dependency.

Eguizábal, Cristina, David Lewis, Larry Minear, Peter Sollis, and Thomas G. Weiss. *Humanitarian Challenges in Central America: Learning the Lessons of Recent Armed Conflicts.* Occasional Paper, no. 14. Providence, R.I.: Thomas J. Watson, Jr. Institute, 1993. Reviews the past decade of humanitarian action in Central America and includes NGOs in its preview. A significant section compares NGOs' performances in three countries and discusses the disadvantages of NGOs' association with governments and certain factions.

Fowler, Alan. "Non-Governmental Organizations as Agents of Democratization: An African Perspective." *Journal of International Development* 5, no. 3 (1993): 325–339. Fowler contends that NGOs in Africa are unlikely to have an impact on political reform. Changing this situation requires that NGOs incorporate civic education in development efforts.

Loescher, Gil. *Beyond Charity: International Cooperation and the Global Refugee Crisis.* New York: Oxford University Press, 1993. Contains a good discussion on NGOs' monitoring and networking activities as well as their coordinating efforts with the UNHCR, claiming that the international community relies on NGOs more and more to alleviate the refugee crisis.

McCoy, Michael, and Patrick McCully. *The Road from Rio: An NGO Action Guide to Environment and Development.* Utrecht, The Netherlands: International Books, 1993. Discusses the significance of the Rio Earth Summit to the NGO community. Summarizing the Earth Charter, Agenda 21, and the biodiversity and climate change conventions, the authors offer NGOs advice about the resulting opportunities and limitations. Though NGOs did not change policies much at Rio, they gained formal recognition and thereby established a precedent for their formal participation in future international events. Furthermore, documents such as Agenda 21 provide NGOs with the touchstone to hold governments accountable and thus heighten NGOs' monitoring abilities.

Mercer, M. A., L. Liskin, and S. J. Scott. "The Role of Non-Governmental Organizations in the Global Response to AIDS." *AIDS Care* 3, no. 3 (1991): 265–270. Describes NGOs' present and potential role in containing the AIDS epidemic and notes that indigenous groups, because of their size, are often at a disadvantage in obtaining funds from large donors.

Princen, Thomas, and Matthias Finger (eds.). *Environmental NGOs in World Politics: Linking the Local and the Global.* New York: Routledge, 1994. Though the book's

purpose is to examine environmental NGOs in world politics, its first three chapters provide a theoretical overview of international NGOs in general. Some NGOs, the World
Wildlife Fund, for example, can wield enough economic clout to change governments'
and other NGOs' behavior; other NGOs such as Greenpeace can command attention on
some issues in ways that few other actors can. Other authors review the differences and
commonality underlying environmental and other NGOs. NGOs became a critical part of
the United Nations Conference on Environment and Development (UNCED) process and
changed as a result of this relationship. UNCED greatly accelerated international environmental NGOs' growth process, which was not a smooth one; tensions between how
states and how NGOs themselves defined their roles resulted in a bargaining process.

Randel, Judith. "Aid, the Military and Humanitarian Assistance: An Attempt to Identify
Recent Trends." *Journal of International Development* 6, no. 3 (1994): 329–342.
Tackles several issues surrounding humanitarian aid, including the trends in expendi-
ture and the collaboration between NGOs and the military. Randel also analyzes the
compatibility of humanitarian assistance with peacekeeping.

Sands, Philippe. "The Role of Environmental NGOs in International Environmental
Law." *Development Journal of the Society for International Development* 2 (1992):
28–32. Four case studies describe environmental NGOs' involvement in both developing legislation and enforcing international compliance through formal and informal
participation.

Starke, Linda. *Signs of Hope: Working Towards Our Common Future.* New York: Oxford
University Press, 1990. Chapter 4 reviews the rise of NGOs and discusses NGOs'
milestones in environmental affairs, listing their participation in international meetings and networks.

Staudt, Kathleen. *Managing Development: State, Society, and International Contexts.*
Newbury Park, Calif.: Sage Publications, 1991. Examines NGOs' national and international participation in development and empowerment.

Steiner, Henry J. *Diverse Partners: Non-Governmental Organizations in the Human Rights
Movement: The Report of a Retreat of Human Rights Activists.* Cambridge: Harvard
Law School Human Rights Program and Human Rights Internet USA, 1991. A basic
discussion of NGOs' human rights activities that is more descriptive than analytical.

Tendler, Judith. *Turning Private Voluntary Organizations into Development Agencies.*
USAID Program Evaluation Discussion Paper, no. 12. Washington, D.C.: U.S. Agency
for International Development, 1982. Evaluates NGOs' shift from relief to development work. Written in 1982, the paper raises timeless issues such as the concept of
PVOs as "precursors" to governments.

Thomas, Caroline. *The Environment in International Relations.* London: The Royal Institute of International Affairs, 1992. Traces the development of environmental issues
on the international agenda, and the momentum gained with the Cold War's conclusion. It then describes the interaction of the UN, international lenders, governments,
and NGOs since the 1972 Stockholm Conference.

Wallace, Barbara. "AIDS Prevention and Care for Refugees and Migrants: The Need for
a Coordinated NGO Response." *Disasters* 14, no. 3 (1990): 259–264. NGOs working
in refugee camps are in a good position to introduce AIDS education and care into the
existing primary health care programs, but few NGOs have done so.

Weissbrodt, David. "Humanitarian Law in Armed Conflict: The Role of International
Nongovernmental Organizations." *Journal of Peace Research* 24, no. 3 (1987):
297–306. Five reasons why NGOs use humanitarian law to protect human rights during periods of armed conflict. Describes the work of the International Committee of
the Red Cross (ICRC), suggesting that other organizations learn from ICRC.

World Health Organization, South-East Asia Region. *NGOs' Role and Involvement in the
Prevention and Control of AIDS: Report of a Regional Workshop, 30 October–November*

1990. SEA/AIDS/22, 1991. This document reviews the various activities of NGOs involved in AIDS prevention and control.

Yudelman, Sally W. "The Integration of Women into Development Projects: Observations on the NGO Experience in General and in Latin America in Particular." *World Development* 15: Supplement (1987): 179–187. Criticizes NGOs' inadequate attention to women and challenges organizations to overcome cultural prejudices in their approaches.

Government Relations

Bebbington, Anthony, and John Farrington. "Governments, NGOs and Agricultural Development: Perspectives on Changing Inter-Organizational Relationships." *Journal of Development Studies* 29, no. 2 (1993): 199–219. Argues that discussions on NGO-government collaboration tend to be overly optimistic. The authors re-examine the costs and benefits of such collaboration in agricultural development, using Latin American, Asian, and African case studies.

Bebbington, Anthony, Graham Thiele, Penelope Davies, Martin Prager, and Hernando Riveros. *Non-Governmental Organizations and the State in Latin America: Rethinking Roles in Sustainable Agricultural Development.* New York: Routledge, 1993. A thorough overview of issues affecting grassroots efforts in Latin America that offers new insights into how the NGO-government relationship assists the democratization of rural society. The authors tackle issues from networking to democratization to NGO typologies.

Clark, John. *The State and the Voluntary Sector.* HROWP Working Paper, no. 12. Washington, D.C.: The World Bank, 1993. Reveals the barriers to good NGO-state relations, citing political jealousy as one, and lists the state's instruments impacting NGOs' operational efficacy.

Dawson, Elsa. "NGOs and Public Policy Reform: Lessons from Peru." *Journal of International Development* 5, no. 4 (1993): 401–414. Traces the experiences of three NGOs working to influence national policymaking and lists the factors that led to the successes and failures of the strategies employed.

Downs, Charles, and Giorgio Solimano. "Toward an Evaluation of the NGO Experience in Chile: Implications for Social Policy and Future Investigation." In Charles Downs, Giorgio Solimano, Carlos Vergara, and Luis Zúñiga (eds.), and Paula Orrn (trans.), *Social Policy from the Grassroots: Nongovernmental Organizations in Chile.* San Francisco: Westview Press, 1989, 199–212. In addition to giving an overview of the various activities of NGOs in Chile, this chapter discusses NGO-government relations.

Farrington, John, David J. Lewis, S. Satish, and Aurea Miclat-Teves (eds.). *Non-Governmental Organizations and the State in Asia: Rethinking Roles in Sustainable Agricultural Development.* New York: Routledge, 1993. A series of country analyses that study NGOs as information intermediaries between people and governments.

Fowler, Alan. "The Role of NGOs in Changing State-Society Relations: Perspectives from Eastern and Southern Africa." *Development Policy Review* 9, no. 1 (1991): 53–84. Analyzes the validity of the idea that a growing NGO sector will strengthen civil society and contribute to the democratization of African countries. Noting that external aid to local NGOs can weaken accountability, exacerbating the fact that most NGOs are controlled by society's elites and exhibit top-down structures, this article also examines how the state's practice of project funding can influence the evolution of NGOs and how NGOs in turn can undermine the state's hegemony.

Friedmann, John. *Empowerment: The Politics of Alternative Development.* Cambridge, Mass.: Blackwell Publishers, 1992. Drawing upon Latin American examples, chapter 7 is a useful listing of ten factors influencing NGOs' relationship with governments.

Organisation for Economic Co-operation and Development. *Directory of Non-Government Environment and Development Organisations in OECD Member Countries*. Paris: Organisation for Economic Co-operation and Development, 1992. Included in this directory is an article entitled "Partnership Toward Global Sustainable Development: Non-Governmental Organisations in OECD Member Countries Active in Development and Environment: A Review of Trends 1970–1992 and Challenges for the 1990s."

Randel, Judith, and Tony German (eds.). *The Reality of Aid '94: An Independent Review of International Aid*. London: Action Aid, 1994. NGOs from twenty-one OECD countries worked together to produce this volume containing a wealth of statistical information on NGOs' financial concerns and illuminating the underlying relationship between NGOs and governments.

Sibanda, Harold. *NGO Influence on National Policy Formulation in Zimbabwe*. IDR Reports, vol. 11, no. 2. Boston: Institute for Development Research, 1994. This paper describes the impact of Zimbabwean NGOs on the government and compares the strategies and resources employed by these two actors.

Smillie, Ian, and Henny Helmich (eds.). *Non-Governmental Organizations and Governments: Stakeholders for Development*. Paris: Development Centre of the Organisation for Economic Co-operation and Development, 1993. The introductory chapter analyzes why NGOs and governments cooperate, casting new light on familiar topics: dependence, accountability, duplication, and competition. The rest of the book contains country profiles printed in both French and English.

Smith, Brian. *More Than Altruism: The Politics of Private Foreign Aid*. Princeton: Princeton University Press, 1990. A historical and theoretical inquiry into the political and economic circumstances that shape and motivate private foreign aid from the North to the South. The nonprofit sector's agenda, at times, extends beyond charity and altruism by helping governments promote their foreign policies, thereby enhancing state stability.

Tandon, Rajesh. *Civil Society, the State, and Roles of NGOs*. IDR Reports, vol. 8, no. 3. Boston: Institute for Development Research, 1991. Discusses the implications of state dominance and a changing civil society on NGOs.

Walker, Peter. "Foreign Military Resources for Disaster Relief: An NGO Perspective." *Disasters* 16, no. 2 (1992): 152–159. Weighing the pros and cons of a military-NGO partnership in disaster relief, this article warns that the military's primary obligation is to uphold its government's foreign policy, which may not coincide with humanitarian needs.

Wolch, Jennifer. *The Shadow State: Government and Voluntary Sector in Transition*. New York: The Foundation Center, 1990. NGOs are not really nongovernmental because the voluntary sector obtains finances and staff support from governments. As government dominance grows, the voluntary sector more and more resembles a shadow state. This book's state-centered approach to the analysis of NGOs contrasts with the vast majority of analyses describing their idyllic independence. This book does not deal specifically with international NGOs, but the analysis has implications for all NGOs.

Networking and Scaling Up

Alfonso, Carlos Alberto. "NGO Networking: The Telematic Way." *Development Journal of the Society for International Development* (1990): 51–54. Provides a concise history of the rise of computer and telecommunications networks as important tools for NGOs and discusses the role of the UNDP as a funder of such network expansion.

Annis, Sheldon. "Evolving Connectedness Among Environmental Groups and Grassroots Organizations in Protected Areas of Central America." *World Development* 20, no. 4

(1992): 587–595. The creation of networks by grassroots and environmental organizations as well as the spread of information and communications technologies help reduce poverty and environmental deterioration.

———. "Can Small-Scale Development Be Large-Scale Policy?" In Sheldon Annis and Peter Hakim (eds.), *Direct to the Poor: Grassroots Development in Latin America.* Boulder, Colo.: Lynne Rienner, 1988, 209–218. Answering the question posed in the article's title, the author contends that state policy largely undermines grassroots growth and that NGOs tend to flourish where the state is strong.

Brown, L. David. "Bridging Organizations and Sustainable Development." *Human Relations* 44, no. 8 (1991): 807–831. A theoretical study of why and how bridging organizations cope with the diversity of NGOs and provide critical horizontal and vertical links that enable grassroots organizations to influence national policymaking.

Brown, L. David, and Rajesh Tandon. *Multiparty Cooperation for Development in Asia.* IDR Reports, vol. 10, no. 1. Boston: Institute for Development Research, 1992. Looking at seven case studies in six Asian countries, this paper attempts to discover when and how certain forms of cooperation work and continue even when initially unsuccessful.

Carroll, Thomas. *Intermediary NGOs: The Supporting Link in Grassroots Development.* West Hartford, Conn.: Kumarian Press, 1992. This theoretical and empirical examination highlights intermediary NGOs' ability to help grassroots organizations effectively deal with the larger environment and includes a review of the literature on intermediary and local organizations. It cautions readers about the literature's antigovernment bias and provides a balanced, realistic, and useful assessment of grassroots organizations.

Cooperrider, David L., and William Pasmore. "The Organization Dimension of Global Change." *Human Relations* 44, no. 8 (1991): 763–787. Contends that existing international relations theories do not adequately describe and explain international NGOs.

Durning, Alan. "People Power and Development." *Foreign Policy* 76 (1989): 66–82. Looks at grassroots organizations' present as well as potential relationships with governments, international donors, and other international actors. Rather than being a destabilizing force of national governments, these organizations foster a true democracy and thereby avert unrest and social instability.

Elliott, Charles. "Some Aspects of Relations Between the North and the South in the NGO Sector." *World Development* 15: Supplement (1987): 57–68. Discusses three areas where international NGOs help capacity building of indigenous NGOs: personnel, technology, and administrative links.

Fisher, Julie. *The Road from Rio: Sustainable Development and the Nongovernmental Movement in the Third World.* Westport, Conn.: Praeger Publishers, 1993. A comprehensive treatment of grassroots organizations and their networks, although no attempt is made to link them to international affairs.

———. "Is the Iron Law of Oligarchy Rusting Away in the Third World?" *World Development* 22, no. 2 (1994): 129–143. Argues that the iron law of oligarchy is not inevitable for NGOs. She examines the horizontal and vertical links that reinforce democratic rather than oligarchic characteristics.

Fowler, Alan. "Building Partnerships Between Northern and Southern Development NGOs: Issues for the Nineties." *Development Journal of the Society for International Development* 1 (1992): 16–23. Raises issues encountered by NGOs in establishing and maintaining partnerships between Northern and Southern NGOs.

Garner, Maria. "Transnational Alignment of Nongovernmental Organizations for Global Environmental Action." *Vanderbilt Journal of Transnational Law* 23, no. 5 (1991): 1057–1084. In response to the current environmental conditions, this article proposes a network of environmental NGOs that should be formally recognized but not controlled by an international organization.

Morgan, Mary. "Stretching the Development Dollar: The Potential for Scaling-Up." *Grassroots Development* 14, no. 1 (1990): 2–11. Examines why and how scaling-up activities occur.

Oliver, Christine. "Network Relations and Loss of Organizational Autonomy." *Human Relations* 44, no. 9 (1991): 943–961. Analyzes neither international NGOs nor the UN, but the theoretical exploration of organizations' propensity to form linking relationships (networks) regardless of a fear of lost autonomy helps illuminate a trend among all NGOs. It also challenges the assumption that possible external influences deter organizations from forming interorganizational attachments.

Padron, Mario. "Electronic Networks and Democracy in Latin America." *Transnational Associations* 1 (1989): 34–35. An overview of the many ways Latin American NGOs are using electronic networks and modern technology to communicate with each other and their European counterparts.

Sikkink, Kathryn. "Human Rights, Principled Issue-Networks, and Sovereignty in Latin America." *International Organization* 47, no. 3 (1993): 411–441. Reviews human rights theories and emphasizes the need to pay particular attention to NGO networks as they challenge state sovereignty through the construction of regimes.

Stremlau, Carolyn. "NGO Coordinating Bodies in Africa, Asia, and Latin America." *World Development* 15: Supplement (1987): 213–225. Written just as NGO umbrella organizations were beginning to form or to develop formal networks of NGOs, this article provides a framework for evaluating NGO networks such as PACT; analyzes coordinating bodies in terms of their formation, membership, roles, functions, and regional locations; and also outlines the relationship between donors and coordinating agencies.

NGOs in the International System, Overview

Amnesty International. *Amnesty International Report 1994.* New York: Amnesty International, 1994. An overview of the human rights situation, including how one leading human rights organization sees its relationship with the UN and other international organizations.

Bhatnagar, Bhuvan, and Aubrey C. Williams (eds.). *Participatory Development and the World Bank.* World Bank Discussion Papers, no. 183. Washington, D.C.: The World Bank, 1992. More than a discussion of the Bank's involvement with participatory development, this volume contains several articles dealing with World Bank–NGO relations and one about UNICEF's long-standing relations with NGOs.

Chui, J. "Working with NGOs." *Populi* 15, no. 4 (1988): 36–45. Examines the role that NGOs play in UNFPA's programs and documents that NGOs receive a significant portion of UNFPA's budget.

Cohen, Cynthia Price. "The Role of Nongovernmental Organizations in the Drafting of the Convention on the Rights of the Child." *Human Rights Quarterly* 12, no. 1 (1990): 137–147. Using the Convention on the Rights of the Child as a case study signifying NGO participation in UN legislative drafting, this article briefly discusses and evaluates the strategies employed by NGOs in dealing with the UN, including cooperative efforts where group consensus overrode individual concerns.

Cohen, Susan A. "The Road from Rio to Cairo: Toward a Common Agenda." *International Family Planning Perspectives* 19, no. 2 (1993): 61–66. Written in anticipation of the Cairo conference, the article presents insights into the dynamics of negotiations on the issues of women and population among UN officials, feminist organizations, and other NGOs.

Dumelie, Roger. "A Forum for NGOs: A Proposal." *Development Journal of the Society for International Development* 1 (1993): 51–53. Briefly discusses the concept of a global civil society, highlights NGOs as important players, and raises interesting questions for further discussion.

Ghils, Paul. "International Civil Society: International Non-Governmental Organizations in the International System." *International Social Science Journal* 44, no. 133 (1992): 417–431. Using a transnational approach to explain INGOs' shaping of international law, this article focuses on INGOs' scope of action as shapers of opinion, autonomous actors, and competitors with states.

Jacobson, Harold K. *Networks of Interdependence: International Organizations and the Global Political System.* 2nd ed. New York: Alfred A. Knopf, 1984. As one of the leading textbooks on IGOs and NGOs in the world political economy, the book examines international organizations in the context of an emerging international society, comprehensively reviewing global networks and their role in eroding state sovereignty.

Korten, David C., and Antonio B. Quizon. *Government, NGO and International Agency Cooperation: Whose Agenda?* Kuala Lumpur, Malaysia: Asian Pacific Development Centre, June 29, 1991. Examining the trends in and strategies of NGO collaboration with governments, businesses, and international lending agencies, this article contrasts the positive attributes of these collaborations with the danger that external funding to NGOs can result in the legitimizing of donor policies and the bureaucratization of NGOs.

Leatherman, Janie, Ron Pagnucco, and Jackie Smith. *International Institutions and Transnational Social Movement Organizations: Challenging the State in a Three-Level Game of Global Transformation.* Working Paper Series. Notre Dame, Ind.: Kroc Institute for International Peace Studies, University of Notre Dame, 1993. Examines some of the main themes and problems in the study of transformational politics and explores the key ways in which transnational social movement organizations (TSMOs) are eclipsing the state as the primary actor in global politics. The authors present several hypotheses, including the theory that TSMOs facilitate states' internalization of global norms adopted by the UN.

Organisation for Economic Co-operation and Development. *Human Rights, Refugees, Migrants and Development: Directory of NGOs in OECD Countries.* Paris: OECD, 1993. This annual publication includes an article entitled "Partners in Development, Democracy and Global Justice: Non-Governmental Organisations in OECD Countries Active in Human Rights, Refugee and Migrant Assistance and Development."

Shaw, Timothy. "Beyond Any New World Order: The South in the 21st Century." *Third World Quarterly* 15, no. 1 (1994): 139–146. Examines the possible future of international relations, arguing that the international community has had to accept the legitimacy of nonstate actors and an emerging global civil society.

Spiro, Peter J. "New Global Communities: Nongovernmental Organizations in International Decision-Making Institutions." *The Washington Quarterly* 18, no. 1 (Winter 1995): 45–56. Traces the rise of NGOs, showing how NGOs are now venturing into areas that were once exclusively under states' control. Though raising the question of how democratic NGOs are, it makes an argument for their further institutionalization in global decisionmaking.

Tolley, Howard, B., Jr. *The International Commission of Jurists: Global Advocates for Human Rights.* Philadelphia: University of Pennsylvania Press, 1994. The history of the International Commission of Jurists reveals both the difficulties and the possibilities of global democratization. As a case study of an NGO's campaign for human rights, the commission's interaction with governments and IGOs tests present notions of a new world order and theories of international relations.

Woods, Lawrence T. *Asia-Pacific Diplomacy: Nongovernmental Organizations and International Relations.* Vancouver: UBC Press, 1993. Broadens international relations theory by analyzing how NGOs contribute to regional diplomacy.

NGOs in the International System, World Bank Relations

Alexander, Nancy C. "Transcending the Vicious Cycle of Debt and Adjustment." In Ved P. Nanda, George W. Shepherd, Jr., and Eileen McCarthy-Arnolds (eds.), *World Debt and the Human Condition: Structural Adjustment and the Right to Development.* Westport, Conn.: Greenwood Press, 1993, 172–192. Argues for a grassroots collaboration with international lending agencies to resolve Third World debt and poverty. Citing the Development Bank Assessment Network as a collection of U.S. NGOs who are working toward poverty alleviation through the multilateral banks, the author asserts that many NGOs are resisting the role of compensating for deficiencies in structural adjustment programs.

Annis, Sheldon. "The Next World Bank?: Financing Development from the Bottom Up." *Grassroots Development* 11, no. 1 (1987): 24–29. Suggests the possibility of the World Bank as a grassroots funder and raises some implications for its relations with NGOs.

Clark, John. "NGO Perspectives on Debt and Adjustment." *Transnational Associations* 2 (1990): 85–90. Portrays some NGOs as watchdogs of the World Bank's structural adjustment policies.

———. "World Bank and Poverty Alleviation: An NGO View." *Transnational Associations* 2 (1990): 74–84. Originally prepared for the 1988 meeting of the World Bank–NGO Committee, this paper covers significant aspects of the debate between international associations and the Bank.

Leach, Richard. "The Inter-American Development Bank and the NGO Community: A Partnership in Support of the Micro-entrepreneur." In Ved P. Nanda, George W. Shepherd, Jr., and Eileen McCarthy-Arnolds (eds.), *World Debt and the Human Condition: Structural Adjustment and the Right to Development.* Westport, Conn.: Greenwood Press, 1993, 205–222. Looks at the important contributions NGOs make to IDB's micro-enterprise programs.

Shihata, Ibrahim F. I. "The World Bank and Non-Governmental Organizations." *Cornell International Law Journal* 25, no. 3 (1992): 623–641. Studying the legal aspects of the World Bank–NGO collaboration, this article outlines the evolution of the Bank's NGO policy.

The World Bank. *Cooperation Between the World Bank and NGOs: FY 1994 Progress Report.* Washington, D.C.: The World Bank, 1995. The annual report analyzes World Bank–NGO collaboration as an important feature of bank-financed projects, including an increased collaboration with local NGOs and the growing diversity in types of NGO collaboration.

NGOs in the International System, UN Relations

Anheier, Helmut K., Gabriel Rudney, and Lester M. Salamon. *The Nonprofit Sector in the United Nations System of National Accounts: Definition, Treatment, and Practice.* Working Papers of the Johns Hopkins Comparative Nonprofit Sector Project, no. 4. Baltimore, Md.: The Johns Hopkins Institute for Policy Studies, 1992. Describes the rationale behind the UN's treatment of the nonprofit sector by studying why the sector is often neglected in national economic reports. The authors painstakingly review the UN system of national accounts and the statistical implications of present policy.

Baehr, Peter R. "Human Rights Organizations and the United Nations: A Tale of Two Worlds." *Paradigms: The Kent Journal of International Relations* 8, no. 2 (1994): 92–110. Baehr sees a tension between NGOs and the UN when they interact in the field of human rights. Amnesty International and the UN have different visions of a Special Commissioner for Human Rights, namely on his or her authority to initiate action.

Boulding, Elise. "Nongovernmental Organizations." *Bulletin of the Atomic Scientists* 41, no. 7 (1985): 94–96. Boulding traces NGOs' involvement in peace and nuclear disarmament issues and lists a short chronology of their participation in international conferences and events.

Chatterjee, Pratap. "Mixed Success for NGOs." *Crosscurrents: An Independent NGO Newspaper on Sustainable Development* 6, no. 1 (1993). Lists NGOs' mixed reactions to the rules of access to the new Commission on Sustainable Development. Some believe they bring more opportunities, while others are skeptical.

Chiang, Pei-heng. *Non-Governmental Organizations at the United Nations: Identity, Role, and Function.* New York: Praeger Publishers, 1981. Though much has changed since the book was written, it remains a useful work on NGOs in the UN system because it raises concerns that still loom today. Chiang carefully documents the NGO-UN relationship since its inception. Describing this relationship as a source of "profound dissatisfaction" for NGOs, Chiang delineates the NGOs' struggle to assert their identity. Since this book was written, ECOSOC has published new guidelines for NGO relations and many more NGOs have acquired consultative status.

Feld, Werner J., and Robert S. Jordan, with Leon Hurwitz. *International Organizations: A Comparative Approach.* New York: Praeger Publishers, 1983. Focuses on IGOs; significant details are the role of NGOs in IGO decisionmaking, their participation in the disarmament debate, and the problems of consultative status. In addition, the first chapter contains a section reviewing the nature and classification of INGOs as well as their growth pattern since the early twentieth century.

Garrison II, John W. "UNCED and the Greening of Brazilian NGOs." *Grassroots Development* 17, no. 1 (1993): 2–11. Describes the impact of UNCED on grassroots organizations and concludes that the former permitted the latter to demonstrate a new maturity and foreshadow the leading role GSOs will play in the development and further democratization of Brazil.

Gunby, Joan. "Partners in Health." *World Health* (January-February 1988): 12–13. Written by a WHO officer, this article claims that the anniversary of WHO signified forty years of working with NGOs, a contrast to other articles that argue that WHO did not utilize NGOs effectively at the start of its program on AIDS.

Haas, Peter M., Marc A. Levy, and Edward A. Parson. "Appraising the Earth Summit: How Should We Judge UNCED's Success?" *Environment* 34, no. 8 (1992): 6–11, 26–32. Focusing on the results of UNCED, the article summarizes the implications of both official documents and NGOs' alternative reports. The authors also provide a brief background on the Stockholm conference and discuss UNCED-inspired institutions.

International Alert, NIRA, and United Nations University. *Preventive Diplomacy: A UN/NGO Partnership in the 1990s.* New York: International Alert, NIRA, and United Nations University, 1993. Identifying information as the key ingredient affecting UN policies, the paper contends that information dissemination has been and can continue to be the best way for NGOs to influence global policies. It summarizes the state of NGOs' involvement in conflict resolution and recommends a future division of labor.

Jönsson, Christer. "International Organization and Co-operation: An Interorganizational Perspective." *International Social Science Journal* 138 (1993): 463–489. Citing efforts to combat AIDS, this article illustrates the problematic IGO-NGO collaboration and sheds new light on international organizations.

Kakabadse, Yolanda N., and Sarah Burns. *Movers and Shapers: NGOs in International Affairs.* Washington, D.C.: World Resources Institute, 1994. Assesses the Earth Summit's impact on NGO-UN relations and offers suggestions to strengthen NGOs' international participation. After outlining various aspects of UN-NGO relationships, including the accreditation process, it highlights opportunities now available to NGOs.

Livernash, Robert. "The Growing Influence of NGOs in the Developing World." *Environment* 34, no. 5 (1992): 12–16. Tracing NGOs' changing goals, the article states that NGOs now rarely focus on one issue because they recognize the need to cross-link gender, development, and environmental issues. It also discusses NGOs in the UN system, highlighting the pattern of NGOs establishing conferences parallel to UN summits.

Mezzalama, Francesco, and Siegfried Schumm. *Working with Non-Governmental Organizations: Operational Activities for Development of the United Nations System with NGOs and Governments at the Grass-Roots and National Levels.* Geneva: Joint Inspection Unit of the United Nations, 1993. JIU/REP/93/1. Outlines the opportunities and problems of collaboration among UN agencies, lending institutions, NGOs, and governments. A quasi-guide to working with NGOs, it acknowledges that the ECOSOC consultation process emphasizes NGO support of the United Nations rather than meaningful dialogue. The paper presents examples of UN agencies' interactions with NGOs.

Olle, Dahlén, Bo Westas, and Duncan Wood. *Peaceful Resolution of Conflicts: Non-Governmental Organisations in the International System.* Life and Peace Research Reports, no. 1. Sweden: Life and Peace Institute, 1988. Though the three essays on the roles of the UN and NGOs in conflict resolution see NGOs working through the UN system as essential to peacemaking, they recognize difficulties. For example, Wood writes that NGOs recognized at an early stage that they would need to defend their consultative status with the UN collectively if they were to continue to enjoy it individually.

Organisation for Economic Co-operation and Development. *Voluntary Aid for Development: The Role of Non-Governmental Organisations.* Paris: OECD, 1988. Reviews such issues as definitions, institution building, appropriate technology, finances, and education. Chapter 4 examines NGOs' cooperation with the UN and the World Bank.

Pérez de Cuéllar, Secretary-General Javier. "Strengthening Collaboration between UN and Cooperatives." *Transnational Associations* 2 (1989): 101–102. This extract from the statement of the Secretary-General delivered to the International Co-operative Alliance (ICA) Congress in 1988 highlights the key roles that NGOs play in the UN system.

Rhodes, Paula, and Eileen McCarthy-Arnolds. "Expanding NGO Participation in International Decision Making." In Ved P. Nanda, George W. Shepherd, Jr., and Eileen McCarthy-Arnolds (eds.), *World Debt and the Human Condition: Structural Adjustment and the Right to Development.* Westport, Conn.: Greenwood Press, 1993, 153–169. Covers NGOs' relations with the UN, the World Bank, and the IMF and suggests that NGOs are more than peripheral participants in the international lawmaking process.

Stairs, Kevin, and Peter Taylor. "Non-Governmental Organizations and the Legal Protection of the Oceans: A Case Study." In Andrew Hurrell and Benedict Kingsbury (eds.), *The International Politics of the Environment.* Oxford: Clarendon Press, 1992, 110–141. Explains why and how NGOs are involved in international lawmaking. Based on a case study of Greenpeace, it provides a background analysis of the UN, international law, and NGOs' participation.

Stanley, Richard H., Ellen Dorsey, and Bruno Pigott. *The UN System and NGOs: New Relationships for a New Era?: Twenty-Fifth United Nations Issues Conference.* Muscatine, Iowa: The Stanley Foundation, 1994. The conference report raises three views of the international system: the traditional state-centered view, the UN-centered view, and the multiple-actor world system view, which predicts NGOs will act as policy shapers and not merely advocates.

Susskind, Lawrence E. *Environmental Diplomacy: Negotiating More Effective Global Agreements.* New York: Oxford University Press, 1994. In discussing strategies of global environmental negotiations, the book addresses the activities of and the relations among UN agencies, governments, citizens, the World Bank, and NGOs. Though the Salzburg Initiative recommended an expanded reflection of nongovernmental interests, the book argues that the UN is reluctant to redefine the role of NGOs in order to avoid the implications of new powers (such as voting) that would subsequently result.

Thakur, Ramesh. "Human Rights: Amnesty International and the United Nations." *Journal of Peace Research* 31, no. 2 (1994): 143–160. In examining the process of norm-generation, monitoring, and enforcement, the article offers a clear example of the complementary roles played by the United Nations and Amnesty International.

Tinker, Irene, and Jane Jaquette. "UN Decade for Women: Its Impact and Legacy." *World Development* 15, no. 3 (1987): 419–427. Discusses the impact of the UN Decade for Women on NGOs and vice versa. The NGO flora encouraged the growth of women's groups and the formulation of networks. These groups in turn pushed governments to recognize the decade.

United Nations, Economic and Social Council of the United Nations. *General Review of Arrangements for Consultations with Non-Governmental Organizations: Report of the Secretary-General.* E/AC.70/1994/2, 1994. An official source on the bureaucratic relationships between NGOs and the UN, outlining the rules and regulations of NGO participation in the UN system.

———. *Report of the Open-Ended Working Group on the Review of Arrangements for Consultations with Non-Governmental Organizations: Report of the Secretary-General.* A/49/50/rev.1, 1994. Summarizes the issues raised at a meeting of NGO representatives, government delegates, and UN officials. Among the issues discussed were the strategies for improving NGO-UN relations, including a revision of current consultative arrangements.

UNESCO and the Standing Committee of NGOs. "First Regional Consultation of Latin American and Caribbean NGOs." *Transnational Associations* 3 (1990): 154–162. A background article on cooperative efforts between UNESCO and NGOs.

Weiss, Thomas G. "Humanitarian Action by Nongovernmental Organizations." In Michael E. Brown (ed.), *The International Implication of Internal Conflicts.* Cambridge, Mass.: MIT Press, 1995. A typology of the operational, educational, and advocacy NGOs that interact with the United Nations system in complex emergencies.

Williams, Douglas. *The Specialized Agencies and the United Nations: The System in Crisis.* New York: St. Martin's Press, 1987. Appendix C explores the origins of IGO-NGO relations since the League of Nations and contends that the growth in the number of NGOs with the concurrent rise of IGOs was more than a coincidence—NGOs encouraged the creation of new IGOs to promote their concerns.

Woods, Lawrence T. "Nongovernmental Organizations and the United Nations System: Reflecting upon the Earth Summit Experience." *International Studies Notes* 18, no. 1 (1993): 9–15. Briefly outlines various proposals to change the relationship between NGOs and the UN and highlights the growing prominence of NGOs, as exemplified by their participation in the Earth Summit; it situates these issues in the context of the study and teaching of international relations and international law.

About the Authors

Martha Alter Chen is research associate at Harvard Institute for International Development and an experienced development practitioner, planner, and researcher. Her areas of specialization are rural development, poverty alleviation, and women in development. She has recently completed a monograph on "Women and Wasteland Development in India" for the International Labour Organisation and is currently engaged in a study of widows in rural India with support from the World Institute for Development Economic Research.

Ken Conca is assistant professor of government and politics at the University of Maryland at College Park. His research and teaching interests include international environmental politics, North-South politics, the role of social movements in world politics, Latin American politics and society, and the political economy of science and technology. He is coeditor (with Ronnie D. Lepschutz) of *The State and Social Power in Global Environmental Politics* and a coauthor (with Wayne Sandholtz, John Zysman, and others) of *The Highest Stakes: The Economic Foundations of the Next Security System.*

Antonio Donini is a senior officer in the Executive Office of the Secretary-General of the United Nations. His field of study is complex emergencies and the relationship between peacekeeping operations and humanitarian assistance. Donini has been involved in interagency coordination efforts in the fields of planning and evaluation, and has conducted several field evaluations of UN system technical cooperation activities in Sri Lanka, Africa, and Morocco while he was a staff member of the Joint Inspection Unit. His last study focused on how to adapt UN system field representation to the challenges of post–Cold War situations. He has also served in the field from June 1989 to December 1991 with the Office for the Coordination of UN Humanitarian and Economic Assistance programs relating to Afghanistan.

Felice D. Gaer is director of The Jacob Blaustein Institute for the Advancement of Human Rights of the American Jewish Committee. Gaer was appointed a public member of the United States delegations to the World Conference on

Human Rights in 1993 and to the United Nations Commission on Human Rights in 1994 and in 1995. She is a member of the Council on Foreign Relations, a member of the board of directors of the Andrei Sakharav Foundation, a member of the core group of the Human Rights Council at the Carter Center of Emory University, and vice president of the International League for Human Rights.

Leon Gordenker is professor emeritus of politics and faculty associate of the Center of International Studies at Princeton University. He is a longtime observer of international organizations and has written extensively on the United Nations and international organizations. Among his recent books is a forthcoming study of international responses to AIDS. He is the author (with Peter Baehr) of *The United Nations in the 1990s* and editor (with Benjamin Rivlin) of *The Challenging Role of the UN Secretary-General.*

Christer Jönsson is professor of political science at the University of Lund, Sweden, and the vice president of Nordic International Studies Association. He is a member of the editorial boards of *International Studies Quarterly* and *International Organization and Global Governance.* His recent publications include *Communication in International Bargaining* and "Cognitive Factors in Explaining Regime Dynamics" in *Regime Theory and International Relations.*

Andrew S. Natsios is vice president of World Vision and executive director of World Vision Relief & Development, the technical arm of World Vision U.S. Natsios was formerly assistant administrator of the Bureau of Food and Humanitarian Assistance for the U.S. Agency for International Development. He is the author of "Food Through Force: Humanitarian Intervention and U.S. Policy" in the *Washington Quarterly.* From 1989 to 1991, he served as president of the Bush-Quayle Senior Executive Service Association.

Cyril Ritchie is president of the Federation of International Institutions in Geneva and holds leadership roles in the Federation of International Institutions in Geneva, InterAid International, the International Conference on Philanthropy, the Society for International Development, the UNICEF NGO Committee, and the Union of International Associations. Ritchie is a member of the International Biographical Association, International Society of Community Development, and Amnesty International.

Peter Söderholm is research associate of political science and a Ph.D./ABD candidate at Lund University, Sweden. His dissertation is entitled "Foundations of Global Governance: Comparing the Politics of AIDS and the Environment." He has been a visiting scholar at the Institute of International Studies at the University of South Carolina, and has recently published "AIDS and the Multilateral Governance," a paper for the United Nations University publication "Programme on Multilateralism and the United Nations System," and *International*

Cooperation in Response to AIDS, co-authored with Leon Gordenker, Roger Coate, and Christer Jönsson (forthcoming).

Peter Sollis is an independent consultant who works on humanitarian relief and development issues. He was senior fellow at the Washington Office on Latin America until 1994. He has served as a consultant for numerous organizations, including PAHO, IDB, the World Bank, and the John D. and Catherine T. MacArthur Foundation. From 1979–1991, he worked at Oxfam-UKI, where he held a number of positions, including field director for the Andean Region, Mexico, and Central America, and desk officer for Central America. He has published extensively on social policy issues, NGOs, and Central America.

Peter Uvin is assistant professor of research at Brown University's World Hunger Program. He has taught and conducted research on a variety of issues, including development cooperation, North-South relations, community development and grassroots organization, and food and hunger. He has worked extensively in francophone Africa for the Swiss Development Cooperation. His latest publications include *The International Organization of Hunger, The Hunger Report 1994,* and *Scaling Up: Thinking Through the Issues.*

Thomas G. Weiss is associate director of Brown University's Thomas J. Watson Jr. Institute for International Studies. He was formerly with UNCTAD, the UN Commission for Namibia, UNITAR, ILO, and the International Peace Academy. His most recent publications include *The United Nations and Changing World Politics* (with David P. Forsythe and Roger A. Coate) and *Humanitarianism Across the Borders: Sustaining Civilians in Times of War* (with Larry Minear). He is the executive director of the Academic Council on the United Nations System.

Index

Abzug, Bella, 144
Advocacy and NGOS, 38–40. *See also* Human
  rights
Afghan Red Crescent Society, 95
Afghanistan, de-mining in, 95–96
Africa Rights, 63–64, 85
Africa 2000 Network, 172
Africa Watch, 85
Aga Khan, Sadruddin, 36
Agenda 21, 105, 113–114, 144, 193
AIDS. *See* HIV/AIDS
Almeida, Walter, 129
Amnesty International, 27, 29, 54–55, 61–63,
  86
An Agenda for Development (UN document), 85
An Agenda for Peace (UN document), 8–10
Analytic dimensions of NGOS, 41–44
Aristide, Jean-Bertrand, 40
Ayala Lasso, José, 55

Bangladesh Rural Action Committee (BRAC),
  30, 164
Bangladesh Rural Advancement Committee,
  160
Biosphere Conference (1968), 105
Blaustein, Jacob, 52, 60. *See also* Jacob
  Blaustein Institute for the Advancement of
  Human Rights
Boutros-Ghali, Boutros, 24, 185
BRAC. *See* Bangladesh Rural Action
  Committee
Brandt, Willy, 36
Brody, Reed, 63
Brundtland Commission, 111; *Our Common
  Future,* 106. *See also* Harlem-Brundtland,
  Gro
Bruyn, Maria de, 133

CARE, 31, 69–72, 87, 91
Carlsson, Ingmar, 36
Catholic Relief Services (CRS), 69–72, 191
Center for Women's Global Leadership,
  145–147
Central America: growth of NGOS in, 190–192;
  political and economic context for NGOS in,
  189–190; political views, governments, and
  NGOS in, 192–196; UNDP and the future in,
  200–203; UN in, 196–200

Centre for Human Rights, 63–65, 86, 126, 147
Centre for Our Common Future, 106–107, 112
Chisholm, Donald, 133
CIREFCA. *See* International Conference on
  Central American Refugees
Cold War, end of: and NGOS, 24, 30
Commission on Global Governance, 18, 27
Commission on Human Rights, 36, 53–56, 60,
  63–64
Commission on Sustainable Development
  (CSD), 84, 105, 107–108, 113–115
Conable, Barber, 109
Conference of Non-Governmental
  Organizations in Consultative Status
  (CONGO), 23, 183
Conference on Popular Participation in African
  Recovery and Development (Arusha),
  168–169
CONGO. *See* Conference of Non-Governmental
  Organizations in Consultative Status
CRS. *See* Catholic Relief Services
CSD. *See* Commission on Sustainable
  Development

DAC. *See* Development Assistance Committee
DAWN. *See* Development Alternatives with
  Women for a New Era
Department of Humanitarian Affairs (DHA) (of
  the UN), 72, 74, 76–78, 87, 91–92
Development Alternatives with Women for a
  New Era (DAWN), 142
Development Assistance Committee (DAC), 32,
  88
Development Program for Refugees, Displaced
  and Repatriated Persons in Central America
  (PRODERE), 197–201
DHA. *See* Department of Humanitarian Affairs
DIACONIA (El Salvadore), 191–192
DONGO. *See* Donor-organized
  nongovernmental organization
Donor-organized nongovernmental organization
  (DONGO), 21, 37; World Bank and, 31

Earth Summit (1992), 166
ECHO. *See* European Community Humanitarian
  Office
Economic and Social Council (ECOSOC),
  21–23, 52–53, 55, 77, 105; NGOS and, 85;

Resolution 1296 of, 83–84. *See also* Commission on Sustainable Development
Education, advocacy, and NGOs, 38–40
Eichelberger, Clark, 52
Emergencies, 67–68; collaborative efforts in, 74–78; future of responses to, 78–80; International Red Cross and, 73–74; NGOs and, 68–72; the UN system and, 72–73
Environmental Defense Fund, 109, 111
Environmental issues, 103–104; global conferencing on, 111–112; specialized agencies for, 108–109; UN system and, 104–108, 114–117; UNEP and, 112–113; World Bank and, 108–110. *See also* Commission on Sustainable Development; Tropical Forestry Action Plan
ESOSOC. *See* Economic and Social Council
EU. *See* European Union
European Community Humanitarian Office (ECHO), 69, 79
European Union (EU), 89, 91, 133

FAO. *See* Food and Agriculture Organization
FFP. *See* Food for Peace
Finances, size, and independence of NGOs, 31–32; in humanitarian relief efforts, 71
Financial transfers among NGOs, 88–92
Food and Agriculture Organization (FAO), 72–73, 77, 85, 104, 108, 160. *See also* Tropical Forestry Action Plan
Food for Peace (FFP), 68–69
Freedom from Hunger Campaign (of the FAO), 85, 190

Garcia Sayan, Diego, 63
General Assembly (of the UN), 77; NGOs and, 84–86
Global Management Committee (GMC), 130–132
Global Programme on AIDS (GPA), 122, 128–131
Global Tribunal on Violations of Women's Human Rights, 146–147
GMC. *See* Global Management Committee
GONGO. *See* Government-organized nongovernmental organization
Government-organized nongovernmental organization (GONGO), 20–21
Governments and NGOs, 30
GPA. *See* Global Programme on AIDS
Grameen Bank, 160, 164
Grassroots organizations (GROs), 159–161; and scaling down the summit, 170–174; scaling up, 161–165
Grassroots support organizations (GRSOs), 159–160
Greenpeace, 40, 106, 111
GROs. *See* Grassroots organizations
Grose, Robert, 128–129
GRSOs. *See* Grassroots support organizations

Haas, Ernst, 133
Hammarskjöld, Dag, 36
Harlem-Brundtland, Gro, 36
HIV/AIDS: emergence of, 121–122; human rights and, 125–127; IGO-NGO responses to, 128–137; medical issues in, 123–125; nature of, 122–123; socioeconomic problem of, 127–128
Human rights: field operations for, 62–64; future of, 64–65; NGOs for, 56–58; NGOs in Central America and repression of, 194–195; role of NGOs and, 55–56; in UN charter, 51–53; UN machinery and abuses of, 53–55; women and, 145–150; World Conference on, 58–61
Human Rights Watch, 29, 61–63
Humanitarian relief efforts. *See* Emergencies
Hyden, Goren, 162

IASC. *See* Inter-Agency Standing Committee
IBRD. *See* International Bank for Reconstruction and Development
ICASO. *See* International Council of ASOS
ICPD. *See* International Conference on Population and Development
ICRC. *See* International Committee of the Red Cross
ICVA. *See* International Council of Voluntary Agencies
IFRC. *See* International Federation of Red Cross and Red Crescent Societies
IGO. *See* Intergovernmental organizations
ILO. *See* International Labour Organisation
IMF. *See* International Monetary Fund
Independent Sectors' Network, The, 107
Ingram, James, 29
InterAction, 26, 70, 79, 86, 91
Inter-Agency Standing Committee (IASC), 77, 86
Intergovernmental organizations (IGOS), 18, 20. *See also* HIV/AIDS
International Bank for Reconstruction and Development (IBRD), 31. *See also* World Bank
International Committee of the Red Cross (ICRC), 21, 31, 40, 67–68, 71–72; in humanitarian emergencies, 73–74, 78; Security Council and, 86
International Conference on Central American Refugees (CIREFCA), 30, 197–200
International Conference on Population and Development (ICPD) (Cairo), 147–150
International Conference on Refugees in Central America, 30
International cooperation: theories of, 32–36
International Council of ASOs (ICASO), 129–130
International Council of Voluntary Agencies (ICVA), 26–27, 29, 79, 86, 91, 182
International Federation of Human Rights, 54, 61

International Federation of Red Cross and Red Crescent Societies (IFRC), 27, 70, 77, 86
International Human Rights Law Group, 61, 63
International Labour Organisation (ILO), 22, 84, 168
International League for Human Rights, 54, 60–61
International Monetary Fund (IMF), 40, 109
International Organization for Migrations (IOM), 67, 77
International Union for the Conservation of Nature (IUCN), 104–105
International Women's Health Coalition, 147–149
International Women's Tribune Center, 142, 146–147
International Women's Year (1975), 140, 142
Interorganizational relations, 25–30
IOM. See International Organization for Migrations
IUCN. See International Union for the Conservation of Nature

Jacob Blaustein Institute for the Advancement of Human Rights, 61
Japanese International Cooperation Agency (JICA), 161
JICA. See Japanese International Cooperation Agency

Kastberg, Nils-Arne, 132
Kouchner, Bernard, 40

Lecomte, Bernard, 162

Mack, Myrna, 195
Mahler, Halfdan, 127
Mann, Jonathan, 124–126, 128–129, 131, 135
Martin, Ian, 63
Médicins Sans Frontières (MSF), 26–27, 36, 40, 68, 85, 87
Morrison, Ken, 129
MSF. See Médicins Sans Frontières

NAPs. See National AIDS Programs
National AIDS Programs (NAPs), 128–129
Nerfin, Marc, 19
Nolde, Ferderick, 52
Nongovernmental organizations (NGOS):
analysing, 41–44; Central American states and, 189–203; concepts of, 97–100; constraints on, 40–41; defined, 18–21, 178–179; educational and advocacy roles of, 38–40; and end of Cold War, 24, 30; environment, UN system, and, 103–117; finances, size, and independence of, 31–32, 179–180; grassroots, 159–165; growth of, and relations of, with the UN, 7–12, 17; HIV/AIDS, IGOS, and, 121–137; human rights and, 51–65; humanitarian emergencies and,
67–80; international cooperation, theories of, and, 32–36; International Women's Movement, the UN, and, 139–153; interorganizational relations of, 25–30; operational coalitions of, 177–188; operational roles of, 37; participation of, in international regimes, 165–170, 209–221; peacemaking efforts of, 87–88; technological developments, resources, and, 25; UN and, 21–23, 83–100
Nyerere, Julius, 36

OFDA. See Office of Foreign Disaster Assistance
Office of Foreign Disaster Assistance (OFDA), 68–69, 71–72, 79
Operational roles of NGOS, 37
Oxfam, 26–28, 31, 69–70, 85, 87, 91, 167, 170

PAHO. See Panamerican Health Organization
Palme, Olaf, 36
Panamerican Health Organization (PAHO), 124, 197
ParinAc. See Partners in Action
Partners in Action (ParinAc), 29, 74
Partners in Development Program, 171, 196
Peacemaking efforts of NGOS, 87–88
Priestley, Michael, 73
PRODERE. See Development Program for Refugees, Displaced and Repatriated Persons in Central America
Proskauer, Joseph, 52

Ramphal, Sonny, 36
Rector, Richard, 129
Red Cross Movement, 78. See also International Committee of the Red Cross; International Federation of Red Cross and Red Crescent Societies
Rich, Bruce, 109–110
Rosenau, James, 20

Sadik, Nafis, 149
Save the Children, 27–28, 69–70, 87, 91
Security Council (UN), 63, 76; NGOS and, 85–86
Shotwell, James, 52
Six-S, 160, 162
Sixth International AIDS Conference (San Francisco), 130
Stettinius, Edward, 52
Strong, Maurice, 106, 113
Sy, El Hadj As, 133

TFAP. See Tropical Forestry Action Plan
Tolba, Mostafa, 103, 113
Tropical Forestry Action Plan (TFAP), 110–111

UN Charter: human rights, NGOS, and, 51–53; humanitarian relief efforts and, 76
UN Conference on Environment and Development (UNCED) (Rio de Janeiro), 23, 84, 103,

105–108, 111–112, 115, 164; women and, 143–144

UN Conference on the Human Environment (Stockholm), 103

UN Decade for Women, 139–142, 150

UN Development Decade, 190

UNCED. *See* UN Conference on Environment and Development

UNCTAD. *See* United Nations Conference on Trade and Development

UNDP. *See* United Nations Development Programme

UNEP. *See* United Nations Environment Programme

UNESCO. *See* United Nations Educational, Scientific, and Cultural Organization

UNFPA. *See* United Nations Population Fund

UNHCR. *See* United Nations High Commissioner for Refugees

UNICEF. *See* United Nations International Children's Emergency Fund

UNIFEM. *See* United Nations Development Fund for Women

Unitarian Universalist Service Committee (UUSC), 167, 170

United Nations: military forces, 96–97; NGO coalitions, conferences, and, 180–186; NGOS in the field and, 92–97; role of, in Central America, 196–200; world conferences, International Women's Movement, and, 139–153. *See also* Environmental issues

United Nations Commission on the Status of Women, 140

United Nations Conference on Trade and Development (UNCTAD), 105

United Nations Development Fund for Women (UNIFEM), 146

United Nations Development Programme (UNDP), 21, 26, 28, 93, 160; in Central America, 200–203; emergency relief efforts and, 72–73, 78; financing of NGOS and, 31; Third World NGOS and, 160–172. *See also* HIV/AIDS

United Nations Educational, Scientific, and Cultural Organization (UNESCO), 84–85, 104–105

United Nations Environment Programme (UNEP), 103, 105, 108, 112–113

United Nations High Commissioner for Human Rights, 60–62. *See also* Human rights

United Nations High Commissioner for Refugees (UNHCR), 27–30, 37, 68, 72–74, 78, 86–87, 89, 91, 160; in Pakistan, 93; in Rwanda, 94

United Nations Human Rights Commission, 52. *See also* Commission on Human Rights

United Nations International Children's Emergency Fund (UNICEF), 29, 36, 72–73, 78, 85–86, 89, 160; in Pakistan, 93

United Nations Office for the Coordination of Humanitarian Assistance to Afghanistan (UNOLA), 95

United Nations Population Fund (UNFPA), 149

United Nations Transition Authority in Cambodia (UNTAC), 29

United States Agency for International Development (USAID), 67–68, 131, 161–162, 191

Universal Declaration of Human Rights (1948), 52

UNOCA. *See* United Nations Office for the Coordination of Humanitarian Assistance to Afghanistan

UNTAC. *See* United Nations Transition Authority in Cambodia

USAID. *See* United States Agency for International Development

UUSC. *See* Unitarian Universalist Service Committee

Van der Stoel, Max, 36

Wapner, Paul, 104

WEDO. *See* Women's Environment and Development Organization

WFP. *See* World Food Programme

Women: human rights and, 145–150; policy agendas and, 150–151; UNCED and, 143–144

Women's Caucus, 144–149

"Women's Declaration on Population Policies," 148

Women's Environment and Development Organization (WEDO), 144, 149

World Bank, 26, 28, 31, 40; environmental issues and, 108–110; Third World NGOS and, 160, 165–166, 168, 170–172

World Conference on Human Rights (Vienna), 51, 58–61, 145–147

World Conferences on Women: First (Mexico City), 139–140; Second (Copenhagen), 141; Third (Nairobi), 141; Fourth (Beijing), 139–140, 152–153

World Food Programme (WFP), 29, 72, 78, 86, 89–90, 160; in Pakistan, 93

World Health Organization, 77, 108, 160. *See also* HIV/AIDS

World Resources Institute (WRI), 106, 110–111

World Vision, 69–71, 87, 91

WRI. *See* World Resources Institute

About the Book

A comprehensive exploration of the role of nongovernmental organizations in the international arena, this collection examines the full range of NGO relationships and actions.

The authors first outline the aims and scope of NGOs and suggest a systematic way of thinking about their activities. These conceptual notions underlie Part 2 of the book, five case studies focusing on NGOs vis-à-vis critical issues in contemporary world politics: AIDS, the environment, human rights, humanitarian relief, and women in development.

In Part 3, the authors concentrate on themes that cut across NGO activities in the realms of education, advocacy, and operations. They conclude with their proposal for an alternative division of responsibilities and labor between intergovernmental and nongovernmental actors, a vision in keeping with the complex mosaic of global governance.

Emerging Global Issues

THOMAS G. WEISS, SERIES EDITOR

Third World Security in the Post–Cold War Era
edited by Thomas G. Weiss and Meryl A. Kessler

The Suffering Grass:
Superpowers and Regional Conflict in Southern Africa and the Caribbean
edited by Thomas G. Weiss and James G. Blight

State and Market in Development: Synergy or Rivalry?
edited by Louis Putterman and Dietrich Rueschemeyer

Collective Security in a Changing World
edited by Thomas G. Weiss

Humanitarianism Across Borders: Sustaining Civilians in Times of War
edited by Thomas G. Weiss and Larry Minear

Changing Political Economies:
Privatization in Post-Communist and Reforming Communist States
edited by Vedat Milor

The Third World Security Predicament: State Making, Regional Conflict, and
the International System
Mohammed Ayoob

The United Nations and Civil Wars
edited by Thomas G. Weiss

NGOs, the UN, and Global Governance
edited by Thomas G. Weiss and Leon Gordenker